ROBERT SOUTHEY
AND HIS AGE

ROBERT SOUTHEY
From a water-colour by Edward Nash

ROBERT SOUTHEY AND HIS AGE

The Development of a
Conservative Mind

BY

GEOFFREY CARNALL

(Quaker author)

OXFORD
AT THE CLARENDON PRESS
1960

Oxford University Press, Amen House, London E.C.4

GLASGOW NEW YORK TORONTO MELBOURNE WELLINGTON
BOMBAY CALCUTTA MADRAS KARACHI KUALA LUMPUR
CAPE TOWN IBADAN NAIROBI ACCRA

920

W3072

PRINTED IN GREAT BRITAIN

There are new things under the sun, . . . new miseries, . . . new enormities, . . . this portentous age produces them.

ROBERT SOUTHEY, *Colloquies on the Progress and Prospects of Society* (1829)

He has passed from one extreme of political opinion to another, as Satan in Milton went round the globe, contriving constantly to 'ride with darkness'. Wherever the thickest shadow of the night may at any moment chance to fall, there is Mr. Southey.

T. B. MACAULAY, Essay on Southey's *Colloquies* (1830)

PREFACE

THIS book deals mainly with aspects of Southey's life and work that have not before been fully investigated. It is based upon an examination of the main collections of Southey manuscripts, as well as of the abundant printed materials. My special concern has been with the development of Southey's political ideas. This development is of considerable literary interest, partly because of the light that it throws on Wordsworth and Coleridge, but also because it helps to bring romantic literature as a whole into sharper focus. Southey's journalism and his correspondence enable one to feel with unusual intensity the stresses under which poems and novels were written, and ideas formed and changed, in the early nineteenth century.

I have not attempted to examine in any detail the question of how far Southey's views differ from those held by his contemporaries, or by modern historians. While such an examination would be well worth undertaking, it would have considerably extended the scope of the present volume. My purpose here has been to describe the reaction of one man to the events of his time—a man whose views were more representative than is often assumed, and who was perhaps the first to use the word 'conservative' in its modern sense.

The following have kindly allowed me to quote from manuscripts in their possession: the Bodleian Library; the British Museum; the Brotherton Library, Leeds; the Fitz Park Museum, Keswick; the Huntington Library, San Marino, California; the Library of the Society of Friends, London (and Mr. Q. E. Gurney); the National Library of Scotland; the National Library of Wales; the Henry W. and Albert A. Berg Collection of the New York Public Library; and the Victoria and Albert Museum. I should like to express my thanks to the staffs of these libraries, and of the Cambridge

University Library and the library of the Queen's University, Belfast, for help of many kinds.

I am also grateful to Mrs. M. B. Colt for making available to me the letters of Southey to Edward Nash, and the two portraits of Southey by Nash which are here reproduced for the first time.

Some of the material used in this book has already appeared in the *Friends' Quarterly*, *Notes and Queries*, and the *Philological Quarterly*. I am indebted to the editors of these journals for permission to reproduce it.

I am grateful to the staff of the Clarendon Press for help in preparing this study for publication. Professor F. W. Baxter and Professor Asa Briggs read the typescript at an earlier stage, and it has benefited greatly from their criticism. Valuable suggestions were also made by Mr. I. R. Browning, Dr. K. H. Connell, Mr. Leo Japolsky, the Rev. S. Senior, Professor T. J. B. Spencer, and Mr. R. J. White. I am indebted to the Earl of Shaftesbury and Professor D. S. Robertson for help in tracking down manuscripts; and to Mr. A. W. Stockwell for permission to read his unpublished thesis on Wordsworth's politics.

Like all students of Southey I owe a great deal to the work of Professor Kenneth Curry and Professor Jack Simmons. Professor Simmons's biography of Southey, in particular, has helped me in innumerable ways. My greatest debt, however, has been to Mr. B. R. Davis of Bristol. From the earliest stages of my work in this field, I have had the benefit of his wide knowledge of Southey's life and writings. His unfailing interest and encouragement have been invaluable.

G. C.

The Queen's University of Belfast
10 March 1959

CONTENTS

LIST OF ILLUSTRATIONS

ABBREVIATIONS USED IN THE NOTES

BL	Bodleian MSS. Eng. Letters.
BM	British Museum.
HM	Huntington Library MSS., Southey–Rickman correspondence.
LC	*The Life and Correspondence of Robert Southey*, ed. C. C. Southey (1849–50).
NLW	National Library of Wales MSS.
NYL	New York Public Library MSS. (Berg Collection).
QR	*Quarterly Review.*
Rickman	*Life and Letters of John Rickman*, by Orlo Williams (1911).
SL	*Selections from the Letters of Robert Southey*, ed. J. W. Warter (1856).

instability of Coleridge, the posturings of Byron, the bitter misanthropy of Hazlitt, and the feverish outpourings of Keats. And yet they ought not to do this without misgivings, for these writers are obstinately representative figures of their time, in a way which more sensible people like Scott, Peacock, or Jane Austen are not.

They are representative because they have clearly felt the shock of a great upheaval. It would be going beyond the scope of the present study to analyse in detail the relationship between the 'Industrial Revolution' and the romantic movement in literature. But the vast economic growth which set in as the eighteenth century came to an end produced at least one consequence which is reflected in the literature of the time. It increased feelings of insecurity, made people feel more uncertain of their relations with others, more isolated. Hence the cult of the solitary—'There is a pleasure in the pathless woods', 'I wandered lonely as a cloud', and (less pleasant)

> Alone, alone, all, all alone,
> Alone on a wide wide sea.

Hence, too, an unusual interest in suicide. The popularity of *Werther* is notorious. How far the literary fascination is reflected in the suicide rate is hard to say, for there are no reliable statistics. But it is remarkable that between 1815 and 1822 three prominent British politicians committed suicide—Whitbread, Romilly, and Castlereagh. This must be a record in parliamentary history. One may observe, too, that the great economic crisis of 1810 was precipitated by the suicide of Abraham Goldsmid, a London banker. Those who did not go the length of suicide could sometimes be the victims of acute depression. Southey's friend John Rickman, secretary to the Speaker of the House of Commons, and a sturdy statistician, is a significantly unromantic example. He was convinced that England had never been so prosperous before in her history. The reign of George III, he said in 1820, had seen an unparalleled increase in the comforts of life. Nevertheless, he could not *feel* the new glories of his country, though he could argue himself into a juster frame of mind. Rickman explained this unreasonable reaction as the poisonous effect of the malignant opposition press. But Southey, who was not likely to feel any more goodwill than Rickman towards newspapers, seems nearer the mark in his assertion that the manufacturing system had increased enormously the activity and wealth of the nation; but it had also, in a far greater degree, 'diminished its happiness and lessened its security'.[1]

The misery and insecurity were specially obvious among the working classes. It was, for example, the labouring man who bore the brunt of the great redistribution of population that took place as a result of the Industrial Revolution, with all the suffering necessarily involved in abandoning one's accustomed way of life. During the Napoleonic War, moreover, and for some years after it, high rents, high rates of interest, the system of taxation, the shortage of coin, and the difficulty of importing food, all worked together to worsen the economic status of labour.[2] Among early nineteenth-century writers, perhaps the most sombrely eloquent of those who described the state of the poor was a medical man, Charles Hall, whose book, *The Effects of Civilization*, appeared in 1805. He lays great emphasis on the social irresponsibility of modern commerce. 'Trade knows no friends or kindred', he says, '—avarice no compassion—gain no bounds.' He is oppressed by an awareness of the 'regular, orderly, silent' processes by which the poor are subdued. The power of the rich, he argues,

is as strong and effective as that of the most absolute monarch that ever lived, as far as relates to the labour of the poor; indeed, probably more so, since it is doubtful whether any power ever existed, in any kind of government whatever, that could impose on

[1] *Rickman*, p. 216. Letter to Southey, 10 Feb. 1820; Southey, *Essays* (1832), i. 111.

[2] *Capitalism and the Historians*, ed. F. A. Hayek (1954), pp. 133–5. This particular essay, by Professor T. S. Ashton, is mainly concerned with showing the improvement in the working-class standard of living after 1821.

the people what is imposed on them by the power of wealth. To condemn so many to the mines; to confine such numbers to such nauseous, irksome, unwholesome, destructive employments—is more than equal to any kingly power on earth. . . .[1]

From the point of view of those who enjoyed this kingly power, such conditions could be exhilarating. As Mr. R. J. White has remarked in a recent study of the period, the will-to-power in man had a greater scope then than it has ever had. In industry there was no government interference, no effective trade unionism, no patents to prevent enterprising young men from picking any brains they chose. 'It was a matter of a large number of men letting loose the life within them into a new field of adventure.'[2] 'Letting loose'—that is the clue to both the high and the low spirits of the time. It was exhilarating to feel identified with this power let loose, and intimidating to feel overwhelmed by it. Neither reaction was *social*, people responding to people.

The sense of insecurity produced in these conditions was expressed not so much by those, like the handloom weavers, who suffered slow extinction as a class, as by those who enjoyed enough privileges to fear losing them. Men who profited from the economic revolution might still feel threatened by the fate of the higher ranks of society in France. Hazlitt might speak of the 'grand whirling movements' of the French Revolution, of its 'tumultuous glow of rebellion' in head and heart.[3] But to Burke these movements were terrifying. They seemed to portend the collapse of all social order. The spirit of the French Revolution, he said, in his second letter *On a Regicide Peace*, 'lies deep in the corruption of our common nature'. The rulers of France have found their resources in crimes. 'The discovery is dreadful: the mine exhaustless.' The doctrine of majority rule, put into practice by the French, loosens all old venerations and attachments,

---

[1] C. Hall, *Effects of Civilization*, ed. J. M. Morgan (1850), pp. 151, 170, 40.
[2] R. J. White, *Waterloo to Peterloo* (1957), p. 58.
[3] W. Hazlitt, *Works*, ed. A. R. Waller and A. Glover (1902–6), iv. 237 (from the essay on Horne Tooke in *The Spirit of the Age*).

leaving society exposed to the untrammelled will of a succession of mob leaders.[1]

Burke's fears belong to a region of experience unfamiliar, in England at least, before the eighteenth century. Shakespeare's Ulysses may express himself in terms which suggest such alarm:

> Then every thing includes itself in power,
> Power into will, will into appetite,
> And appetite, an universal wolf,
> So doubly seconded with will and power,
> Must make perforce an universal prey,
> And last, eat up himself.

But it is arguable that Shakespeare could not even imagine the intensity of panic that seized Burke. To Ulysses, disorder is only an episode. The heavens themselves, the planets and this centre observe degree, priority, and place; and however much the planets may wander in evil mixture to disorder, the glorious planet Sol remains enthroned and sphered in noble eminence. It is obvious that the orthodox doctrine of hierarchy, as stated by Ulysses, is put under a severe strain both in the play where it appears, and elsewhere in Shakespeare. But broadly speaking, although it sometimes looks as though humanity must perforce prey on itself, like monsters of the deep, the vile offences which are committed receive their punishment. Macbeth might be willing to let the frame of things disjoint, but his willingness is only a sign of the disorder which is within himself, by which he will soon be destroyed.[2]

The disturbing novelty of the situation in the later eighteenth century can be appreciated if one compares Burke on the French Revolution with Clarendon on the Great Rebellion of the seventeenth century. To Burke, the revolutionaries were outlaws of the human race. Clarendon saw his opponents simply as factious and malicious men. The rebellion, he

---

[1] Burke, *Works* (1852), v. 321, 341; iv. 471–2.
[2] See *Troilus and Cressida*, I. iii; *King Lear*, IV. ii; and *Macbeth*, III. ii.

thought, arose from the interaction of infinitely various temperaments and qualities—

the pride of this man, and the popularity of that; the levity of one, and the morosity of another; the excess of the court in the greatest want, and the parsimony and retention of the country in the greatest plenty; the spirit of craft and subtlety in some, and the rude and unpolished integrity of others, too much despising craft or art; like so many atoms contributing jointly to this mass of confusion now before us.[1]

Clarendon here comments on a fact of political life in which Burke too was interested. The purposes of individuals may find issue in joint action that was far from any one man's intention. In his *Appeal from the New to the Old Whigs*, Burke describes how whole bodies of men may be hurried into schemes of politics through 'a careless and passive assent . . . a sort of activity of inertness', strengthened by 'the fear of differing with the authority of leaders on the one hand, and of contradicting the desires of the multitude on the other'.[2] Burke feels himself hustled by the course of events. Clarendon, however, always makes one feel that matters could have been kept under control with a shrewder policy and a little more good fortune. If the Short Parliament had not been dissolved, if Sir Thomas Gardiner could have been Speaker in the Long Parliament, if the Earl of Bedford had not died so unseasonably, disaster might have been avoided. This underlying assurance is not to be found in Burke. He saw himself sinking under the attacks of atheists, and for him the only question was how he might arm himself against them before it was too late.[3]

The sense of powerlessness in the face of events impressed many observers of the French Revolution. John Stuart Mill, for example, in his admirable review of Walter Scott's *Life of Napoleon*, described the revolution as a force independent of

---

[1] Clarendon, *History of the Rebellion*, ed. Macray (1888), i. 4.
[2] Burke, *Works* (1852), iv. 476.
[3] Ibid., vi. 100.

party interests, class interests, personal interests, depravity,
virtue, or genius—these things appearing to influence the
course of events only when they fell in with it and added force
to the current, proving impotent when they found themselves
thrust into opposition.[1] Joseph de Maistre made the same
observation, though from an entirely different standpoint.
The more one examined the career of the leaders of the
revolution, he said, the more passive and mechanical
their activity appeared to be. They did not lead the revolution; they were mere tools of the revolution.[2] Maistre saw
proof in this that God used the revolution to punish the
French for their irreligious presumption. But even those who
were concerned to vindicate the revolution were obliged to
acknowledge the part played in it by this terrifying force.
Thus, James Mackintosh said that the burning of châteaux and
other riotous acts of this kind were something that the National
Assembly could not repress without either provoking a civil
war or putting arms into the hands of their enemies. 'Placed
in this *dilemma*, they were compelled to expect a slow remedy
from the returning serenity of the Public mind. . . .'[3] This is a
reasonable defence, but of course a great deal might happen
before the public mind returned to serenity. Thomas Paine,
for one, was astonished that the National Assembly had been
able to restrain so much of the confusion—'beyond the controul of all authority'.[4] Paine argued, indeed, that the outrages
committed by the Paris mob were no more the acts of the
French people than the outrages of the London mob in the
Gordon Riots of 1780 were the acts of the whole people of
England. But the parallel could be used against Paine, for
the Gordon Riots had shown, on a small scale, what could
happen when normal loyalties broke down and the mob took
control. Recalling the 'dreadful fermentation' of that time,

[1] *Westminster Review*, Apr. 1828, p. 255.
[2] J. de Maistre, *Considérations sur la France* (Paris, 1821), pp. 5–10. First
published in 1797.
[3] J. Mackintosh, *Vindiciae Gallicae* (1791), p. 181.
[4] T. Paine, *Rights of Man*, ed. H. B. Bonner (1949), p. 23.

Burke described how 'wild and savage insurrection quitted the woods, and prowled about our streets in the name of reform. Such was the distemper of the public mind, that there was no madman, in his maddest ideas, and maddest projects, who might not count upon numbers to support his principles and execute his designs.'[1] Fortunately the cry of the mob had been 'No Popery!'—which was a little more favourable to the established order than 'The Rights of Man!' If it had been otherwise, Burke thought that England might have begun the democratic revolution instead of France.

Comparatively few people viewed the French Revolution with the desperate passion that possessed Burke. If he looked like a man who was going to defend himself against murderers, Fanny Burney, who tells us this, tells us also that she 'feared not with his fears', though tacitly assenting to his doctrines.[2] This, however, does not make Burke unrepresentative, as is shown by the way he crystallized English opposition to France in 1792. What other people were haunted by as an occasional bad dream, was for him a habitual nightmare.

Southey, too, was subject to nightmares. They drove him from the radicalism of his earlier years into a fervent conservatism. In considering this change, it is useful to recall some wise words of his son Cuthbert. Some people, he said, might consider his father's apprehensions at the time of the Reform Bill of 1832 exaggerated and unfounded; but we should remember that 'we are often apt to think lightly of our own fears and those of others when the danger has passed by'.[3] It is a salutary exercise to reconstruct the perspective in which Southey and his contemporaries saw the events of their time. It is easy for us, looking back on the evolution of British institutions in the nineteenth century, to feel superior to Southey's gloom and panic. His opposition to parliamentary reform and Catholic emancipation has, as the phrase goes,

[1] Burke, *Works* (1852), v. 220 (from *A Letter to a Noble Lord*, 1796).
[2] *Diary and Letters of Mme d'Arblay* (1854), v. 267–8, 18 June 1792.
[3] *LC*, vi. 172.

been proved wrong by 'history'. The citadel of the constitution was not taken by assault, as Southey believed it would be, and Lord Shaftesbury is remembered as a factory-reformer, not, as Southey further predicted, for his part in a counter-revolution.[1] Even when Tory prophecies have come true, they seem less dreadful to us than to the original prophets. Many modern conservatives would agree with Rickman that universal suffrage has led to 'an organised Robbery of the Upper Classes'; but they seem to take this robbery philosophically enough. Still more striking is an accurate prediction in the *Courier*, at the time of Lord Grenville's election as Chancellor of the University of Oxford. Grenville was a leading advocate of Catholic emancipation, but he had none the less secured the votes of certain bishops. 'They have conspired', said the *Courier* with bitter sarcasm, 'to throw open the gates of the University to persons of every religious persuasion *whatever*.' The highest academic posts might well in future be given to Socinians and Catholics.[2] This prophecy has been fulfilled to the letter. It would have been even more remarkable if the *Courier* had added atheists to the list, but doubtless it did not wish to exaggerate. It had appalled its readers enough already. Even today it should be possible to appreciate that the prospect conjured up must have appeared monstrous and intolerable. To the Duke of Wellington, the consequences of parliamentary reform seemed no less appalling. He preferred, he said, to fall in defence of the unreformed British Constitution rather than endure 'the lingering operation of a modern revolutionary system', such as would be established by the Reform Bill.[3]

There is, in fact, nothing necessarily eccentric or unbalanced about Southey's reaction to the events of his time. His state of mind was similar to those who nowadays wish to

---

[1] NYL, 7 Nov. 1831, 28 May 1832.

[2] *Courier*, 22 Dec. 1809. For Rickman on the Reform Bill, see Chap. III, p. 186, below.

[3] Arthur, Duke of Wellington, *Despatches, etc.*, supp. ser. vii (1878), p. 470. Letter to Lord Cowley, 15 July 1831.

make a firm stand against communism, or Titoist revision-
ism, or the encroachments of the coloured races. The un-
compromising resister of shifts in the balance of power may be
wrong, but he is not abnormal.

II ∾ JACOBIN

1. THE YOUNG RADICAL

Robert Southey was born a few minutes before half past eight in the morning of Friday, 12 August 1774. The time was ill-chosen. The eccentric poet William Gilbert, who drew up his horoscope, told him that he would get a pain in his bowels at the age of thirty, and that Jupiter was his deadly antagonist. In compensation, however, he was given 'a gloomy capability of walking through desolation'.[1] Whether the first part of the horoscope was fulfilled remains obscure, but Jupiter was certainly a deadly antagonist through much of Southey's life. One can understand why Shelley affected him as the ghost of his own youth when he appeared in Keswick in 1811. In his younger days Southey contended with Jupiter in the character of Prometheus. Later he exchanged this role for that of Saturn. 'In the end', he wrote in 1819, referring to the political conflicts of that time, 'they will make it a struggle between youth and age, and then the weakest must go to the wall.'[2]

Southey would be a good subject for a psycho-analytical biography. He was for a long time in the care of a maiden aunt, Miss Tyler, and the effects of her peculiar discipline were doubtless great. Psycho-analysis is beyond my competence, however, and it will be enough to mention here a childhood dream that would have pleased Freud. 'I thought

[1] *LC*, i. 23. Letter to G. C. Bedford, 30 Sept. 1797.
[2] BL, d. 47, f. 174. Letter to same, 5 Nov. 1819. The astrological reader will note with interest that Jupiter was Wordsworth's 'own beloved Star' (*Prelude*, iv. 247). Also that Shelley was born under the same sign of the Zodiac as Southey—Leo.

my head was cut off for cursing the King—and after it was
done I laid my head down in my mothers lap—and every
now and then lookd up and cursed him.'[1] Southey took to
sedition at an early age.

But it would be a distortion to explain the development
of Southey's character and opinions purely in terms of his
experiences in early childhood. These experiences may have
made him vulnerable to the strain of life in the England of
his day, but the strain of life was considerable. To take what
may at first seem a trivial example, Professor Jack Simmons
has plausibly suggested that Southey's later pugnacity was
nourished by the bullying that went on at the school he
attended in Bristol when he was six years old. And the bullying school was a characteristic part of the dangerous world in
which young Southey found himself. In the same year that he
went to this school, the Gordon Riots broke out in London,
when for days the capital was in the hands of a mob which
pillaged and burned with impunity. The riots had repercus-
sions in Bath and Bristol. At Bath the Catholic chapel was
burnt, together with the houses adjoining it, and a mob prepared to march on Bristol. Nor was this an isolated instance of
violence. The spring of 1783 was a hard time for the poor
because of the scarcity of food, and there was in consequence
'a frightful increase of crime, especially of burglaries and
highway robberies'.[2] Southey himself was never directly
affected by these outbreaks, but one thing which he recalled is
perhaps related to them. When he was about nine years old
—that is in 1783—a reading of Shakespeare's history plays
convinced him that a state of civil war still existed in his own
time. He therefore thought that if he wished to become a
great man like the Earl of Warwick he ought to begin securing
partisans. The method he chose was to convince his schoolfellows that he could interpret dreams, and then, when they
came to him to have their dreams interpreted, he referred

[1] BL, c. 23, f. 21. Letter to G. C. Bedford, 30 Sept. 1797.
[2] J. Latimer, *The Annals of Bristol in the Eighteenth Century* (1893), p. 454.

them all to 'great civil wars and the appearance of the very
great man who was to appear—meaning myself'.[1] Southey
evidently did not share Shakespeare's abhorrence of civil war.
It is a curious scrap of evidence in support of Tocqueville's
contention that in the ten or fifteen years before the French
Revolution the human mind was abandoned throughout
Europe to 'strange, incoherent, and irregular impulses', very
alarming if their significance had been understood.[2]

In 1788 Southey was sent to Westminster School. There
his life was complicated by the capricious tyranny of some of
the older boys. His boarding house was under the tyranny of
one William Forrester—'a great brute,' said Southey, 'as
great a one as ever went upon two legs'. But he at least
saved the house from another bully, Brice, who was mean and
malicious, which Forrester was not. It is clear that Southey
had something of an admiration for Forrester. 'He would have
made a good prize-fighter, a good buccaneer, or, in the days
of Coeur de Lion or of my Cid, a good knight, to have cut
down the misbelievers with a strong arm and a hearty good
will.'[3] Southey was himself fond of striking down his literary
and political enemies with 'a hearty good will', and there may
have been a half-conscious recollection of Forrester in his
mind whenever he used the phrase.

Later in his school career Southey developed into a rebel
against authority. By the time of his expulsion in 1792 his
sensibility had been fed by a diet of Rousseau and *Werther*,
and his freethinking exercised by Voltaire and Gibbon. He
had written a theme for the Headmaster, Dr. Vincent, in
which he had abused Burke—presumably the Burke of the
Reflections, for Dr. Vincent objected. He took part in a school
'rebellion', and may have helped in cutting off the nose of
Major André's statue in Westminster Abbey. (André was

---

[1] BL, c. 23, f. 22. Letter to G. C. Bedford, 30 Sept. 1797.
[2] A. de Tocqueville, *The State of Society in France before the Revolution of
1789*, trans. H. Reeve (1888), p. 192.
[3] *LC*, i. 150. The names of Forrester and Brice may be found in the MS.
Recollections of his Early Life, letter 17 (Fitz Park Museum, Keswick).

a hero of the American War of Independence—on the wrong side.) One can learn a good deal about Southey's schoolboy rebelliousness from a prose romance, *Harold*, which he composed in the summer of 1791. It is a story of the days of Robin Hood and Richard Coeur de Lion. Richard is a democratic monarch who approves of the rebellious activities against church and state carried on by the outlaws in Sherwood Forest. How different, Southey observes, are the rulers of England in his own day. Perhaps the most revealing part of *Harold* is an inset episode in the twenty-second book. It is what purports to be the genuine story of Crispus, the son of Constantine the Great whom his father caused to be executed. Southey probably read about Crispus in Gibbon, and would have found the subject peculiarly attractive. It enabled him to show the ruler who first united church and state as an evil despot. It gave ample opportunities to display the sufferings of the young and innocent. And, since Crispus's popularity was one cause of his father's jealousy, a democratic flavour could easily be given to the story. According to Southey, Constantine was jealous of Crispus not only because his son was more popular than he, but because he wanted to seize his concubine, Thaeana. Constantine offers her the choice of yielding to his lust or suffering death. Crispus finds this out from Thaeana herself, and she offers to commit suicide. He stops her.

Hold Thaeana hold, by our mutual love I charge thee, attempt not thy life. The name of Crispus is beloved by the people—in such a case as this 'twere madness to retain one spark of filial duty. I will hasten from this accursed spot, I will proclaim my injuries aloud, and the inhuman Constantine shall know that they who have[1] so largely contributed to seat him upon his throne, can pull him down.[2]

Unfortunately Constantine comes in soon enough to frustrate this plan, and Crispus has to watch Thaeana and their child being executed while Constantine gloats over his agony. 'I

---

[1] The MS. reads 'has'.
[2] Bodleian MS. Eng. misc. e. 114, f. 177.

rushed at this spectacle upon my murdrous father, seized him
by the throat, and should certainly have slain him, had not
those fell members of his cruelty who were nigh preserved
him.'[1] Crispus himself is condemned to death by starvation,
and while he is starving composes the memoirs which are
inserted into *Harold*. Southey relates that Richard Coeur de
Lion was moved to tears by the story. 'I wish that Villain
Constantine was now living', he remarked. 'I would proclaim
a Crusade against him.'[2] A pleasant comment on the first
Christian Emperor!

Southey's final act of insubordination at school was to
write a paper against corporal punishment, which formed the
fifth number of *The Flagellant*, a school periodical begun by
Southey and his friend Grosvenor Bedford. The paper argued
that corporal punishment was an invention of the Devil,
proving this on the authority of Herodotus, Plutarch, Cicero,
Seneca, Lucian, Athanasius, Jerome, and Hugo Grotius.

How virulently does Moses exclaim against idolatry and against
idolaters! 'Ye shall destroy their altars, and break down their
images, and cut down their groves, and burn their graven images
with fire'; and again, 'If thou do walk after other gods, and serve
them and worship them, I testify against you this day, that ye shall
surely perish.' Thus pointedly does Moses express his detestation,
and denounce the anger of the Deity against whosoever shall serve
the Devil.[3]

To introduce sacred texts in such an irreverent manner was
bad enough, but to use them to prove the perilous spiritual
condition of schoolmasters who flogged was unpardonable.
Southey was expelled in April 1792.

'I am not conscious of having acted wrong', he told Bedford at this time. 'My future welfare may or may not be
affected by malicious envy but the firm assurance of rectitude
cannot.' Assurance of rectitude never deserted him, certainly,
but it served as a defence against an unmanageable emotional

---

[1] Bodleian MS. Eng. misc. e. 114, f. 180.   [2] Ibid., f. 181.
[3] *The Flagellant*, No. 5, p. 85.

insecurity. He could write that he had undergone enough to break a dozen hearts, and was given to indulging in suicidal wishes. 'Should I be rejected at Oxford', he told Bedford, 'the grave is always open—there at least I shall not be molested.'[1] His early letters reveal a giddy oscillation between defiance and submission. He thinks of himself as the oak in Aesop's fable, torn up by the roots, and says that he must learn to be a reed; and this immediately after an avowal of republican sentiments in the bold language of Tom Paine.[2]

At this time, he tells us, his head was perilously full of *Werther* and Rousseau. What kind of attraction did they exercise on him? *Werther* is chiefly known as a glorification of suicide, and the novel is of considerable interest as a study in its causes. Goethe seizes on the isolation of the suicide, the sense of being forsaken in a bewildering labyrinth. In Southey's opinion Rousseau's *Confessions* showed 'the cravings of a heart that wanted and deserved an equal companion',[3] and the sensuality into which Rousseau plunged was no compensation for this companionship. It was evidently the loneliness of Werther that made an appeal to Southey. Although Southey himself had deep and rewarding friendships, they meant so much to him partly because he was oppressed by the desolate solitariness of human life in general—his horror of the 'common, hollow, cold, lip-intercourse of life'[4] was no mere literary convention. Friendship and domestic comfort was one support to him; the stoicism of Epictetus was another. The latter enabled him to control the sensibility which might otherwise have overwhelmed him. It helped him to keep a belief in the ultimate goodness of nature. Rousseau's optimism was useful here. Southey especially admired the letter which Rousseau wrote to Voltaire, replying to the latter's poem on the great Lisbon earthquake. Such catastrophes, said Rousseau, rather

---

[1] BL, c. 22, f. 9. Letter to G. C. Bedford, 16 Apr. 1792; *SL*, i. 8. Letter to T. P. Lamb, ? Sept. 1792.
[2] BL, c. 22, f. 27. Letter to G. C. Bedford, 21 Oct. 1792.
[3] *SL*, i. 54. Letter to John May, 6 Apr. 1798.
[4] *LC*, i. 336. Letter to Mrs. Edith Southey, 4 June 1798.

suggested that it was wrong to live in cities than that man was
only born to suffer and to die.[1]

When Southey went up to Balliol College, Oxford, in
January 1793, Europe was enduring the first main shocks of a
political earthquake. In the previous autumn France had been
invaded by an army under the Duke of Brunswick, with a view
to restoring the old order. The revolutionaries in their turn
deposed the French king and held him for trial, and the
notorious September massacres marked the first stage of the
reign of terror in Paris. By early October the Duke of Brunswick was compelled to retreat, and this reverse for the
'coalesced tyrants' put new heart into sympathizers with the
revolution on both sides of the English Channel. In parts of
the north of England and in Scotland there were boisterous
celebrations, and riotous assemblies were reported as late as
the end of November. An English National Convention was
talked of. In Sheffield, a stronghold of radicalism, 'the late
successes of the French armies' were celebrated 'in the most
signal manner'. An ox was roasted whole, divided into
quarters, and drawn through the streets to the firing of cannon
and the cheers of the crowd. Three of the quarters were left
in different parts of the town for distribution to the poor.
The remaining quarter was sent to the debtors in jail.[2] The
London Corresponding Society sent a congratulatory address
to the French National Convention, saying, 'Frenchmen, you
are already free, and Britons are preparing to become so.'[3]

Southey shared this excitement. He wrote to Grosvenor
Bedford from Bristol on 21 October 1792 and said that
that city seemed to be preparing for a 'republic system'.
He refers to a pamphlet, printed locally, proposing the
abolition of the corporation—an unconstitutional and arbitrary body—and hinting that other corporations should be
abolished too. 'These little attacks upon the outworks sap

[1] *Correspondance générale de J.-J. Rousseau*, ed. T. Dufour (Paris, 1924–34),
ii. 303 et seq.
[2] *London Chronicle*, 3 Dec. 1792.
[3] *Memoir of Thomas Hardy* (1832), p. 21. Address of 27 Sept. 1792.

the foundations of the citadel. If France models a republic and enjoys tranquillity who knows but Europe may become one great republic and Man be free of the whole?'[1] It was in this somewhat fevered atmosphere that the French National Convention's decree was issued on 19 November, declaring support for movements of liberation in all lands.

The following day, however, a counter-movement was launched in London which in a short time checked the English jacobins decisively. The initiative was taken by John Reeves, a lawyer just returned from Newfoundland, where he had been Chief Justice. At a meeting in the Crown and Anchor Tavern in the Strand on 20 November, he formed an association for protecting liberty and property against republicans and levellers. Within a fortnight, men of property could feel tranquil again. As late as 29 November the *London Chronicle* was noting that many alarming rumours were in circulation. 'Foreign quarrels, and domestic commotions, are painted in terrific colours, to dismay the monied men.' But on 7 December *The Times* could report that a complete change had occurred in the political situation. The previous four days had seen general dejection and dismay turn into joyful confidence. The machinations of Britain's enemies had been defeated by 'the energy of public opinion'.

This energy was manifested in every part of the country by an extraordinary number of loyal associations, formed on the model provided by John Reeves. Some are mentioned in the papers of the Poole family. Thomas Poole of Nether Stowey in Somerset, a tanner by trade, was a friend of Coleridge and Southey, and, like them, a democrat in his sympathies. So was his brother Richard, who lived in the neighbouring county of Dorset. Richard did not, however, stand out against the local loyal association. On the contrary he hastened to sign its declaration of 'attachment to the present Establishment in Church and State, which was agreed to by the inhabitants of Sherborne, and patronized by Lord Digby'.

[1] BL, c. 22, f. 27. Letter to G. C. Bedford, 21 Oct. 1792.

A similar declaration of loyalty was arranged in Bristol, and is referred to in Charlotte Poole's diary for 18 December, 1792. In Leicester there were the same protestations of loyalty, the same closing of party ranks. In that town leading Whigs joined an association to discover the authors, publishers, and distributors of seditious writings, and to assist the civil authority in case of riot. A hundred and twenty-eight innkeepers 'declared their intention to permit no subversive meetings or disloyal expressions in their houses'.[1] One could prolong a list of these signs of enthusiastic conformity into several pages. It will be enough to mention that *The Times* at this period contains many notices of loyal associations in and around London. Mile End, West Ham, Southwark, Lambeth, Camberwell, Hampstead, Highgate, Finsbury, Hackney, and Clerkenwell are among the places mentioned. Everywhere effigies of Tom Paine were burnt, and at Waltham Abbey free porter was supplied to those of the populace who assisted at the celebration. Waltham Abbey was probably not unique.

The columns of *The Times* contain paragraphs that help one to understand why Richard Poole was so earnest in his declaration of constitutional principles. 'Every good, every loyal, every constitutional subject', we are informed, 'is loudly called upon at this time narrowly to watch those whose principles lead to a Revolution, and whose words and actions correspond with that idea.' Such people should be arrested, for the sake of the happiness and welfare of the kingdom. Noted reformers, even if they were not as yet arrested, had a difficult time. Samuel Favell, a Southwark tradesman, had his shop stuck over with insulting printed bills, and was so hooted by street boys that, according to an exultant paragraph in *The Times*, he preferred to stay indoors. Moderate reform was suspected as much as radicalism. 'The

---

[1] Mrs. Henry Sandford, *Thomas Poole* (1888), i. 35, 64; A. Temple Patterson, *Radical Leicester* (1954), pp. 70–71. Cf. Frida Knight, *The Strange Case of Thomas Walker. Ten Years in the Life of a Manchester Radical* (1957).

appearance of moderation is a very convenient mask for our internal enemies' was the comment of *The Times* on 30 November; loyal men should not be lulled into security by cajoling language. Sometimes even the most militant loyalty did not ensure protection from other loyalists. For example, George Harcourt of Ankerwyke wrote to *The Times* explaining that he had been grievously misunderstood. On 20 November he had attended the Haymarket Theatre, and while he was there the song of 'God save the King' was called for. After it had been sung, he writes, 'I heard seditious voices from the gallery repeat *ça ira*, which I hissed: at that moment the call for the air of '*God save the King*' was likewise repeated, and many supposed I was inimical to that air being played, and in mistaking my real intentions behaved improperly to me.'[1] One hopes that this letter to *The Times* was enough to clear Mr. Harcourt's good name.

These things represented a powerful social pressure that either had to be compromised with or resisted. Southey attempted the latter course, but at the price of an intense uneasiness and priggish hostility. He is a striking contrast to Wordsworth, and one finds in his letters nothing of the confidence

> That, if France prospered, good men would not long
> Pay fruitless worship to humanity.[2]

The difference between the two men was partly one of temperament. It was also one of age and experience. Wordsworth was four years older than Southey, and knew France and the practical aims of the revolution at first hand. Southey spoke the language of philanthropy not so much because he felt the sufferings of the common man but because that was the proper language of 're-publicans and sinners', who will not take their hats off when 'God save the King' is sung, will not have their hair powdered, and will not shoot game because of the barbarity of the amusement. He was sympathetic to the

[1] *The Times*, 29 Nov., 1, 4, and 5 Dec. 1792.
[2] *Prelude*, x. 258-9.

cause of the French because those who administered corporal punishment were hostile. After expelling Southey, William Vincent had settled down to write *A Discourse addressed to the People of Great Britain*,[1] in which he recommended sound education as a remedy for dangerous and delusive principles. Southey could not help feeling an attachment to any principles which Vincent regarded as dangerous and delusive. But the predominant note in Southey's letters in 1792 and 1793 is one of anxiety. He identified the persecution to which *The Flagellant* incident had exposed him with that which pursued Tom Paine.

> To hope that Truth would shelter me how vain
> When Truth and Eloquence both faild for Paine![2]

He felt himself to be 'the most insulated being existing',[3] and although he was fond enough of quoting the appropriate verse of Horace—'iustum et tenacem propositi virum', &c.— he evidently found the stoic fortitude difficult to assume. On 3 December 1792 he went to the theatre at Bristol and saw 'that compilation of turgidity and bombast the Grecian Daughter'. It contained many passages of loyalty, royalty, and freedom, and, says Southey, party feeling ran high and 'God save the King' was sung. 'Philosophy like Imlac was swept silently down the stream.' One strong-minded democrat attempted to adhere to his principles. Although he judged it prudent to take off his hat for 'the King', he was the last of the audience to do so. His obvious unwillingness brought on him insults from the rest of the audience, and during the interval he was cold-shouldered. Southey could not rise to such a demonstration himself, but with an effort he brought himself to countenance the demonstration of his fellow-democrat. He

---

[1] First preached as a sermon on 13 May 1792 at St. Margaret's, Westminster.

[2] BL, c. 22, f. 41. Letter to G. C. Bedford, 30 Dec. 1792. Paine was tried for seditious libel (in his absence) on 18 Dec. 1792. He was defended by Erskine. So strong was the feeling against Paine that the jury found him guilty without hearing the prosecution's reply to Erskine's defence.

[3] BL, c. 22, f. 61. Letter to G. C. Bedford, 14 July 1793.

went across to him and struck up a conversation. Even this
was difficult. 'When I am agitated', he told Bedford, 'every
nerve trembles, but at those moments when a bystander
would think me palsied with some fear I could leap to pluck
bright honor from the palefaced moon. I could write an ode
and stand to be shot at.'[1]

His correspondence at this time shows the same shrinking
from human contact that is specially noticeable after the failure
of the Pantisocracy scheme. Pantisocracy itself—the plan for an
equalitarian community in one of the back-settlements of the
United States of America—seems to have grown out of an unwillingness to come to terms with the hostile England of 1793
and 1794. For example, on 22 December 1793 he wrote to
Bedford that occasionally he was able to indulge in optimistic
speculations, 'but more frequently the visions of futurity are
dark and gloomy—and the only ray enlivening the scene beams
on America'.[2] At this time he had seriously begun to entertain
the idea of following the example of the unitarian radical Dr.
Priestley and leaving Britain altogether. As an idle speculation
some such notion had long attracted him. Indeed, before he
was six he and two schoolfellows had planned to go and live by
themselves on an island. 'We were to have one mountain of
gingerbread and another of candy.'[3] While still at Westminster,
Bedford and he had planned a *Flagellant* paper on the *Bounty*
mutineers. Otaheitee, he said, had many attractions independent of its women (whom Captain Bligh thought to have been
the chief cause of the mutiny)—attractions not only for the
sailor but the philosopher. 'He might cultivate his own ground
and trust himself and friends for his defence—he might be truly
happy in himself and his happiness would be increased by com-
municating it to others. He might introduce the advantages
and yet avoid the vices of cultivated society.'[4] These words

---

[1] BL, c. 22, f. 33, 4 Dec. 1792. Presumably *The Grecian Daughter* was the
play of that name by Arthur Murphy.
[2] BL, c. 22, f. 91, 22 Dec. 1793.
[3] BL, c. 23, f. 22. Letter to G. C. Bedford, 30 Sept. 1797.
[4] BL, c. 22, f. 48, 8 Feb. 1793.

were written in February 1793, when the release offered by
emigration began to be more than idly attractive. He was
maintained at Oxford by his uncle, the Rev. Herbert Hill, who
wanted him to be a clergyman of the Church of England. But
from the beginning he was troubled by doubts about whether
he could accept the Thirty-Nine Articles, and from time to
time he seems to have felt that he was in an intolerable position. At first he hoped to compromise by practising the
virtues inculcated by the Athanasian Creed while not reflect-
ing on the mysteries it contained. 'Of the sanctity of those
mysteries I know nothing—their incomprehensibility is
evident—Athanasius the reputed author of that stumbling
block confessed he understood them not. Tillotson wished the
creed expunged from the liturgy—yet the one was a Saint and
the other an Archbishop.'[1] Why, after all, should anyone be
asked to believe more than Tillotson did? Southey evidently
gained confidence in the pursuit of his clerical career from his
friendship with Edmund Seward. Seward intended to become
a clergyman himself. He was somewhat older than Southey,
and seems to have been exceptionally solemn. He sympathized
with some at least of Southey's levelling sentiments. On 7
February 1793, in a debate, Southey, Seward, and another
candidate for ordination called Lewis, supported the view that
clerical incomes should never exceed £200 a year. It was in
such demonstrations of practical Christianity that he sought to
quiet his misgivings about 'speculative points of faith'. (It
was also consistent with such jacobinical questions as 'Had
any of the Apostles ten thousand a year?') The arguments of
Seward may also perhaps be traced behind Southey's statement to Bedford that religion, even when not to the taste of
the philosopher, should be respected for the sake of the miserable, for whom it is the one remaining consolation. The study
of philosophy did nothing to undermine his faith, or to con-
firm it. Hume's arguments against religious belief he felt
able to dismiss without reading them. In June 1793 he told

[1] BL, c. 22, f. 45, 19 Jan. 1793.

Bedford that more morality had been 'distilled from the waters of Helicon than ever was procured from the withered skulls of metaphysicians or Philosophers'.[1] In spite of the influence of Seward, however, Southey was unable to accept Christianity as anything more than the purest of moral systems, and his disquiet about having to subscribe to the Thirty-Nine Articles at ordination continued to oppress him.

In the autumn of 1793 he did not go to Oxford but remained in the west of England. It was at this time that he read Godwin's *Political Justice* and seriously began to think of emigration as a way out of his awkward situation. His letters to Bedford during these months show that his religious unorthodoxy was becoming more extreme. On 30 October he announced that he was working on an essay arguing that Superstition was a greater evil than Impiety, and the train of thought which this essay started in his mind was not what one would expect of a candidate for ordination.

How very little have the doctrines of Christ been understood! We find neither bishops of 10,000 a year—jugged Jews or roasted heretics—or church and state—or test act in the whole gospel. . . . Those damned monks who smuggled and monopolized the scriptures for so many years—pieced them and patchd them from the Alexandrian Platonists—the Oriental fictions and Jewish Cabbala— till we read of persecution—metaphysics—scarlet whore and eating books—in the book of life of benevolence and simple truth.[2]

After this outburst he admits that Edmund Seward would not approve, but adds that he cannot accept everything that Seward believes, much though he has learnt from him.

A fortnight later he speculates gloomily about the merits of suicide and tyrannicide—the two things being closely linked in his mind—and among other things has this to say about religion. 'Religion—the word is so prostituted that I am sick of it. Instead of a benefit as intended by an all good and all

---

[1] Ibid., f. 47, 8 Feb. 1793; ibid., f. 65, July–Aug. 1793; ibid., f. 57, 12 June 1793. See also *LC*, i. 174.

[2] BL, c. 22, f. 72, 30 Oct. 1793.

wise creator it is degenerated into a curse. Nay the very scriptures at the same time that they contain the most important truths, may be alledged in vindication of every vice.'[1] At that moment he was unusually depressed. Brissot and twenty-one other Girondins had recently been executed, the news of which, he said, completely harrowed up his faculties. He looked round the world and everywhere found the same mournful spectacle: 'the strong tyrannising over the weak, man and beast; the same depravity pervades the whole creation'. Virtue, he thought, could only aspire to be content in obscurity, and he was ready to quarrel with his friends for not bringing him up to be a carpenter.[2] Two days later we find him telling Grosvenor Bedford's brother Horace that he would like to retire to America, as the poet Cowley wanted to do, and there 'till the earth and provide by honest industry the meal which my wife would dress with pleasing care'.[3] Ten days after this comes the first indication that Southey had been reading Godwin. He had borrowed *Political Justice* from the Bristol Library Society on 25 November, and evidently began to read it at once. On the 26th he wrote to Grosvenor Bedford in an enthusiastic vein: 'I am studying such a book! Talk of morality in—Potiphar's wife and Solomon's song! Democracy, real true democracy is but another word for morality—they are like body and soul.'[4]

It is easy to see why *Political Justice* should have overwhelmed Southey when he read it. The first edition in particular is written with a calm but exhilarating radicalism, which sets the whole moral world in a new perspective. Gratitude, for example, is proved to be a vice, and one is continually coming across sentences like the following: ' "But what becomes of the great duty of secrecy," ' Godwin imagines an objector saying, ' "which the incomparable Fenelon has

---

[1] BL, c. 22, f. 76, 14 Nov. 1793.

[2] *LC*, i. 189–90. Cuthbert Southey gives the date of the first part of the letter only. This passage was written on 14 Nov. 1793.

[3] This section was written on 16 Nov. 1793. BL, c. 22, f. 79. Cf. *LC*, i. 194.

[4] BL, c. 22, f. 80.

made a capital branch in the education of his Telemachus?"
It is annihilated.'[1] Godwin's criticism of 'things as they are'
is that of a thorough democrat, and monarchy and aristocracy
are subjected to a severe analysis. But this jacobinism is
combined with an unruffled dignity and restraint which would
have had a special appeal for Southey. Every man is bound to
resist every unjust proceeding on the part of the community,
he would learn, and if for the time being his resistance has no
visible effect he must wait without giving way to infantine
impatience. The doctrine of necessity would teach him to be
superior to the tumult of passion, and he will learn to 'reflect
upon the moral concerns of mankind with the same clearness
of perception, the same unalterable firmness of judgment,
and the same tranquillity as we are accustomed to do upon
the truths of geometry'.[2] Godwin's first edition breathes a fine
confidence in the ultimate triumph of reason. He deprecates
violence precisely because 'the phalanx of reason is invulner-
able; it advances with deliberate and determined pace; and
nothing is able to resist it'.[3] This alone was sufficiently
intoxicating, but Southey would have specially appreciated
the importance which Godwin attached to literature. Very
early in the first edition Godwin insisted on the influence
of literature in subverting tyranny and usurpation. A truth,
once discovered, is everlasting. And later, while criticizing
political associations, he describes them as

the expedients of men who do not know that truth is omnipotent.
It may appear to die for a time, but it will not fail to revive with
fresh vigour. If it have ever failed to produce gradual conviction,
it is because it has been told in a meagre, an obscure or a pusillani-
mous manner. Ten pages that should contain an absolute demonstration of the true interests of mankind in society could no otherwise
be prevented from changing the face of the globe, than by the
literal destruction of the paper on which they were written.[4]

Godwin had philosophical literature in mind here, but as he

[1] *Political Justice* (1793), i. 247.   [2] Ibid., pp. 316–17.
[3] Ibid., p. 203.   [4] Ibid., p. 211.

believed that there had often been more truth in the incidental observations of imaginative writers than in the systematic treatises of philosophers, Southey could feel that his poetic ambitions had a firm utilitarian justification.[1]

The doctrine of necessity was so evidently a vital part of Godwin's system that *Political Justice* temporarily converted Southey to a belief in the importance of metaphysics. In June and July 1794 he wrote to Grosvenor Bedford laboriously explaining the evidence for necessity—'an abstruse subject, but of the utmost importance'.[2] But although Southey could be carried away by Godwin for a time, the fundamental difficulty of his position remained, and continued to depress him. He was supposed to be studying to be a clergyman, and he could not conscientiously become one. 'To obtain future support—to return the benefits I have received, I must become contemptible infamous and perjured.'[3] In the early months of 1794 he brought himself to a resolution either to secure some honest employment or to emigrate. And then, some time about 11 June, Coleridge visited Oxford and met Southey for the first time. The fruit of their conversations was the scheme of Pantisocracy. No longer was emigration merely a picturesque way of committing suicide. ('Whilst life can be of service to one existing being', he told Horace Bedford in December 1793, 'it is criminal to quit it. What but this witholds me either from seeking happiness in France in America or in the grave?'[4]) In the idyllic colony in Kentucky or Pennsylvania, motives to vice would no longer exist, and Man would shine forth in his natural goodness.

As we know from *Biographia Literaria*, Coleridge owed much to the deep impression made on him by Southey's uprightness and integrity. And it is evident that Southey was equally responsive to the warm high spirits, the volatile intellectual excitement, that could make Coleridge's company so ex-

---

[1] *Political Justice* (1793), appendix to Book III, chap. vi.
[2] BL, c. 22, f. 113.
[3] Ibid., f. 82. Letter to H. W. Bedford, 11 Dec. 1793.
[4] Ibid., f. 83, 11 Dec. 1793.

hilarating. The tone of greater optimism and enterprise that is to be found in Southey's letters in the later part of 1794 is very striking. Part of this was the consequence of feeling that at last his future was settled. In a letter written in October he tells Grosvenor Bedford that life was desirable to him—'I am exalted in my own eyes—I am of consequence to others.' While getting ready to emigrate, the Pantisocrats acquired a remarkable reputation in Bristol. No longer was Southey an insulated being living in a city 'peopled with rich fools'. He was 'at once the object of hatred and admiration: wondered at by all; hated by the aristocrats; the very oracle of my own party'.[1] The excitement caused by the pantisocratic enterprise was remembered for many years. In 1818 James Jennings, a druggist who had worked in Bristol in the 'nineties, wrote an article defending Robert Owen's plans for the establishment of co-operative settlements for paupers. There he recalled the co-operative scheme projected by 'a few choice spirits of the year 1794, warm from the groves of Rhedycina and Granta'. Elsewhere, more imaginatively, Jennings describes how in those days in Bristol

> . . . rebel thought 'gainst Superstition rose,
> And many a mystic custom: all within
> Was wonder; and awakening, as from some
> Mysterious trance, I heard the hymnings high
> Of FREEDOM, big with hope and holiest love.[2]

Another of the Bristol jacobins wrote to the *Monthly Magazine* in 1819 to protest against Coleridge's denial in *Biographia Literaria* that he had ever been a 'democrat'. The Pantisocrats, this writer insisted, were 'positively and decidedly democratic'. *The Fall of Robespierre* was much read by 'the hot-headed and youthful democrats of Bristol, amongst whom I am not, like Mr. Coleridge, ashamed to say that I was

[1] Ibid., f. 132, 14 Oct. 1794; ibid., f. 82, 11 Dec. 1793; *LC*, i. 231, 8 Feb. 1795.
[2] *Monthly Magazine*, Jan. 1818, pp. 499–501; J. Jennings, *Poems* (1810), pp. 208–9.

one'. He attended the lectures which Coleridge gave in
Bristol in 1795, and gives an alarming extract from the first
which will not be found in the pages of *Conciones ad Populum*,
the authorized text.[1]

Animated by Pantisocracy and universal benevolence (a
benevolence, of course, not so universal as to include kings,
priests, and other pests), Coleridge and Southey caused much
alarm. Their visit to Nether Stowey in August 1794 was long
remembered in the neighbourhood.[2] The news of Robespierre's death arrived while they were there. Southey was
reported to have said that he would rather have heard of the
death of his own father, and even that Robespierre was 'a
ministering angel of mercy, sent to slay thousands that he
might save millions'. No doubt their main motive was to
shock the respectable, much as Becky Sharp exclaimed *Vive
Bonaparte!* in despite of Miss Pinkerton and to the horror of
Amelia. Not long after the visit to Nether Stowey, however,
Southey argued quite seriously in defence of Robespierre in a
letter to Horace Bedford. Coleridge, he said, had thought the
man one whose actions were great and bad; but he was now
inclined to agree with Southey that the actions of a man so
situated could not be judged by common laws, 'that Robespierre was the benefactor of mankind—and that we should
lament his death as the greatest misfortune Europe could
have sustained'.[3]

The Fall of Robespierre, the 'historic drama' which Coleridge

---

[1] *Monthly Magazine*, Oct. 1819, pp. 203–5. This article is signed 'Q', and
the address given as 'Park-street, Grosvenor-square'. It closes with a threat
which was unhappily never carried out. 'It is my intention, if I have leisure,
to commit to paper, as matter of history, not only the piquant sayings, the
amusing metaphors, and other *bonae*, of several wits and politicians, who had
temporary residence in Bristol in the years 1794, 5, and 6, but also many facts
which these *Pantisocrats*, as they were pleased to call themselves, think are
quite forgotten, and that no eye or ear witness to them now exists: that witness,
however, I am. . . .' It would be interesting to know who 'Q' was. I suspect he
was the 'Avonian' who in 1825 contributed two articles to the *Monthly* on the
poetry of Bowles.

[2] Mrs. Henry Sandford, *Thomas Poole* (1888), i. 100–6.

[3] BL, c. 22, f. 127, 22 Aug. 1794.

and Southey wrote between them at the end of August, does not enforce the moral that Robespierre was the benefactor of mankind. According to the concluding speech, put into the mouth of Barère, Robespierre's fall proves that France, regenerated, will never wear the despot's yoke, and will survive to liberate the world. On the other hand, while he is on the scene, Robespierre is presented with some sympathy. Southey would have felt for any man who said

> I stand here
> An isolated patriot—hemmed around
> By factions noisy pack.

When the younger Robespierre defends himself against charges of mercenary conduct, the tone is equally sympathetic. The main impression left by *The Fall of Robespierre*, however, is not one of sympathy for one party or another, but a confused hubbub of factious conflict. Coleridge inserted in the first act a song—

> Tell me, on what holy ground
> May domestic peace be found?

which indicates where the deepest sympathies of both poets lay.[1] For the genuine note of jacobinism, one must turn to the wholehearted indignation of *Wat Tyler*.

This poetic drama is mainly known because of its inconvenient publication in 1817, when Southey was an ardent supporter of the government. It would be difficult to claim much for it as a poem, but it has a freshness about it which is too often lacking in Southey's verse. 'Oh, with what glee I wrote it', he exclaimed to Grosvenor Bedford in 1817;[2] and the glee communicates itself. The play tells the story of the Peasants' Revolt in the fourteenth century. Southey probably got most of his facts from Burke and Paine. Burke had poured scorn on the medieval 'jacobins' in his *Appeal from the New to the Old Whigs*, and Paine had taken up the challenge in the

---

[1] *The Fall of Robespierre* (Cambridge, 1794), pp. 18, 21, and 13–14. See also C. Tilney, 'An Unpublished Southey Fragment', *National Library of Wales Journal* (1955), ix. 149–56.   [2] *SL*, iii. 59, 22 Feb. 1817.

second part of the *Rights of Man*. He vindicated Wat Tyler as
a man who had checked the rage and injustice of taxation in
his time. He was intrepid and disinterested; and the proposals
which he put to King Richard

were on a more just and public ground than those which had been
made to John by the Barons, and notwithstanding the sycophancy
of historians and men like Mr Burke who seek to gloss over a base
action of the court by traducing Tyler, his fame will outlive their
falsehood. If the Barons merited a monument to be erected at
Runnymede, Tyler merits one in Smithfield.[1]

Doubtless what made this theme irresistible to Southey was
the fancy that Wat Tyler was one of his ancestors. (His
maiden aunt, it will be remembered, was a Miss Tyler.) He
used to call the old rebel his uncle Wat, and thus inspired he
proceeded with unusual vigour.

> While the peasant works,—to sleep,
> While the peasant sows,—to reap,
> On the couch of ease to lie,
> Rioting in revelry;
> Be he villain, be he fool,
> Still to hold despotic rule,
> Trampling on his slaves with scorn!
> This is to be nobly born.[2]

John Ball's sermon on equality can still rouse a sympathetic
reader to enthusiasm, and even the treachery of the court is
presented with a full-blooded cheerfulness. John Ball goes to
his death with genuine unconcern, confident that truth will
have its hour, when it will blaze

> with sun-surpassing splendour,
> And the dark mists of prejudice and falsehood
> Fade in its strong effulgence.

The play closes with a high-spirited fling at courtly hypocrisy.

[1] *The Rights of Man*, ed. H. B. Bonner (1949), pp. 209–10. The story of
Wat Tyler was often retold in chap-books down to the beginning of the
nineteenth century.

[2] Southey, *Poetical Works* (1837–8), ii. 33–34.

Richard orders the troops to spare the rebels and take them prisoner.

> Let the blood-reeking sword of war be sheathed,
> That the law may take vengeance on the rebels.[1]

Southey insists on the rebels' moderation. They demand justice, not vengeance. The implication is that their moderation was a mistake. John Ball acknowledges that he was deceived by 'the seemly voice of pity', and the mighty movement he had led was in consequence ruined.

> I fear me I have been like the weak leech,
> Who, sparing to cut deep, with cruel mercy
> Mangles his patient without curing him.[2]

At that moment one can hear the voice of Robespierre's apologist.

Wat Tyler was written in the summer of 1794, when Southey's democratic fervour was at its height. By the autumn he seems to have taken fright a little at the violence of jacobinism. He was frightened, perhaps, at the violence in himself which found expression in jacobin sentiments. One motive for leaving England was his fear of civil war. In the summer of 1794 Hardy, Horne Tooke, Thelwall, and other democrats were under arrest and awaiting trial for high treason. When Southey told Bedford to come and join in the 'aspheterizing system' in America 'when the storm bursts on England',[3] one may suppose that he had the raging of Pittite tyranny in mind. But the acquittal of Hardy in November does not seem to have pleased him as much as one would expect. Nearly three weeks after Hardy's acquittal, and just before the acquittal of Horne Tooke, he wrote to Bedford pleading with him to avoid the storm that was coming. 'There are bad men and mistaken men in England who do not know that revolutions should take place in mind. Let the violence of either

[1] Ibid., p. 54.
[2] Ibid., p. 49.
[3] BL, c. 22, f. 120, 20 July 1794. 'Aspheterism' was a Coleridgean term for the renunciation of private property.

party prevail and the moderate will be equally proscribed.'[1] Southey may have been alarmed at the character of the rejoicing that greeted the acquittal of the English jacobins. The rejoicing had only been in certain places and in certain circles; but in London it had been general enough for Hardy to be drawn in triumph through the streets—a great change from the temper of December 1792 when Paine was found guilty with such inattention to legal forms. Erskine, the defending counsel, had compared himself then to the countryman arguing with Jupiter: 'I cannot fight against the thunder of authority.' In the same way, Erskine went on, 'I cannot fight against the universal voice of England.' Now, in 1794, there was something of Jupiter's thunder in Erskine's defence.

Pantisocracy was an escape from Jupiter in any possible incarnation. 'I shall regret those I leave', Southey told Horace Bedford, 'but you must all come when the fire and brimstone descends. Away runs Lot. Come to us in Kentucky.'[2]

This plan to leave the City of Destruction came to nothing, however. The failure was a trying experience for both Coleridge and Southey, and the latter began to revert to the misanthropic depression from which the American scheme had saved him. He had not now quite the same material reason for depression. Some money could be made by lecturing. He had had at least one article accepted by the *Telegraph* newspaper, and he was revising the text and correcting the proofs of his epic poem *Joan of Arc*, for which Joseph Cottle (a Bristol bookseller and publisher) had given him fifty guineas. Moreover, his school friend Charles Wynn offered him an annuity of £160 a year, and it was becoming clear that in one way and another he would be able to support himself and perhaps a wife and family. Indeed, this may well have been the decisive influence in cooling his zeal for pantisocratic emigration. Coleridge began to ask him reproachfully why he wrapped himself up 'in the Mantle of self-centering *Resolve*'.

---

[1] BL, c. 22, f. 138, 22 Nov. 1794.
[2] Ibid., f. 123, 1 Aug. 1794.

Southey, for his part, withdrew from company as much as possible, preferring solitary thought to uncongenial acquaintances. 'I am grown an acute observer of men', he told Grosvenor Bedford, 'and agree with Burns that "they are an ugly squad".'[1] His jacobinism finds utterance in outbursts against aristocracy. He longs to marry—he is in love with Edith Fricker, who is devoted to him but penniless—and he has to endure the thought that 'fools are squandering away daily what would make us happy'. He could curse them, himself, and the destiny which made him. He was in no mood to make himself agreeable to influential people. He was indignant that his friends should want him to seek the notice of Charles Wynn's brother, Sir Watkin Williams Wynn, or of Lord Carysfort. 'Sir!—the very idea of a great man disgusts me.' As for Lord Carysfort, he was a poet, true enough; but he was also a peer, and that was enough to make Southey decide not to visit him. Bedford had told Southey that 'the notice of *such a man* as Lord C. you must not despise'; and Southey commented that it was 'an odd sentence to address to me'. Already, moreover, Southey had formed the opinion of William Pitt that he was to keep all his life. 'It is not possible to express the contempt and abhorrence I feel for that man.'[2]

Something of this misanthropic jacobinism is expressed in *Joan of Arc*, written originally in 1793, and prepared for the press during 1795. There are attacks on the mighty ones of the earth and their ridiculous priests—

> prime ministers of death,
> Who stalk elated o'er their fields of fame,
> And count the thousands they have massacred,
> And with the bodies of the innocent, rear
> Their pyramid of glory!

Joan and her follower Conrade speak like disillusioned Pantisocrats.

---

[1] S. T. Coleridge, *Letters*, ed. E. L. Griggs (Oxford, 1956), i. 150, 19 Jan. 1795; BL, c. 22, f. 149, 13 May 1795.

[2] BL, c. 22, f. 147, 9 Feb. 1795; ibid., f. 150, 26 May 1795; ibid., f. 163, 1 Oct. 1795.

Along the weary pilgrimage of life
Together will we journey, and beguile
The dreary road, telling with what gay hopes
We in the morning eyed the pleasant fields
Vision'd before; then wish that we had reach'd
The bower of rest!

The subject of *Joan of Arc* was itself a striking innovation.
It was an English epic hostile to England, with a woman as
its main character. None the less, the general impression made
by the poem is not aggressively jacobin, as *Wat Tyler*, with
its firm, brutal rhythms and clear construction, undoubtedly
is. *Joan* is seriously weakened by decoration. Southey believed that a poem could be improved by setting out to
'spangle' it with similes. In *Joan of Arc* one can see him con-
sciously trying to achieve novelty, as when he extends the
range of the Miltonic simile by using Mexican or Muslim
references.

Such ardor for the fight
Burnt in each bosom, as young Ali felt
When to the assembled tribe Mohammed spake,
Asking for one his Vizier.[1]

Although (as the *Monthly Review* pointed out) a Crown
lawyer who wanted to make out a list of treasonable innu-
endoes would find plenty of scope for his talent in the poem as
a whole, it was still the work of a clever young poet rather
than that of a clever young jacobin. It is not altogether surprising that the aristocracy behaved with great liberality to
Joan. And Southey's comment on their liberality is significant. 'If they will favour me by forgetting that I have ever
meddled too much with public concerns, I will take care not
to awaken their memories.'[2]

For a time, at least, Southey was more eager to come to
terms with society than the other Pantisocrats, and Coleridge

---

[1] *Joan of Arc* (Bristol, 1796), pp. 166, 265–6, 198; NLW, 4812 D 162.
[2] *SL*, i. 30. Letter to Charles Wynn, May 1796.

accused him of deserting the cause of equality and virtue. 'O God!' he exclaimed, 'that *such a mind* should fall in love with that low, dirty, gutter-grubbing Trull, WORLDLY PRUDENCE!!'[1] In the autumn of 1795 Southey agreed to spend the winter in Portugal with his uncle, Herbert Hill, who was chaplain to the British Factory at Lisbon. He departed in November, and married Edith Fricker secretly, just before he left. He had renounced political enthusiasm, and was determined to look for the holy ground of domestic peace in some place nearer than the banks of the Susquehanna River.

Naturally enough he renounced Godwin too, or felt that he had outgrown him. 'The frequent and careful study of Godwin', he told Bedford in October, 'was of essential service—I read and all but worshipped. I have since seen his fundamental error—that he theorizes for another state, not for the rule of conduct in the present. I despise the man—I can confute his principles—but all the good he has done me remains.'[2] Southey does not go into detail about the permanent good that Godwin has done him. It may be that his enduring belief in the virtue of free and fearless speaking was confirmed by Godwin's insistence upon absolute sincerity. One thing, however, would certainly have appealed to him with even greater force than before. In the last chapter of *Political Justice*, Godwin refers to Addison's *Cato*: 'It probably happens, much oftener than we are willing to imagine, that "the post of honour", or, which is better, the post of utility, "is a private station".' It was in a private station that Southey had now resolved to live.

2. THE MISANTHROPIC REFORMER

The Rev. Herbert Hill probably hoped that a visit to Portugal would help his nephew to grow out of his youthful radicalism. The experience certainly had some effect on him.

---

[1] S. T. Coleridge, *Letters*, ed. E. L. Griggs (Oxford, 1956), i. 171, 13 Nov. 1795.
[2] BL, c. 22, f. 163, 1 Oct. 1795.

'I have learnt to thank God that I am an Englishman', he told
Wynn. Portuguese squalor and superstition made him feel
that though everything in England was not quite so well
ordered as in El Dorado, it was a better country to live in than
any other.[1] The visit did two things that were to be important
for Southey in the future. It interested him in the literature
and history of Spain and Portugal, and it gave him a strong
antipathy to Roman Catholicism.

He returned to England in May 1796 and settled down to
the study of law. It was an uncongenial profession, for Southey
did not like the idea of being concerned in criminal cases
that might be capital, nor did he relish taking part in law-
court debates. However, these things might be avoided in the
quieter parts of legal practice, and in the meantime he could
continue writing poetry. As he put it to Grosvenor Bedford at
this time, 'I have been in the crowd and have had my corns
trod upon, and therefore I chuse to take a snug bye path for
the future'.[2] He was, however, still very much of a radical. He
paid visits in radical circles in London,[3] and was a violent
anti-militarist. The anti-militarism may be illustrated by an
outburst prompted by the news that his friend T. P. Lamb had
become a soldier. Military officers, said Southey,

are the most ignorant impertinent and debauchd members of this
execrable state of society. If ever I were disposed to get out of the
world, I should prefer being shot for beating an ensign. I have
known so many horrible acts [of] oppressive barbarity exercised
by those liveried murde[rers] that I feel a most honest and hearty
hatred for [?] the gang.[4]

This sustains the misanthropic mood that accompanied the
break-up of Pantisocracy. Resentment, Southey observed once,
is the best antidote to vexation.[5] Jacobins had reason to be
vexed in the last four years of the eighteenth century. Their
hopes in the French Revolution itself were dashed, and reac-

---

[1] SL, i. 23, 26 Jan. 1796.   [2] BL, c. 22, f. 203 ,31 July 1796.
[3] For example, see LC, i. 305–6.
[4] BL, c. 22, f. 210, 25 Sept. 1796.
[5] SL, i. 259. Letter to Miss Barker, Feb. 1804

tion seemed firmly established at home and abroad. Repressive laws made political agitation difficult or impossible. The career of John Thelwall shows what reformers had to contend with. He was one of the men tried for treason in 1794, and acquitted. He resumed his political activities, but had to abandon them altogether when the 'Two Acts' of the winter of 1795–6 were passed. These made political meetings illegal unless specially authorized, and extended treason to cover speaking and writing as well as treasonable acts. For a time he tried to give historical lectures, but they were broken up by loyal mobs, and in the end he decided to retire to the country and take up farming. He visited Coleridge in Somerset, and while he was in the west country wrote some lines which expressed his weariness of the 'vain effort to redeem a Race enslav'd because degenerate'.

> Ah! let me then, far from the strifeful scenes
> Of public life (where Reason's warning voice
> Is heard no longer, and the trump of Truth
> Who blows but wakes The Ruffian Crew of Power
> To deeds of maddest anarchy and blood)
> Ah! let me, far in some sequester'd dell,
> Build my low cot. . . .[1]

He obtained a farm in Brecknockshire, at Llys-Wen, but was not a successful farmer. He achieved prosperity in the middle years of his life when he took up speech training.

At about the same time as Thelwall was uttering his despondency in Somerset, the *Morning Post* (in those days a paper with jacobin sympathies) remarked that the British public in general was cold and apathetic. 'Nothing seems to move us; events that are prosperous do not rouse us to joy; occurrences that are adverse do not incite us to sorrow.'[2] In this atmosphere the best that the English jacobins could do was to wait and hope for better days. The hope was not very

---

[1] J. Thelwall, *Poems chiefly written in Retirement* (1801), p. 129. This poem is dated 27 July 1797. For Llys-Wen, see Wordsworth's *Anecdote for Fathers*.

[2] *Morning Post*, 11 July 1797.

strong. John Aikin wrote an interesting analysis of this state
of mind in an article for the *Monthly Magazine*, published in
January 1799. He was one of a group of liberal dissenters who
contributed a great deal to science and literature in the later
eighteenth century. They welcomed the French Revolution
with enthusiasm, and some of them suffered for their beliefs,
notably Dr. Joseph Priestley in the Birmingham riots of 1791.
Aikin's article was one of a series called 'The Enquirer', and
his inquiry concerned the probability of the 'future melioration of the state of mankind'. He pointed out the apparently
unavoidable evils of life in manufacturing cities, the evident
hopelessness of abolishing war, the rivalries and enslavement
produced by the spirit of commerce. It was true that there had
been some improvement. Superstition had been weakened and
knowledge diffused—but only in Europe. What of China,
Africa, Turkey, Arabia, Persia, India? Only conquest could
effect their improvement, 'and what a Pandora's box does
that word *conquest* comprise!' The temper of Aikin's article is
best illustrated by quoting what he says about the reform of
abuses prevalent under absolute monarchs, and (one infers)
constitutional monarchs too. Such rulers will never pursue a
policy which jeopardizes their own power. Only the people
will reform abuses which spring from the exercise of sover-
eign authority.

But here is the great difficulty. How is it possible that the mass of
a nation should ever, in the hands of their old masters, become
enlightened enough to comprehend their evils, and the remedies
of them—should be able peaceably to deliberate about them, and
take proper steps for their relief—should avoid the snares of crafty
demagogues, and pursue steadily the right objects by the wisest
means; and, finally, amidst the unjust opposition they would be
sure to meet with, should preserve their minds from that irritation
which will in the end break out in acts of the most dreadful violence?

It is not enough to say that the people must first be enlightened, for rulers do their utmost to prevent enlightenment.
Aikin's conclusion is sombre:

The melioration of mankind by means of political revolutions is, indeed, a noble subject of speculation; and I am far from asserting that the hopes of patriots on this head are futile and visionary; but, for my own part, I have only the *wish* left—the *confidence* is gone.[1]

One can feel the full weight of Aikin's pessimism if one compares this article with a once-celebrated revolutionary tract, the Comte de Volney's *Ruins*. This, a survey of the rise and decline of civilization, was first published in Paris in 1791, and published by Joseph Johnson in an English version in 1795. It sold well, mainly as a popular handbook of infidelity. But it is not its arguments against Christianity that concern us here. In the earlier part of the book, Volney, visiting the ruins of Palmyra in the Syrian desert, is moved to meditate on the transience of earthly prosperity. Will not the fate of Palmyra also be the fate of Paris and of London? He is reproved by a spirit who tells him that the decline of civilization is the consequence of man's folly. This is no consolation to Volney, who sees no likelihood of the human race abandoning its follies.

To dissolve these fatal shackles, a miraculous concurrence of happy circumstances would be necessary. It would be necessary that a whole nation, cured of the delirium of superstition, should no longer be liable to the impressions of fanaticism; that, freed from the yoke of a false doctrine, it should voluntarily embrace the genuine system of morality and reason; that it should become at once courageous and prudent, wise and docile. . . .[2]

He is finally converted to optimism by a vision of the French Revolution—or rather of that universal revolution which the National Convention so confidently expected in November 1792. By the latter half of the nineties, however, it was difficult to regard the revolution as the 'miraculous concurrence of happy circumstances' which it seemed to Volney. Nothing was left but the pessimism from which Volney was only rescued by his vision.

That pessimism achieved its most notable statement in the Rev. T. R. Malthus's *Essay on the Principle of Population*,

[1] *Monthly Magazine*, Jan. 1799, p. 11.
[2] Volney, *The Ruins*, translated from the French (1795), p. 122.

first published anonymously in 1798. In spite of Malthus's later reputation as a callous reactionary, it could only have been written by one who had been brought up as a liberal. If the tenderness with which he speaks of the optimism he cannot share is partly a pose, it is a pose which no disciple of Burke could have adopted convincingly. The book was published, moreover, by Joseph Johnson, the friend of Paine and Blake, the publisher of Volney's *Ruins*, the man who spent the later months of 1798 in prison for printing a seditious pamphlet by Gilbert Wakefield. (Wakefield himself, by the way, was for a time Malthus's tutor.) Malthus's *Essay* will be considered more fully later, when Southey's objections to it are considered. It will be enough here to note that the *Essay* was an answer to Godwin's arguments in favour of human perfectibility. Malthus contended that sexual desire would always tend to produce more children than there was food for, and the population of the world was therefore inevitably subject to famine, disease, war, and vice. Malthus does not want to disbelieve in the possibility of human improvement. Within narrow limits some genuine improvement is possible. But, he argues, it is useless to slur over difficulties which are really there, and are insuperable. To ignore this is to invite the fate of Sisyphus, to condemn oneself to endless frustration.

Even Godwin had been a little disturbed by the myth of Sisyphus. His revision of *Political Justice*, published in 1796, shows that he has become aware of what he calls 'the principle of flux and reflux in human affairs'. Revolutions may lead only to the riveting anew of the chains of despotism.[1] Godwin, of course, does not allow himself to be dispirited by obstacles to improvement. All will be well at length. Men of good will must insist on freedom of inquiry, and gradually illumination will become general. It was probably some such faith as this which sustained the more determined jacobins in the last years of the century.

One agent of illumination was the *Monthly Magazine*. John

---

[1] *Political Justice* (1796), i. 277–83.

Aikin was the literary editor, and both Malthus and Godwin occasionally contributed. It was started in 1796 by Richard Phillips, not long after he had completed a prison sentence for selling Paine's *Rights of Man*. The magazine's prospectus made clear that it was going to make a stand for liberal principles against the encroachments of conservative obscurantism. In its first years of publication, Southey often contributed to it, mostly on literary subjects or in the form of miscellaneous poems. Naturally enough, he sympathized with the magazine's politics, and on one occasion he supplied it with a useful story. In 1797 his brother Tom, who was serving in the navy, had been taken prisoner by the French. He had been quite well treated, and Richard Phillips suggested to Robert Southey that he should get an account of the imprisonment to be published in the magazine. Presumably this was to offset the tendency to regard the French as revolutionary barbarians. 'For my own part', Southey wrote to his brother, 'I think the behaviour you received there cannot be too generally known.'[1]

In the *Monthly Magazine* the jacobins made a successful attempt to come to terms with a largely hostile society. By the comparative excellence of its non-political contributions, it found its way into the hands of those who were hostile to its principles. In a similar way, Southey's interest in antiquities, travels, and oriental literature enabled him to build up a reputation which extended beyond the circle of dissenters and other radical groups. This interest served to muffle the jacobinism which had hitherto often been perceptible in his published work. The muffling can be observed in the second edition of *Joan of Arc*, which appeared in 1798. He omitted two attacks on National Fasts, one in the fourth book, the other in the eighth. But he added many historical notes which served to emphasize the antiquarian rather than the political flavour of the poem. Thus, in the fifth and eighth books, he

---

[1] *SL*, i. 35, 9 Aug. 1797. The article appears in the *Monthly Magazine* for Aug. 1797, pp. 87–88.

inserted a number of notes to illustrate medieval warfare. At one point a prayer for heavenly aid is expanded, in order to allow for a long note on St. Aignan, the tutelary saint of Orleans.[1] Southey's motive in doing this sort of interpolation was simple historical curiosity. But the curiosity was itself stimulated by a desire to avoid the contentions of current politics.

Southey's jacobinism may have been moderated in other ways too. It would be interesting to know his precise reaction to a piece of literary task-work that he performed in April 1797, a translation of the second volume of Necker's book on the French Revolution. He worked at high speed, but the effort of translation (and it is a spirited piece of work) must have compelled him at any rate to attend to Necker's arguments. They were like Burke's. Necker insisted that the radical vice of the revolution was its tampering with the natural moral order. 'It is by permitting ourselves to be restrained by duty, by observing the great rules of morality, that we can acquire a confidence and firmness which may enable us to rule others and to govern ourselves.'[2] The last section of this volume is an essay on equality—the pursuit of which, says Necker, is incompatible with order, liberty, morality, or even individual happiness. It is a solvent of traditional social ties. The book is not impressively argued, and it certainly did not overturn Southey's levelling principles. This is clear from a sentence in a letter to Horace Bedford, written on 11 June 1797. 'I would destroy Greatness and Wealth because I wish to annihilate Poverty and all the vices that arise from want.' In its context, however, this sentiment sounds rather less revolutionary. It should be explained that at this time Southey and his wife were staying at Christchurch in Hampshire. On Sunday, 11 June, he went to church, and afterwards met the local clergyman, who evidently impressed him very

---

[1] *Joan of Arc* (1798), v. 24.
[2] J. Necker, *On the French Revolution*. Translated from the French (1797), ii. 27.

favourably. Writing to Horace Bedford the same day, he said that the best effect of a church establishment was that it placed in every village a man who had had the education of a scholar and generally had the manners of a gentleman. This last word made him wince a little, for he added:

I hate the word gentleman, it has been so prostituted to puppies—but what can one substitute? Under the new order of things this advantage ought to be preserved, and public instructors scattered over the country. I hoped at one time to have seen something like the Grecian schools of philosophy revived in France—but France has disappointed me in her internal conduct, and if it be true that Babœuf be put to death—she has now no man left whom we may compare with the Gracchi. For me I attack not establishments because their titles disgust me. I would destroy Greatness and Wealth because I wish to annihilate Poverty and all the vices that arise from want.[1]

The admiration for the Church by law established is something new, and significant for the future. In the previous September, for example, he had confided to Grosvenor Bedford that the life of a country clergyman with a tolerable income was an enviable one—but only because he lived in the country where he could have solitude. And Southey immediately exclaims: 'Would to God his creed was such as a contemplative man could with truth profess!' But, he says, he believed too firmly in the faith of Jesus Christ to become 'the perjured defender of its corruptions'.[2] For one reason or another his point of view had shifted slightly during the next nine months. And clearly the Southey who saw advantages in an established church was not quite the Southey who, when lecturing in Bristol in the spring of 1795, apostrophized Paine as the 'hireless Priest of Liberty! unbought teacher of the poor! Chearing to me is the reflection that my heart hath ever acknowledged—that my tongue hath proudly proclaimed—the Truth and Divinity of thy Doctrines!'[3]

[1] BL, c. 22, f. 194, 11 June 1797.   [2] Ibid., f. 209, 25 Sept. 1796.
[3] BM MSS. Adds. 30,927, f. 5. Letter to Tom Southey, 9 May 1795. This, at least, is what Southey *said* that he said.

Even in 1797, however, Southey admired Babeuf, and
Babeuf was a more extreme jacobin than Paine. He had engaged in a conspiracy against the Directory and was arrested
in May 1796. He was a radical equalitarian, and attacked the
Directory as a betrayal of the revolution. He was inspired by
the communistic ideals held by Robespierre and Saint-Just,
and shared their view that only the 'proletariat'—*les gens
gueux*—were trustworthy revolutionaries. To defeat the
bourgeois, unite the people. Mary Wollstonecraft had known
Babeuf, and said that she had never seen anyone of greater
ability or equal strength of character. Southey met Mary
Wollstonecraft in London in 1797, and she may have inspired
him with her enthusiasm for Babeuf. He certainly knew one
of the published collections of Babeuf's papers which were
seized at the time of his arrest, because in a notebook which
Southey kept at this time there is a passage transcribed from
the first Mandate of the Secret Committee, directed to each of
the principal agents of the conspiracy. Southey gave it the
title 'Duty of insurrection'. It is an eloquent vindication of
the right of those inspired by liberty to make themselves the
coercive saviours of their fellow-citizens.[1] It is difficult to
believe that Southey ever seriously assented to this doctrine.
But it would appeal to him in moods when he wished he was the
Exterminating Angel. He agreed with another former Pantisocrat, Robert Allen, that man was a beast, and that a year's
crusade to benefit mankind would cure anyone of prejudices in
their favour. Even so, he did not concur in the mysterious
'gunpowder plot' which Allen proposed for 'the improvement
of a rascally public'. The world must be mended by the total
reorganization of society, he said; and it was part of his level-
ling-Christian faith that such reorganization was inevitable.[2]

[1] See *Common-Place Book*, 4th ser. (1850), p. 65. Transcribed from a notebook in the Fitz Park Museum, Keswick, dated 2 Jan. 1797–16 Aug. 1798.
Cf. *Copie des Pièces saisies dans le local que Babœuf occupoit lors de son arrestation*
(Paris, an V [1797]), p. 173. For Mary Wollstonecraft's opinion, see *QR*
(1831), xlv. 177.
[2] BL, c. 22, f. 201, 26 July 1796; ibid., f. 215, 8 Dec. 1796.

The letter which Southey wrote at the time when he heard the rumour of Babeuf's death shows some disappointment with France, and one may guess that he was chiefly attracted to Babeuf because of his cry of 'the Revolution betrayed!' In matters of foreign policy, however, Southey's sympathies remained with the French rather than with his own government right up till the end of 1799. In the October of that year the French achieved some remarkable victories. The British expedition in Holland was compelled to withdraw, and Masséna wrested control of Switzerland from the Russian army. In Italy, France was paramount; and although the French expedition to Egypt had come to nothing, this was offset by Bonaparte's dramatic escape. On Tuesday, 15 October, the *Morning Post* was reporting a serious fall in the Funds, and the issue for that day contained an editorial paragraph on the 'alarming change in the affairs of the Allies'. On Wednesday the 16th the same paper commented scornfully on officially inspired rumours of peace negotiations. 'In the hour of victory Ministers disclaim peace, unless signed at Paris, at the head of a Russian army, with a French monarch.' If a reasonable peace were to be obtained, it would be a striking instance of the moderation of the French, not of the wisdom of the British Government.

The *Morning Post* detested Pitt, as is indicated by its publishing *Fire, Famine, and Slaughter* and *The Devil's Thoughts*.[1] In the spring of 1798, however, it became anti-gallican as well. There was fear of an invasion of Britain, while Switzerland was actually incorporated into the French continental system. When the fear of invasion had subsided, however, and the Swiss had shown little inclination to rise against their French conquerors when they had the opportunity, the anti-gallican sentiment became less militant. In the autumn of 1799 the *Morning Post* was not especially hostile to France, though it was not friendly. Southey reacted to the good fortune of the

[1] See *Poetical Works of S. T. Coleridge*, ed. E. H. Coleridge (1912), pp. 237–40, 319–23.

French with wholehearted sympathy, however, if one may judge by a letter to Humphry Davy, dated 18 October. 'Massena, Buonaparte, Switzerland, Italy, Holland, Egypt, all at once! the very spring-tide of fortune! It was a dose of gaseous oxide to me, whose powerful delight still endures.'[1] The *Morning Post* might speak of the Directory's ambition and insolence. Southey made no such reservations.

It is not easy, on the evidence available, to plot the course of Southey's political sympathies between 1797 and 1799. Something can be learnt from Charles Lloyd's novel *Edmund Oliver*, partly because Southey was closely associated with Lloyd when he was writing the book, partly because of the obvious portrait of Southey given in the character of Charles Maurice.[2] Maurice utters anti-military sentiments and condemns commerce. So far he is a disciple of Rousseau. But he is also a critic of the moral experiments of 'modern philosophy', and argues that human happiness must be built upon the domestic affections. He is opposed to the radical Mr. D'Oyley's sanguinary attacks upon Ministers, for though they are evil, they cannot help themselves. 'We make monstrous situations', he tells D'Oyley, 'and then complain if monsters fill them.' However, Maurice is more of a leveller than D'Oyley, although he believes in gradual methods—very gradual. No good effected by force can be lasting. Therefore Maurice desists from meddling with political bodies and, conforming to a system of complete passiveness, winds himself into the bosoms of his neighbours. He attacks the root of the evil, 'the selfishnesses of human nature'.

I would excite my friends to follow the example, and trusting that the process of amelioration thus begun, would make a *sure* though *slow* advancement, I would consider myself as a co-operator with infinite benevolence, and should look forward with hope to the glorious day when all wars and fightings, and their necessary

---

[1] *Fragmentary Remains of Sir Humphry Davy*, ed. J. Davy (1858), p. 39.

[2] 'Lloyd's book comes on but slowly', he told Tom Southey on 15 Mar. 1798; 'I now correct the proofs for him, the second volume is only advanced 88 pages.' BM MSS. Adds. 30,927, f. 31.

causes, distinction of rank and person, should be banished from the earth!

Maurice, indeed, believes that ardent and active spirits who are stung to rage by pity have a contribution to make to the improvement of society. But they cannot do without the solid, constructive labours of 'patient, persevering, and subdued virtue'.[1]

If Charles Maurice is a picture of Southey as he saw himself, one must allow that it is confirmed, in outline at least, by the poems he was composing at this time. These were written as contributions to the *Morning Post*.[2] Southey visited London in the winter of 1797–8, and arranged with Daniel Stuart, the editor of that paper, to contribute verses regularly. The temper of the greater part of his contributions is one of calm and sober sentiment, but emotions are sometimes expressed which show that it would be incorrect to describe Southey simply as a cheerful 'co-operator with infinite benevolence'. Naturally enough, the tone is sometimes strongly democratic. He writes an inscription for a monument in Smithfield for Wat Tyler, such as was suggested by Paine; he condemns the 'guilty patience' of the oppressed people; and hopes that the time would soon come when

> The rich, the mighty tyrants of the earth,
> Shall hide them in the mountain dens, and call
> Upon the mountain rocks to fall on them. . . .[3]

He writes poems in praise of Charlotte Corday and Joseph Gerrald the Scottish reformer.[4] As late as 1803, indeed, he wrote lines in praise of the Irish rebel, Robert Emmet, though his praise then was rather for his latent loyalty than for his actual rebellion. These were democratic heroes, but it

---

[1] C. Lloyd, *Edmund Oliver* (Bristol, 1798), i. 178–87.
[2] Nearly all his contributions are anonymous, and it is difficult to be sure always that a poem is Southey's, especially when it is satirical. The tone of his serious effusions, however, is usually unmistakable.
[3] *Morning Post*, 12 Feb., 27 Feb., and 2 Apr. 1798.
[4] Ibid., 13 July 1798 and 9 Feb. 1799.

was not their democratic hopes that stirred Southey's imagination. He warms (if that is the word) to their stoical endurance.
He thinks of Gerrald banished to Australia:

> Long captivity
> Subdu'd his mortal part, but not his mind,
> Th' unconquerable mind: for chains to him,
> And banishment, and what the world thinks shame,
> These were his triumphs.

The modern reader will recall the conclusion to Wordsworth's
sonnet on Toussaint L'Ouverture, the West Indian patriot.

> There's not a breathing of the common wind
> That will forget thee; thou hast great allies;
> Thy friends are exultations, agonies,
> And love, and man's unconquerable mind.

The 'unconquerable mind' derives ultimately, I suppose, from
the 'unconquerable will' of Milton's Satan, but the warm and
cheerful confidence of Wordsworth's poem makes the Stoic-
Satanic associations of the phrase seem strangely remote.
Southey, however, shows his 'gloomy capability of walking
through desolation'. The same quality is equally evident in
the poem commemorating the execution of Charlotte Corday.
She died in vain. Her sacrifice was useless because her lot
was cast in a bad world. Fortunately, Southey remarks, she
did not know this.

> Thou didst not live
> To see so fair a morning overcast,
> To see thy dearest hopes all overthrown,
> Yea, with most painful wisdom, to be taught
> Man's abject state and utter worthlessness.

Jacobins are justified because, like the rats who devoured Bishop
Hatto, they are destroyers of the 'pests of mankind'.[1] Their
names will be preserved in immortal verse (by Robert Southey)

---

[1] 'God's Judgment on a Wicked Bishop' was published in the *Morning Post*,
27 Nov. 1799. The exceptionally bad weather of the summer and autumn of
1799 is clearly referred to in the opening stanza, so that it has a plain contemporary reference. The sixth stanza seems to refer to Malthusianism.

to admiring generations, but not on grounds that would have appealed to an optimistic philosopher. Even when the martyr's blood is fruitful, as in 'Telemachos', Southey's mood is not optimistic. Telemachos was the monk whose self-sacrificial descent into the arena brought about the ending of the gladiatorial games at Rome. This is how Southey describes his action:

> Now turn your eyes on him,
> O ye, whose honest hearts
> Revolt against the vices of mankind,
> Who cry aloud against iniquity!
>
> View the mad multitude—
> Behold your fate in his!
> Hark to their yells, their execrating cries,
> That drown the murder'd Hermit's pray'r of death.
>
> He fell—so ever fall
> Th' amenders of mankind.
> Awaken'd wrath forbade the accursed sports,
> For never flow'd the Martyr's blood in vain.[1]

It would have been reasonable to attribute the ending of the sports to remorse felt by the multitude when their tempers had cooled. It is characteristic of Southey, in this mood at least, that he should mention only 'awaken'd wrath'.

Southey recognizes that his 'painful wisdom' is not consistent with an active jacobinism, and many of his poems in the *Morning Post* praise retirement. One published on 11 April 1798 illustrates the tone of many such pieces. 'Ah me!' he exclaims, addressing the River Avon,

> that thus might flow
> My noiseless tide of life thro' some calm vale!
> That down the stream my little bark might sail,
> Glide quietly towards that shoreless sea,
> Then fearless launch upon eternity!

It seems that when he was pressed for subjects, Southey

---

[1] *Morning Post*, 7 Aug. 1799.

resorted to translation. Some of the poems he selected (mainly from Spanish and Portuguese) appealed to him because they praised a withdrawal from the active life. There is a sonnet on the abdication of Charles the Fifth, for example, a suitable subject for a sermon on contempt for worldly glory.[1] Individual action, indeed, seemed important to Southey. In a poem published on 4 October 1798 he addressed a friend who had complained of melancholy. His advice is to 'build th' historic pile' (presumably meaning to write history) and to visit the haunts of wretchedness.

> Relieve the widow, and the orphan bless,
> And find, in active virtue, happiness.

Southey's deeds of active virtue were many. At the end of 1797 he was engaged in planning with his friends John May and Anthony Carlisle a convalescent home for poor people, a scheme which led him to discover that charitable funds were often misappropriated to an extraordinary extent.[2] He tried to persuade his friends not to eat sugar—an economic boycott of the slave trade. He had little success, which astonished and disheartened him. What, he asked John May, 'can be expected from those, who will not remedy so horrible an iniquity, by so easy an exertion?' He published an edition of Chatterton's works for the benefit of the poet's sister and niece, and took some trouble to obtain money for the family of a midshipman who was killed on his brother Tom's ship.[3] He wrote a poem about this man's death, which appeared in the *Morning Post* for 22 June 1798, and is reprinted in his collected works with the title of 'The Victory'. It conveys the contrast between public rejoicing and private sorrow with a poignancy which is not here too seriously weakened by the declamatory style. Southey is often at his best on this theme, as is shown by 'The Battle of Blenheim'. Another striking example is an un-

---

[1] *Morning Post*, 25 July 1798.

[2] Ironically enough, it was Southey's great foe Henry Brougham who did more than anyone to end these abuses.

[3] *SL*, i. 53, 55–56; *LC*, i. 318–19.

reprinted 'eclogue', 'The Battle of Bosworth'.[1] Its diction is conventional and occasionally ludicrous, but this does not spoil the pathos of the desperate mother's impossible questions to the man who has travelled by the battle-field where her son has fought. Southey never approaches the achievement of Wordsworth in this kind of subject—in 'The Ruined Cottage', for example, the poem that was afterwards incorporated into *The Excursion*, Book I. The main reason is that Wordsworth suffers far more intimately with poor Margaret than Southey ever could. Southey's tendency to declaim suggests a man standing apart from the objects of his pity. He thought that the chief cause of 'the incalculable wretchedness of society' was that 'the rich are strangely ignorant of the miseries to which the lower and largest part of mankind are abandoned'.[2] In some of his poems he does his best to stir the imagination of his readers. But 'The Complaints of the Poor' (to take one instance) explicitly observes the sufferings of poor people from the point of view of the well-to-do man who walks through the streets in a warm great-coat. Southey's objections to Wordsworth's 'Idiot Boy' are revealing. He complained that the subject was trivial and certainly not worth 500 lines. 'No tale less deserved the labour that appears to have been bestowed upon this. It resembles a Flemish picture in the worthlessness of its design and the excellence of its execution.'[3] He wrote a poem himself on an idiot, which was published in the *Morning Post* for 30 June 1798. This was about an idiot whose mother died. He was unable to understand what had happened, and dug her body up again on the night of the funeral, seeking to warm it in front of the fire.

> Why, mother, do you look so pale,
> And why are you so cold?

Southey, in short, could appreciate the pathos of the bereaved idiot, but could not enter into the intense joy and pain of

---

[1] Some lines of it are reproduced in *Notes and Queries*, Feb. 1956, p. 82.

[2] *LC*, i. 317. Letter to John May, 26 June 1797.

[3] *Critical Review*, xxiv. 200. Southey's review of *Lyrical Ballads*.

mother-love which is the main strength of Wordsworth's poem. On the other hand, Southey liked the 'Female Vagrant'. She, after all, was a deserving object of charity.

There is little joy in Southey's poetry. When one turns from him to Wordsworth, it is the warmth and tenderness which is more welcome than anything. Southey is obsessed with in-security and death—the obsession makes his idiot poem extremely powerful. Occasionally he can be really harrowing. One instance is the poem on the evacuation of Toulon.[1] It describes the separation of husband and wife when they are trying to escape with the British fleet. The man succeeds in scrambling into a boat, but his wife does not and in despera-tion throws her baby to him. She does not throw it far enough, and it drowns before her eyes. She plunges after it, and is drowned too. The opening passage had described the Toulon rebels as base betrayers of their struggling country. Now France has her revenge, and Southey exclaims:

> The wheels of destiny roll on, and woe,
> Woe to the mortal arm that would impede
> Their irresistible way!

No doubt it was in this frame of mind that Southey could sympathize with Robespierre and Babeuf.

It does not look as though Southey shared to any great extent the revulsion of feeling against the French that many reformers experienced in the spring of 1798. As was noted earlier, the *Morning Post* became quite sharply anti-gallican for a time, and Coleridge published in it the poem generally known as 'France, an Ode'. Its original title was 'The Recantation'. Southey's poetical contributions at this time show little sign of patriotic feeling, although in July he did send in a poem on 'The Spanish Armada'.[2] This is written in a spirit of general defiance against would-be invaders of Great Britain. But it is anti-Catholic, not anti-gallican, and it is worth recall-ing that 'The Battle of Blenheim' was published a fortnight later.

---

[1] *Morning Post*, 7 Feb. 1799.   [2] Ibid., 26 July 1798.

Southey would not have cared to have a poem of his published under the title of 'recantation'. A signed 'Inscription
for a Monument at Merida' makes this clear.

> If thou hast walk'd
> Uprightly through the world, proud thoughts of joy
> Will fill thy breast in contemplating here
> Congenial virtue. But if thou hast swerv'd
> From the right path, if thou hast sold thy soul
> And serv'd, a hireling, with apostate zeal,
> The cause thy heart disowns; oh! cherish well
> The honourable shame that sure this place
> Will wake within thee. . . .[1]

But a marked change occurred at the end of 1799. Bonaparte
had placed himself firmly in power by the *coup d'état* of the
18th Brumaire (10 November). In the last days of the year
the constitution of the Abbé Sieyès was published, and was
somewhat brutally reviewed by Coleridge in the *Morning
Post* for 26 and 31 December. It marked the end of liberty
in France, he argued, for from henceforth all power would
derive from Bonaparte. Southey's reaction to the new constitution is indicated in a postscript to a letter written to
Grosvenor Bedford on 1 January 1800. 'Damn the French!—
that came heartily from the depths of a Jacobine heart.'[2] By
1801 he had mournfully conceded that France had played the
traitor with liberty. He was sorry for it, because Bonaparte
had had his honest days. 'Why had not the man perished
before the walls of Acre in his greatness and his glory? I *was*
asked to write a poem upon that defeat, and half-tempted to do
it because it went to my very heart.'[3]

At the same time as Southey lost faith in France, he became
more acquiescent in the actions of the British Government. He
even secured a temporary appointment under the government
in 1801, as private secretary to Isaac Corry, Chancellor of the
Irish Exchequer. He would have been indignant if anyone had

[1] Ibid., 30 Mar. 1798.   [2] BL, c. 23, f. 80.
[3] *SL*, i. 180. No date given, except 'London, 1801'. Probably November.

suggested that he had sold his soul, and served, a hireling, the cause his heart disowned. All the same, it is unlikely that he would actually have composed a poem like the Merida 'Inscription' while acting as Corry's secretary. On his way to Dublin he wrote to Miss Barker that he was become acquainted with a character with whom he had been long at variance— Mr. Worldly Wiseman. Some days later, he wrote in high spirits to Grosvenor Bedford. He was no richer for his appointment, he said, 'but my shoulders are lighter, Grosvenor. Look at the picture in the Pilgrim's Progress! What happened to Christian when he saw the cross? *He* put nothing in his pocket either.'[1] Southey had not passed through Bunyan's wicket gate, and Evangelist would have had some severe things to say about Southey's confidence that he would from henceforth live by honest neighbours in credit and good fashion. He was now an accepted member of society. No longer, as in 1795, did withdrawal from the world seem to offer the only tolerable future.

3. THE BELLICOSE DEMOCRAT

Southey's youthful jacobinism was turning into something a good deal more conformist. Probably the most important reason for this was the loss of direction suffered by radical politics after 1795. Unless one were simply to support the French, there was no hope to sustain those who had been excited by the prospect of a total renovation of society opened up by the French Revolution. The state of mind that resulted from this loss of hope was analysed with great acuteness by William Godwin, in *Thoughts occasioned by Dr Parr's Spital Sermon* (1801). He points out that many of those who were identified with revolutionary principles in 1797 had since become supporters of the established order. This was not because of any increased distaste for the proceedings in France: the Directory was far more civilized than Robespierre.

[1] *SL*, i. 172–3, 10 Oct. 1801; ibid., p. 176, 20 Oct. 1801.

It was certainly not an increase in the danger of revolution in Britain. But radical zeal requires hope. Since the hope had disappeared, the influence of prevailing institutions was bound to transmit itself more widely.

It is seldom that we are persuaded to adopt opinions, or re-persuaded to abandon them, by the mere force of arguments. The change is generally produced silently, and unperceived except in its ultimate result, by him who suffers it. Our creed is, ninety-nine times in a hundred, the pure growth of our temper and social feelings. The human intellect is a sort of barometer, directed in its variations by the atmosphere which surrounds it. Add to this, that the opinion which has its principle in passion (and this was generally the case with the opinions of men on the topic of the French revolution) includes in its essence the cause of its destruction.[1]

It was the passage containing these words that moved Coleridge to feel remorse at having ever spoken unkindly of Godwin. The copy of the pamphlet in the British Museum contains a note in Coleridge's hand which asserts that he can remember few passages 'that contain more just philosophy in appropriate, chaste, and beautiful diction than the five following pages. They reflect equal Honor on Godwin's Head and Heart.' Coleridge recognized the justice of Godwin's analysis—and Godwin is stating with his usual trenchancy the tragedy of his and Coleridge's generation. He states it again later when discussing Malthus's *Essay on Population*.

The intercourse of the world has a powerful tendency to blunt in us the sentiments of enthusiasm, and the spirit of romance; and, whatever truth we may suppose there to be in the doctrine of the progressive nature of man, it is so far remote from the transactions of ordinary life, and the feelings which impel us in such transactions to bend to the routine of circumscribed and unspeculative men, that it can with difficulty preserve its authority in the midst of so strong a contagion.[2]

So remote from the transactions of ordinary life. It was *Caleb Williams* that showed Things as they Are; and the world presented in that novel is a long way from the Reign of Mind.

[1] W. Godwin, *Thoughts*, &c. (1801), pp. 8–9.   [2] Ibid., p. 61.

Southey provides a fine example of the process of reconciliation to the established order, as Godwin describes it—gradual, and unperceived except in its ultimate result by him who suffers it. In 1801 he could still feel a most radical hostility to William Pitt; and it is only fair to remember that when Southey accepted a post under the government, Pitt was no longer Prime Minister. He had resigned in February 1801, and his place was taken by Henry Addington. In retrospect, Southey associated his greater goodwill for England with this change of Ministers. It cannot be said of him that this goodwill was bought with a salary, for he found the work of private secretary to Isaac Corry exasperatingly futile, and resigned in the spring of 1802. Southey was impressed by the Addington ministry's genuine desire for peace, which brought about the settlement at Amiens in 1802. He also admired its unwillingness to make use of extraordinary powers. (Habeas Corpus, suspended since 1798, was restored in 1801.) Southey's attachment to England was also strengthened by disquieting developments in France which he would have read about in the *Morning Post*. In January 1802 that paper criticized Bonaparte for behaving in a dispute with the Legislature more like a general with his army than the first magistrate of a free country. On 22 July it noted Bonaparte's preoccupation with military affairs—his leading object was to foster the martial spirit. In August he made himself First Consul for life, and took it upon himself to 'restore liberty and equality to the earth'. This prospect gave the *Morning Post* little pleasure: 'We know what his Liberty and Equality would be, the subjection and ruin of every country, to extend the controul and raise the greatness of France; the slavery and ruin of France, when they are necessary to exalt his power and diffuse his glory.'[1] The *Morning Post*'s apprehensions were increased by the report (published on 25 August) that the French government had ordered the seizure of all English newspapers and forbidden

[1] *Morning Post*, 9 Aug. 1802.

their future circulation. The official French newspaper, the *Moniteur*, had earlier in the month attacked the Addington ministry for permitting the British press to foment rebellion in France. Certainly the *Morning Post*'s references to the proposed changes in the French constitution were not respectful. Southey found it easy to share this anti-gallican sentiment. 'I grow more John-Bullish every time I look into a newspaper', he told Wynn in October 1802.[1] Still, he evidently agreed with the *Morning Post* that the evils of the French government did not justify going to war with France. As late as 12 May 1803, when the Peace of Amiens was clearly breaking down, he wrote to his brother Tom that war seemed inevitable, 'and yet God knows what it is all about'. War was declared later in the month, and by 30 May Bonaparte was already 'that damned Corsican rascal'. On 7 June Southey was fiercely hoping that offensive measures would be taken against France. 'Defensive war will not do. It offers no hope, and would break the spirit of the nation.'[2]

Southey was now swept away by the military enthusiasm of the time, which was doubly reinforced by the threat of a French invasion. 'I am damning the French impudence like everybody else', 'I could shake hands with Mr Wyndham'— these cordial expressions of national unity are something new in Southey's correspondence.[3] The unity seems to have been very general. Southey claimed that the anti-gallican spirit raged most violently among those who were most hostile to the previous war, and there was some truth in this, at least under the impact of the invasion scare. The Foxite opposition, which had given a qualified support to the government at the time of the invasion alarm of 1798, now joined wholeheartedly in defence measures. Even Richard Phillips of the *Monthly Magazine* suggested that long bayonets should be issued to the troops so that they could resist the invaders more

[1] NLW, 4811 D 92. Cf. *SL*, i. 207–8. Warter has dated the letter incorrectly.

[2] BM MSS. Adds. 30,927, ff. 86 and 88; NLW, 4811 D 103.

[3] NLW, 4811 D 102, 103, 26 May, 7 June 1803.

efficiently. Hazlitt, though a life-long admirer of Napoleon, seems to have been at one with his more loyal fellow-country-men in uniting to fight the French should they attempt to land. It is true that, if one may judge from the many pamphlet and broadside exhortations published at this time, some of the poorer people were apathetic because they felt they had nothing to lose by a French invasion. The Mayor of Leicester thought there was something more perilous than apathy affecting the common people. He informed the Home Office that if there should be a scarcity of bread, 'a fourth of the population would join the French Standard if they had an opportunity'.[1] Some such sullen hostility may have accounted for the indifference which Henry Cockburn detected behind the bustle of amateur soldiering in Edinburgh in 1803. His own comment was that people simply could not imagine the consequences of an invasion. 'But thinking men were in a great and genuine fright, which increased in proportion as they thought.' War in a country like Great Britain would give the whole system a dreadful shock.[2]

Under the stress of these apprehensions, Southey expressed some surprisingly conservative sentiments. He told William Taylor of Norwich, who was a most emphatic radical, that his own politics approached more nearly to Windham's than to Taylor's. Taylor was curious to know just what he meant by this, and if he meant more than that he sympathized with the anti-jacobin Windham's national spirit. Perhaps Southey did not mean more than this. But it is curious to find him saying that if he had held the religious opinions in 1794 that he did in 1803, he would not have scrupled to become a minister of the Church of England.[3] Later correspondence, and Southey's contributions to the *Annual Review*, make it quite clear that Southey had not in fact become an orthodox Angli-can, and that he still held strong views on the pernicious effects

[1] J. L. and B. Hammond, *The Town Labourer* (1925), p. 80.
[2] H. Cockburn, *Memorials of his Time* (Edinburgh, 1856), p. 196.
[3] J. W. Robberds, *Memoir of William Taylor* (1843), i. 460–5, 23 June and 3 July 1803.

of the Thirty-Nine Articles. What happened in 1803 was that he was swept away by an emotional impulse of national unity which made his jacobin opinions, political and theological, seem unimportant.

The patriotism endured, but soon took an anti-Ministerial turn. By November 1803 poor Addington's government was 'a *Duncery*',[1] and naturally he had nothing but contempt for the new administration formed by Pitt in 1804. In September 1803 he went to live in Keswick, and soon settled down to a life of 'clockwork regularity' in which the alarms of war seemed very distant. Southey told Charles Danvers that Dr. Edmundson had raised eighteen volunteers only. 'The truth is we are safe by situation, and so want the French to land —that the newspapers may not be quite so intolerably stupid.' (Wordsworth, it will be recalled, was disgusted with the apathy of the Keswick people. At Grasmere they turned out almost to a man.[2]) In this atmosphere of security, Southey's jacobinism reappeared. His ideas at this time can be most conveniently studied in his contributions to the *Annual Review*. For several years his work for this journal provided him with a substantial part of his income. He regarded it as wearisome drudgery, but there was one compensation. Reviews of historical works, at least, gave him an opportunity of getting at his own opinions, and bringing them into some order in a first sketch.[3] Some of the articles are written with obvious zest. In the number for 1804, for example, he wrote a spirited attack on an *Address from the Society for the Suppression of Vice*. The vice they suppress, he pointed out, was exclusively that of the lower orders. Take sabbath-observance, for example. It is only the poor who have any motive to buy and sell on Sundays, because for them six days are usually too little for the work which they are compelled to do. To prosecute small shop-keepers and street-vendors who sell provisions on a Sunday is

[1] NLW, 4811 D 115. Letter to Charles Wynn, 11 Nov. 1803.

[2] BM MSS. Adds. 30,928, ff. 37–38, 7 Nov. 1803; Wordsworth, *Early Letters*, ed. E. de Selincourt (Oxford, 1935), p. 341, 14 Oct. 1803.

[3] *SL*, i. 321. Letter to John Rickman, 1 May 1805.

in effect to make poverty a penal offence. Even the Inquisition was not so mean as this, for it made no distinction between rich and poor. 'It so happened that this catholic society never forbade hot meat on a Sunday, but if they had, they would have put out my lord's kitchen fire as well as the public oven.'[1]

Southey's democratic tendencies appear also in a review of Villers's *Essay on the Reformation*. Southey insists that Villers does not do justice to the 'jacobins of the reformation'. The manifesto drawn up by Münzer for the German anabaptists is far closer to the genuine spirit of Christianity than the Augsburg Confession. There were excesses committed by these 'jacobins', it is true, but

> when we execrate the excesses of the peasants in Germany, and of the jacquerie in France, the heaviest portion of the curse should fall upon the oppressors who provoked them. The insurrections in our own country, under Wat Tyler and John Ball, were disgraced by no such enormities. England *was* free from the reproach of national cruelty till the accursed proceedings in Ireland.[2]

Clearly it would have caused Southey no embarrassment if someone had published *Wat Tyler* in 1805.

The most important statement of Southey's democratic views at this time, however, was a review of the second edition of Malthus's *Essay on Population*. Much of this review closely follows notes made by Coleridge, but one must not exaggerate Southey's indebtedness. For one thing, Coleridge's notes are confined to the first thirteen pages of the book. He probably skimmed through the rest, but the notes on later pages in the British Museum copy are in Southey's hand. Moreover, perhaps the weightiest argument against Malthus which is made in the article is based on an observation of Southey's, to be found on page 358 of the *Essay*. For 'the physical constitution of our nature', said Southey, Malthus should read 'in the existing system of society'. Malthus, he said in the review, has not exaggerated the vice and

---

[1] *Annual Review for 1804*, pp. 225 et seq.
[2] *Annual Review for 1805*, p. 181.

misery of the world in the slightest degree. But the reason
for the vice and misery is the imperfect social system. Why is
there such a difference in the population density in Australia,
England, and China? The three degrees of density are mainly
the consequence of man's own social institutions in these
three countries.[1] Malthus's show of scientific method is
merely a device to excuse callous indifference and com-
placency. Southey indignantly objects to Malthus's writing
advice to the poor for the rich to read. The man demands no
sacrifice from the rich. On the contrary, he proposes to relieve
them of the burden of the poor rates. He recommends
nothing to them but that they should harden their hearts.
They have a place at the table of nature. Others have not,
which is unfortunate and unavoidable. If people cannot get subsistence from their parents, and their work is not wanted, they
have no right to the smallest portion of food, and in fact have
no business to be alive at all.[2] So, at least, argued Malthus.

Until the unhappy consequences of the French Revolution
'shook the liberties and morals of Europe', Southey claims, no
wise man ever doubted that the condition of humanity could
be improved. People like Godwin brought perfectibility into
disrepute, and now Malthus has made himself an extraordinary
reputation by refuting Godwin. 'Mr Malthus could not have
obtained more credit in the eighth century for laying the devil,
than he has in the eighteenth for laying Mr Godwin.' By his
argument that population must necessarily tend to exceed the
means of subsistence, Malthus 'triumphantly destroys all
arguments for all amelioration of the state of the human race'.[3]
Malthus's system implies a universe of blind conflict, and it
was this that Southey seems to have found especially offensive.
It is well known that the *Essay on Population* suggested
to Charles Darwin the concept of the evolution of species
through 'natural selection' or 'survival of the fittest'. Malthus

---

[1] *Annual Review for 1803*, pp. 297–8.
[2] Ibid., p. 301. Malthus later omitted the table of nature.
[3] Ibid., pp. 292–5.

occasionally uses rather Darwinian language. For example, in
the first edition of the *Essay*, he had occasion to discuss the
formidable power of shepherd nations. If one tribe came into
conflict with another, 'the contest was a struggle for existence'. In the course of these conflicts for room and food,
there must have been a prodigious waste of human life; but
the power of population was always able to supply the
deficiency. The final result was that northern Asia was
peopled by 'brave, robust, and enterprising' barbarians.[1] Out
of the struggle for existence, in fact, the fittest had survived.
The laws of nature which this account discovers are applied
to the English poor. The man who finds himself in want
should have no assistance; he has only himself to blame. 'He
should be taught to know that the laws of nature, which are
the laws of God, had doomed him and his family to starve for
disobeying their repeated admonitions.'[2] Southey questioned
whether these were the laws of nature. One of his favourite
writers was Bernadin de St. Pierre, whose *Études de la
Nature* asserted the reality of Divine Providence against the
objections of naturalistic philosophers. Southey was well
acquainted with these objections, as is shown by a poem which
appeared in the *Morning Post* for 8 September 1798.

> All to you
> Is dark and cheerless; you in this fair world
> See some destroying principle abroad,
> Air, earth, and water full of living things
> Each on the other preying; and the ways
> Of man, a strange perplexing labyrinth,
> Where crimes and miseries, each producing each,
> Render life loathsome, and destroy the hope
> That should in death bring comfort.[3]

These lines may have been suggested by a striking passage in
Werther. Werther's heart was wasted by the thought of
that destructive power which lies concealed in every part of uni-

---

[1] *Essay on Population* (1798), pp. 47–49.
[2] See *Annual Review for 1803*, p. 300.
[3] Reprinted in Southey's poetical works as 'Autumn'.

versal nature. Nature has formed nothing that does not consume itself, and every object near it; so that, surrounded by earth and air, and all the active powers, I wander on my way with aching heart, and the universe is to me a fearful monster, for ever devouring its own offspring.[1]

Southey's poem shows that he has no wholly convincing answer to the doubts which this vision of nature casts upon the providence of God. The lines are addressed to one 'William', who sounds like Southey himself in his moods of depression. It is an interior colloquy, or rather monologue, in which the optimistic Southey is trying to strengthen his faith that Death still produces Life, and evil works its own destruction. He wishes that William could behold

> The strifes and troubles of this troubled world
> With the strong eye that sees the promised day
> Dawn through this night of tempest!

Then he would feel God in all things. That Southey's consolation is willed rather than felt is suggested by the phrase 'the *strong* eye'. During the night of tempest one can set one's teeth and wait for the dawn. But no eye, however strong, can see the dawn before it comes. It may be relevant here to recall the pathetic letter that Southey wrote to Charles Wynn after his mother's death in 1802. Her body, he said, had so utterly the appearance of death that 'the first feeling was as if there could have been no world for the dead; the feeling was very strong, and it required thought and reasoning to recover my former certainty, that as surely we must live hereafter, as all here is not the creation of folly or of chance'.[2] It was thought and reasoning that subdued the feeling, and the feeling was always liable to break from its restraints. Malthus pressed on a very sensitive nerve.

Southey is a striking contrast to Keats in this respect. The younger poet saw the 'eternal fierce destruction' of nature and could not forget it, and yet was none the less able to see

---

[1] Goethe, *Novels and Tales*, trans. R. D. Boylan (1854), p. 289.
[2] *LC*, ii. 181, 9 Jan. 1802.

the world as a 'vale of soul-making'. Keats was anticipated by
Malthus himself, who devised a similar theological formula.
In the last two chapters of his first edition he put forward
the view that evil was necessary to stimulate exertion: 'and
exertion seems evidently necessary to create mind'. The
world, he says, is not a state of trial but the means which
God has chosen to create mind: 'a process necessary, to
awaken inert, chaotic matter, into spirit; to sublimate the
dust of the earth into soul; to elicit an æthereal spark from
the clod of clay'.[1] Keats's emphasis is more on the schooling of
an 'intelligence' by a world of pains and troubles in order to
make it into a soul, and the tone of the letter in which he
expounds this idea is very different from anything in Malthus.
Keats is involved in the suffering he observes. As he makes
Moneta say in the revised version of *Hyperion*,

> None can usurp this height . . .
> But those to whom the miseries of the world
> Are misery, and will not let them rest.

It might be unfair to Malthus to say that he was unconcerned
about the miseries of the world, but no one would claim that
these miseries made him lose any sleep. He looked at the
world with the feelings of a man who was assured of his
place at the table of nature. The poet in *Hyperion* has to pass
through an experience of death before he can mount the steps
of the altar.

Southey was like Keats and unlike Malthus in understanding the condition of those who had no place at Nature's table.
If the rich cast off their responsibility for the poor, the
responsibility of the poor to the rich is also dissolved. 'You
have had your turn at the table long enough, gentlemen,' they
would say, 'and if those who have no places are to starve, we
will have a scramble for it at least!'[2] In some moods Southey
was able to enjoy the prospect of the oppressed rising up
against their oppressors—

---

[1] *Essay on Population* (1798), pp. 360, 353.
[2] Southey, *Essays* (1832), i. 94.

Justice shall yet unclose her eyes,
Terrific yet in wrath arise,
And trample on the tyrant's breast,
And make Oppression groan opprest.[1]

The Romans, he said, in a review of a pamphlet on the slave trade, did not dare let their slaves wear a badge for fear that they should recognize their numerical strength. The slaves in the West Indies have an unmistakable badge in their colour. The slave-holders 'can neither keep their slaves ignorant of their strength, nor conceal themselves from their fury when the day of retribution arrives'.[2] That day of retribution gives Southey much satisfaction.

The West Indies were a long way off. A day of retribution in England would not be so enjoyable. But there seemed every reason to believe that one was coming. *Letters from England*, supposedly translated from the Spanish of Don Manuel Alvarez Espriella, provide some of the evidence. This book, first published in 1807, contains what must be one of the earliest literary exposures of life in industrial England. The thirty-eighth chapter describes the use of child labour in Lancashire, where the children, overworked and badly kept, either die or grow up 'without decency, without comfort, and without hope, without morals, without religion, and without shame, and bring forth slaves like themselves to tread in the same path of misery'.[3] In the thirty-sixth chapter there is an account of life in Birmingham, with its miserable workmen doing tasks that ruin their health, and liable to be thrown out of employment by a slight change in the market. It is not surprising that the Birmingham mob showed itself to be ferocious in 1791. Later in the book, when Southey considers the whole question of the effects of the manufacturing system, he argues that an industrial society is bound to create a

[1] 'To the Genius of Africa', *Poems, by Robert Southey* (1797), pp. 42–43. This stanza was omitted in the second edition because Coleridge objected to the last line.
[2] *Annual Review for 1804*, p. 648.
[3] *Letters from England* (1808), ii. 88.

populace which is always ripe for rioting or revolution. They have no local attachments, they feel the full weight of taxation, they naturally consider that their interests are incompatible with those of their rulers; they are aware, moreover, of their strength in numbers. In consequence, a country that founds its prosperity upon manufactures sleeps upon gunpowder. It will be well for England, he concludes, 'when her cities shall decrease, and her villages multiply and grow; when there shall be fewer streets and more cottages'.[1]

The thought of a brutalized populace, willing to try any change in the hope that it might be a change for the better, alarmed Southey very much; although he thought that the middle class and the soldiers between them would stand a good chance of suppressing any rebellion. Sometimes he was able to persuade himself that a revolution might be long deferred. Thus, in a letter to Charles Danvers in 1806, he said that for himself it would be best if the old order lasted out his time, as he supposed it would, though change was inevitable and desirable.

Being a tenant of an old house, I would rather suffer its inconveniences and its vermin, than be at the trouble and expense of repairs. But, for the country, I have only to say that the fable of the Phoenix looks like a political emblem, and that old governments must be cut up and put into Medea's cauldron.[2]

This philosophical mood was only possible, however, when the immediate situation was not threatening. He was alarmed by the temper shown by the London mob at Colonel Despard's execution and funeral. Despard was convicted of plotting to assassinate the King. At his execution he protested his innocence and said that he died a martyr to his zeal for liberty. 'What is most extraordinary', says Southey, commenting on the event through the mouth of Don Manuel, 'is, that the mob applauded him while he spoke, took off their hats as if in respect when he suffered, and hissed the executioner when he

---

[1] *Letters from England* (1808), iii. 111, letter 61.
[2] *SL*, i. 358, 3 Feb. 1806.

held up his bloody head.'[1] Despard's funeral was given the honours properly reserved for public characters. He was certainly not regarded as a traitor ought to be.

The temper of the populace was also apparent in their religion. Southey was especially interested in this, as is shown by the amount of space he gives to the religious underworld of his time in *Letters from England*. At first sight his interest might seem to be that of an antiquarian preserving contemporary oddities for the benefit of future antiquarians. Thus, in his account of Joanna Southcott, it is the boisterous absurdities of her dialogue with the devil which appeal to him. These absurdities show the credulity of the English, which Don Manuel, being a Catholic, attributes to the want of a true religion. In no age or country, indeed, he says, are the conditions more favourable for the success of imposture or the growth of superstition than in contemporary England. It is the social power which these crudities have which fascinates and frightens Southey. The tracts which fanatics circulate never come to the notice of what is called the public. But they are read by an astonishing number of people with consuming zeal. The quackery of William Huntington, the absurd prophecies of Richard Brothers, may be despised, but they tell one much about the undercurrents of society, and the undercurrents, he told Grosvenor Bedford, carry more water than the upper stream. He thought that this credulity would ultimately lead to a general reconversion to Catholicism by way of a methodistical usurpation of the Church Establishment. Southey told Grosvenor Bedford of a system carried on in the north of Germany to convert people to Roman Catholicism. They bring people to believe in Böhme, and then they can believe anything else. (Southey had this on the authority of Coleridge, who claimed the acquaintance of the director of this propaganda in Rome.)[2]

The more immediate danger, that of a Methodist ecclesiastical

---

[1] *Letters from England* (1808), iii. 97–98, letter 61.
[2] Ibid., 259, 197–8, letters 70, 68; BL, c. 24, f. 45, 5 May 1807.

polity, seemed to him to be rapidly increasing. The Methodists really did exercise pastoral care over their congregations. The good which they did in producing sobriety and orderliness among the lower classes was very great, and this in itself tended to increase the strength of the Methodists. Meanwhile, Southey believed, the system of tithing by which the Church of England was supported was being undermined, and the time would come when the clergy would become salaried ministers. This weakening of their economic position would expose them still further to Methodist attacks, and in the end nothing would be left of the Establishment.[1]

Southey's objections to Methodism are fervently stated in his review of Myles's *Chronological History of the Methodists*, which appeared in the *Annual Review for 1803*. He denounces the practice of group confession, censorship of books, and the insistence on hell-fire. The drabness of Methodist religious discipline appalled him. 'Oh! if superstition is again to triumph and to reign, let us rather be harlot-tempted than hag-ridden.' (Rome, of course, is the harlot.) Above all he is afraid of the fanatical intolerance of Methodism, especially of the Calvinist kind. They would burn heretics if they could, he told Charles Danvers, 'and no holocaust would raise up to them so sweet a savour as a roasted Socinian'.[2] Roasted Robert Southey, in fact. Atheism and infidelity are not dangerous to society, because man is naturally religious, and the appetite for faith cannot be denied. They are valuable, indeed, for in Portugal he believed that it was the cold water of scepticism which had put out the fires of the Inquisition for ever. Perhaps Voltaire had saved the life of many a poor Jew.[3] At worst, infidelity was a counter-poison. Southey's views on infidelity were to change when he became aware that it too could become a popular movement. The popular character of Methodism was in itself a source of alarm. Methodist

---

[1] *Letters from England* (1808), ii. 352–4.
[2] *Annual Review for 1803*, pp. 201 et seq.; BM MSS. Adds. 30,928, f. 19, 10 Jan. 1804.
[3] *SL*, i. 107. Letter to Danvers, June 1800.

preaching is a means by which the lowest sort of tradesmen
—bakers, barbers, tailors, even servants and labourers—are
promoted to social eminence. These people find themselves
in positions of influence for which 'by birth, education,
knowledge and intellect' they are quite unfit.[1] This dislike of
the democratic character of Methodism is reinforced by the
political analogies that Southey detected between it and
the Corresponding Societies and the United Irishmen. The
Methodists, he told Charles Wynn, are 'literally and precisely speaking, an Ecclesiastical Corresponding Society—a
set of United Methodists'.[2] Not all those of methodistical
opinions were bakers, barbers, or tailors. But the fact that
people like Wilberforce and Hannah More, 'Church Evan-
gelicals', were an influential party in the state was in itself
frightening evidence of the social power of intolerant religion.

The reader may well ask how Southey reconciled the
undemocratic sentiments of the article on the Methodists with
what he said about Malthus or Villers or the Society for the
Suppression of Vice. No doubt a reconciliation could be
devised. While one must do full justice to the poor and uneducated, the poor and uneducated must recognize their
limitations. Yet such a reconciliation would miss the real
point of the contrast between Southey the anti-Methodist and
Southey the apologist of Wat Tyler. He was a democrat when
he felt himself to be at one with the populace who were being
maligned and persecuted. But as soon as he felt that the malign-
ing and persecuting power was embodied in the populace, he
became anti-democratic.

It is certain that Southey exaggerated the infidel-burning
tendencies of early nineteenth-century evangelicalism. His
fears of violence betray the violence of his own temperament.
It is characteristic of him that the compliment he valued most
was the one bestowed on him in 1817 by Mrs. Piozzi, at the
time of the *Wat Tyler* controversy. 'Oh', she cried, 'how I

---

[1] *Annual Review for 1803*, p. 210.
[2] *SL*, i. 249, Dec. 1803.

delight to see him *trample* upon his enemies!'[1] All the same, it
is clear that there was some violence for him to respond to,
though it is difficult to assess exactly how much. Thus,
Southey claimed to have read a Methodist apology for Calvin's
part in the burning of Servetus, and it seemed a natural
inference that Methodism might at some time revive the
fires at Smithfield. An evangelical magazine, the *Christian
Observer*, objected that it knew of no such book; but that the
reference might be to a book which argued that Calvin was
not responsible for the burning of Servetus. If so, the inference
which Southey drew was quite unjustified. I have not been
able to trace the book to which the *Christian Observer* refers.
But one can get an idea of the kind of book it was from a
pamphlet published in Belfast in 1854: a *Defence of John
Calvin, in the case of Michael Servetus*, by Dr. W. D. Killen.
It was prompted by a defence of Servetus and an attack on
Calvin by the minister of the Rosemary Street Unitarian
Church—an attack violently supported by a local newspaper,
the *Northern Whig*. The pamphlet takes the line that Servetus
was a licentious, untruthful, blaspheming fellow. In the
sixteenth century any party would have thought it quite
proper to burn him; and since Calvin did in fact try to mitigate the sentence an attack on him in this matter is particularly
unfair. One can see the point of the *Christian Observer*'s
comment on a book of this kind, but one can also see that
Southey has a point too. Dr. Killen explicitly disavows the
persecution of heretics, and in vindicating Calvin merely
exercises his historical imagination. But it is an exercise
which he performs with considerable zest.

On the other hand, the *Christian Observer* managed to find
one clear example of Southey's temperament playing tricks
with his memory. Southey had alleged that Hannah More
referred to heretical opinions as 'Egyptian points of doctrine
which are to be cut off by the edge of the sword'. The *Christian*

---

[1] Bodleian MS. Don. d. 86, f. 11. Letter to Robert Gooch, 13 Dec. 1824.
Cf. *SL*, iii. 474.

Observer pointed out that Southey was almost certainly thinking of a quotation from Francis Bacon in Hannah More's *Hints to a Princess*. The intention of the passage was to recommend charity to those who differ from us in theological matters. The *sword* is the *sword of the spirit*—the Bible.[1]

Southey saw the Church Establishment as a bulwark against fanaticism. It had among its bishops Richard Watson, to whom he was introduced in 1806. Watson was 'a staunch Whig, and would as willingly see the Athanasian Creed and half a dozen other absurdities struck out of the liturgy as I should'.[2] Southey thought that the Establishment might save itself if it developed on Watsonian principles. The review of Myles's *History of the Methodists* modestly suggests that the Thirty-Nine Articles might be abolished, African and Genevan interpolations removed, and theological dogmas not to be found in the Bible abandoned. 'Open the doors of the church, that they who feel and love the gospel may enter in, that zeal may be opposed by zeal, ignorance by knowledge, enthusiasm by virtue.'[3] Watson was the Bishop of Llandaff to whom Wordsworth addressed his republican letter in 1793, censuring him for his abandonment of reforming principles. He was also well known as the man who replied to Paine's *Age of Reason*, in terms which annoyed both Hannah More and William Blake, though for different reasons. (Hannah More found him too polite to Paine, while Blake thought him an impudent State-trickster and pharisee.) Although Watson was liberal and 'advanced', he was most emphatically a friend to order. It is a sign of some degree of conservatism in Southey's views in 1806 that he could find the bishop congenial company.

It should not be thought, however, that an admiration for

---

[1] *Christian Observer* (1810), ix. 762–3. Cf. *QR*, ii. 327. The passage was revised in the second edition of this volume of the *Quarterly*. 'We have been warned against Egyptian points of doctrine, which, in language of rather ambiguous import, are to be cut off by the spiritual sword.'

[2] BM MSS. Adds. 30,927, f. 118. Letter to Tom Southey, 28 July 1806.

[3] *Annual Review for 1803*, p. 213.

the Church Establishment was confined to those who inclined towards conservatism. In June 1808 Leigh Hunt's *Examiner* supported a Bill for bettering the condition of curates on the ground that it would strengthen the Establishment against intolerant Calvinists and gloomy Methodists who were swarming through the land.[1] And Southey himself was a partisan of the Church during years when he could be described as an 'almost-Quaker'.

Southey's interest in the Society of Friends dates from 1803, when he went to live in Keswick. There he became acquainted with Thomas Clarkson, the slave-trade aboli-tionist, for whom he had an unbounded admiration. 'If there be one man living', he wrote in 1806, 'who has laboured more earnestly than all others, for the good of his fellow creatures, Thomas Clarkson is that man.'[2] Clarkson had been an Anglican clergyman, but he had given up this office, and inclined towards Quaker beliefs. He never actually joined the Society of Friends himself, but was exceptionally well informed about its history and practice, and when Southey met him was writing his *Portraiture of Quakerism*. The first results of their meeting may be seen in Southey's review of Myles's *History of the Methodists* which he wrote late in November or early December 1803. In this article he compares the characters of John Wesley and George Fox, to the disadvantage of Wesley. Wesley was 'a pharisaic instituter of forms and ceremonies', Fox 'an Israelite indeed, in whom there was no guile'. 'A worse danger than the spread of methodism can scarcely be apprehended for England; a greater blessing for mankind cannot be desired or devised, than that the system of George Fox should become the practical system of the Christian world.'[3] Until Southey met Clarkson, he does not seem to have taken much interest in Quakerism. He regarded it as one of the enthusiastic sects which might provide amusement for an idle hour. In the summer of 1803 he had gleefully reported

---

[1] *Examiner* (1808), i. 369.   [2] *Annual Review for 1806*, p. 595.
[3] *Annual Review for 1803*, p. 207.

his discovery on a bookstall of John Perrott's *Battering Rams against Rome*, an account of a mission to convert the Pope to Quakerism; 'the rarest jewel in all the Bibliotheca Fanatica', Southey called it. He had not felt any deeper interest nine years before, when he visited the father of his friend Robert Lovell. Old Lovell, he said, was 'the most primitive of Quakers, but withall an affable intelligent pleasant man'. He offered to lend Southey a 'good book written by William Dell'. The offer was accepted, and Southey set about reading 'a large octavo full of mysticism'. In 1794 Southey was not much inclined to take mysticism seriously. One suspects that for him the word was in practice synonymous with 'nonsense'. It is true that on one occasion he spoke of himself as likely to find his place in heaven 'among a whole herd of Frenchmen, Revolutionists, and a sort of Quaker-Christians who have a mortal antipathy to regimentals'. But this implies no more than a newspaper-acquaintance with the Society of Friends.[1]

What chiefly attracted Southey to the Quakers when he became better informed about them was their combination of warm religious feeling with a freedom from dogma. They abstained from defining what had been left indefinite in the Bible, and did not regard the Bible itself as a final revelation. This fitted well with Southey's own belief that Christianity was not an historical religion but a perpetual revelation.[2] They avoided such theological horrors as the doctrine of eternal punishment and the impossibility of salvation outside the Christian fold. Their discipline of life appealed to Southey, for they were truly Christian stoics. 'They show to the world', he said in a review of Clarkson's *Portraiture of Quakerism*, 'that all angry passions may be subdued, and that a body of men may exist, acting upon the principles of peace on earth, and good will towards men.' The Pennsylvania experiment proves that Quaker principles of peace are quite

---

[1] NLW, 4811 D 109. Letter to Charles Wynn, 29 July 1803; BL, c. 22, f. 105. Letter to Grosvenor Bedford, 26 Apr. 1794; ibid., c. 23, f. 53. Letter to Grosvenor Bedford, 3 Jan. 1799.
[2] BL, c. 24, f. 122, 30 Oct. 1809.

practical. It is, he believes, true that 'a people whose principle it is never to resist evil, and always to bear testimony against it, cannot be crushed by any exertion of human power short of universal massacre'.[1]

Southey's admiration is qualified by a distaste for some details of the Quaker discipline. He thought that their objection to paying tithes was foolish. He found nothing spiritually perilous in playing cards. He saw no need for the plain dress, and much affectation in the 'plain speech'. He was not disposed to ridicule even these things, however, if one may judge from his suppression of a note which Coleridge made for his review of Malthus in the *Annual*. This was a reference to the Quakers' 'silly' objection to *you* when *thou* is meant. It followed quite naturally in the train of argument, but Southey left it out.[2] Again, although Southey is disposed to laugh at the excesses of some of the early Quakers, he is careful to point out that the prohibition of violence ensured that their fanaticism hurt no one but themselves. He was, however, clearly relieved that in his own time there were no more prophecies uttered in the streets, or testimonies borne in sackcloth and ashes. He was thankful that the Grand Turk had latterly been abandoned to his misbelief, 'and the Pope, notwithstanding their concern for him, given up as irreclaimable'.[3]

There was no Quaker meeting in Keswick in Southey's time; otherwise he would have taken his seat in it, without, however, conforming himself to the full rigour of the sect. He once expressed the wish that his son Herbert should be brought up a Quaker. Quaker influence probably lay behind his proposal (made in a letter to Charles Wynn in 1807) that capital punishment should be entirely abolished. 'The reverence for life which it would exhibit in the law would tend to produce or strengthen the same reverence in the people.' It

[1] *Annual Review for 1806*, pp. 596, 606.
[2] The text of Coleridge's note may be found in *PMLA* (1936), li. 1064–5. It is quoted by G. R. Potter in an article on Coleridge's marginalia in Malthus's second edition. Cf. *Annual Review for 1803*, p. 295.
[3] *Letters from England* (1808), iii. 60, letter 57.

is true that Beccaria, the eighteenth-century Italian penal reformer, whose book on crimes and punishments Southey had read in 1793, argues on the same lines. But in early nineteenth-century England, even the movement to restrict capital punishment to the most serious crimes was regarded as dangerously unpractical. That movement, by the way, may be said to have begun in the summer of 1808, when William Allen, Richard Phillips, Basil Montagu, and others founded a society for the diffusion of information about the punishment of death. Two years later Sir Samuel Romilly made the first of his attempts in the House of Commons to restrict the death penalty. Thus, in proposing total abolition to that unsentimental Whig M.P. Charles Wynn in 1807, Southey showed himself to be among the most radical of social reformers.[1] Still more remarkable is a suggestion which he made, quite seriously, in 1810 when writing on prison reform in the *Edinburgh Annual Register*. Here he actually proposed handing over the prisons to the management of the Society of Friends. This audacious proposal was made three years before Elizabeth Fry had even *visited* Newgate.[2]

Since Southey believed that Quakerism was probably the true system of the Gospel, he naturally enough believed that they were the best missionaries. He reviewed a pamphlet which described two attempts to do welfare work among American Indians, and pointed out that this was in the excellent tradition started by William Penn. The Quakers begin in the right way. By teaching the Indians to hoe and plough their fields, to enclose them, to raise cattle, build comfortable houses, do blacksmith's work, spinning, cheese-making, &c.,

---

[1] *SL*, ii. 68, 11 June 1808; NLW, 4813 D 513, Nov. 1807. Wynn replied to Southey on 9 Nov. 1807: 'In your wish for the entire suppression of capital punishment I am much enclined to concur, though I have grave doubts as to it's ever being practicable in this country and am convinced that if ever effected it can only be done gradually. The mind of the public must be prepared for it and it is only by seeing that other punishments are sufficient to check the less heinous offences, that men can be persuaded to part with what appears to be the protection of their lives and their security.' Ibid. 4814 D 29.

[2] *Edinburgh Annual Register for 1808*, part i, p. 160.

they do something of immediate benefit. This will prepare the
Indians

to embrace opinions, of which they have already witnessed the
excellent effects. It is absurd to go to savages with tales of mysteries, the true method of converting them is by showing them,
like the old blind man in Madoc, how little difference there is in the
basis of our faith.

> 'Know ye not him who laid
> The deep foundations of the earth . . .?'
>   '. . . We also know,
> And fear, and worship the Beloved One.'
> *'Our God'*, replied Cynetha, *'is the same,*
> *The Universal Father.'*

Such language the Quakers may hold with perfect truth: in fact,
it is the language which they have held to the Indians, and which
the Indians understand. Let them go on in doing good to them, and
time and example, and the Universal Father, will bring about the
rest.[1]

Inasmuch as evangelical work was a means of civilizing
savage races, Southey could sympathize even with missionaries who insisted on theology. When reviewing the
reports of the Baptist Missionary Society in the *Annual
Review for 1802*, he pointed out that he did not share these
missionaries' belief that there was no salvation outside the
Christian Church. He agreed with a Brahmin who told one of
the Baptists that there were rivers from the east, west, north,
and south, which all met in the sea; 'so', he argued, 'there
are many ways among men, but all lead to God'. None the
less, Southey believed that the moral institutes of Christianity were 'calculated to produce the greatest possible good'.
They would end polygamy, human sacrifice, infanticide, and
practices of self-torture. Christianity, moreover, laid firm
foundations for British rule. Unless a vigorous policy were
adopted of introducing Christianity into the East Indian
territories, he told Wynn, 'I prophesy that by the year 2000

---

[1] *Annual Review for 1806*, p. 593.

there will be more remains of the Portugueze than of the English Empire in the East'. (This prophecy stands some chance of coming true.) Southey had no anti-imperialist scruples. It would be insulting the reader's intelligence, he said in another review of missionary reports, to argue the case for the right to conquer the South Sea islands—'the right of conquering cannibals and child-murderers! the right of preventing human sacrifices by force!'[1] He felt as confident about Britain's mission in South Africa. Between 1802 and 1806 the Dutch colony at the Cape of Good Hope, which had been seized by the British during the French Revolutionary war, was restored to Holland. Southey strongly disagreed with this restoration, arguing that it ought to be seized again, for the benefit of the Hottentots if for nothing else. A more gentle and docile race does not exist, he says, and they are cruelly oppressed by the Boer farmers. These Boers, indeed, would be difficult to educate, and the only practical suggestion he could make would be an importation of hangmen 'for their especial benefit'.[2]

Although one can see why Quaker faith and practice appealed to Southey, one cannot help being astonished that they should have appealed to him so much. He may have given his assent to the principle that all angry passions may be subdued; but he made little attempt to reconcile this with his delight in trampling on his enemies. Nor is it easy to see how he was able to hold 'almost-Quaker' opinions alongside his strongly held conviction that the war against France must be carried on with aggressive vigour. He recognized the importance for Friends of their pacifism, and, when his mind was warmed with Quaker narratives, accepted its validity. But once he turned to his newspaper he reverted to a belligerent attitude. Were it not for Bonaparte, he told Charles Wynn, he would have little hesitation in declaring his

---

[1] *Annual Review for 1802*, pp. 207–18; NLW, 4813 D 514, Oct. or Nov. 1806; *Annual Review for 1803*, p. 200.
[2] *Annual Review for 1804*, pp. 27–33.

conviction that Quakerism was the true system of the Gospel;
'that is, my reason is convinced, but I want to have the
invasion over before I allow it to be so'.[1] The only way one
could sum up his attitude would be in the formula: Morality
is the best policy—but not yet. In a single letter he can tell
Charles Wynn that he is in all essential points very nearly a
Quaker, and then go on to say that nothing can redeem
Ireland but such measures as 'none of our statesmen—except
perhaps Marquis Wellesley—would be hardy enough to
adopt—nothing but a system of Roman conquest and colonization—and shipping off the refractory savages to the colonies'.[2]

The Marquis Wellesley (the elder brother of Arthur
Wellesley, the famous Duke of Wellington) seems to have
been in Southey's eyes one of the manifestations of William
Forrester, the 'great brute' at Westminster School. Southey
admired James Paull for his pertinacity in pressing charges of
misgovernment in India against Wellesley, but on the other
hand he wished that those charges had concerned any man but
Wellesley, for he had great abilities and was as ambitious as
Bonaparte himself. He would throw open the ports of South
America, seize Mauritius and other French islands in the
East, expel the French from the West Indies, annex Sicily and
Sardinia, and garrison Alexandria. 'If he cannot be sent over
in chains to India and hung in presence of Embassadors from
the court of every native Prince, and then his skin stufft and
sent round the country,—I would give him the rein at home.'[3]
A month after he had written this, he again declared his
confidence in Wellesley's wholesome ambition. 'Nothing will
so well reconcile the people to the burthens they must bear as
glory.'[4] There is a portentously Tory flavour in this remark.
It reminds one of Hannah More's joy when, after the news of
the Battle of Camperdown in 1797, the poor people actually
ran to the clergyman and said they were now willing to be

[1] *SL*, ii. 31, 3 Dec. 1807.
[2] NLW, 4812 D 194, Apr. 1807.
[3] BM MSS. Adds. 30,928, f. 73. Letter to Charles Danvers, 6 Nov. 1806.
[4] NLW, 4812 D 184. Letter to Charles Wynn, 13 Dec. 1806.

taxed double.[1] However, as William Cobbett showed in the early days of his conversion to radicalism, it was possible to combine fervency in war with jacobinism at home.

William Pitt died at the beginning of 1806, and was succeeded by the 'ministry of all the Talents', a coalition predominantly Whig. Wordsworth was almost indifferent to the change, believing that there was no true honour or ability on either side—

> a servile band,
> Who are to judge of danger which they fear,
> And honour which they do not understand.[2]

Southey was more sympathetic, although disheartened by what he called the 'damned scramble for places', and disappointed by the similarity between the new policies and the old. The Whigs had to forgo the bold speaking natural to opposition. '"What shall we hear *unsaid* tonight?" was the triumphant sneer with which the New Opposition used to enter the House of Commons.' Still, Southey whole-heartedly supported their efforts to end the slave trade—efforts which were successful before the fall of the ministry in 1807—and he agreed with Windham's army reforms. He disagreed with the policy of concessions to the Catholics, a policy which was generally unpopular, and led directly to the fall of the ministry. He felt, however, that it was not their political errors which made 'the Talents' unpopular, but the good that they had done. Thus, the Army Bill was 'an experiment, an innovation; things more annoying to the sons of darkness, than day-light to the birds of night'. Catholic emancipation, he told Wynn, was merely the pretext for ejecting the Whigs. Their real sin had been the abolition of the slave trade.[3]

[1] Letter to Mrs. Boscawen, 27 Dec. 1797. See William Roberts, *Memoirs of the Life of Mrs Hannah More* (2nd ed. 1834), iii. 28.

[2] Wordsworth, *Poetical Works*, ed. E. de Selincourt and H. Darbishire (Oxford, 1940–9), iii. 122; cf. *Letters, The Middle Years*, ed. E. de Selincourt (Oxford, 1937), i. 10.

[3] *SL*, i. 382, 22 May 1806; *Edinburgh Annual Register for 1808*, part i, pp. 5–6; NLW, 4812 D 193, 27 Mar. 1807.

Wynn had been an under-secretary in the Whig administration, and before the Whigs withdrew he was able to secure
for Southey a pension of £200 a year (less income-tax) as a
man of letters. The idea of his being a court pensioner amused
him. 'Who says I am a Jacobine', he asked his brother Henry,
'except I myself? *Quis Diabolus* would ever have foreseen that
I should have a pension . . .?'[1] Certainly the pension had
no immediate effect on his politics. In the recriminations
which followed the fall of 'the Talents', no party's reputation
came out particularly well. Southey said that the debates
reminded him of the first scene of Ben Jonson's *Alchemist*,
and modern government seemed aptly foreshadowed in the
figure of Spenser's Duessa. Politics, he told Grosvenor Bedford on 21 April 1807, 'are very amusing, and go to the tune
of *Tantara-rara*'—the rogues' march.[2] Even his confidence in
the good cause of Britain against Bonaparte was shaken by
the seizure of the Danish fleet and the bombardment of
Copenhagen in 1807 (Denmark then being neutral). 'An
everlasting and ineffaceable infamy' he called it. He told Miss
Barker that Britain had chosen to fight Bonaparte with his own
weapons of cruelty and tyranny. Thus the strength that comes
from fighting in a good cause was forfeited. 'Woe be to the
nation, and to the individual who believes that any thing
which is wrong can ever be expedient!'[3]

If anything, Southey's politics in 1807 were becoming more
radical. The depression that had overcast the English jacobins
for a decade was coming to an end, and a new impulse towards
political change began to be perceptible. De Quincey met
Southey for the first time in November 1807, and was shocked
by the disloyal things that he and Wordsworth uttered in
conversation. The two poets agreed that no good was to be
hoped for in England until the royal family should be expatri-
ated; 'and Southey, jestingly considering to what country
they could be exiled, with mutual benefit for that country

[1] *SL*, ii. 111, 14 Nov. 1808.   [2] *LC*, iii. 81, 21 Apr. 1807.
[3] *SL*, ii. 25–26, 26 Oct. 1807.

and themselves, had supposed the case—that, with a large allowance of money, such as might stimulate beneficially the industry of a rising colony, they should be transported to New South Wales'. Southey then composed *extempore* a verse petition addressed to the King, of which the last three lines ran as follows:

> Therefore, old George, by George we pray
> Of thee forthwith to extend thy sway
> Over the great Botanic Bay.

De Quincey's sense of propriety was not proof against this, and he laughed 'with a sense of something peculiarly droll in the substitution of the stilted phrase—*"the great Botanic Bay"*, for our ordinary week-day name *Botany Bay*, so redolent of thieves and pickpockets'.[1]

Southey's radicalism was not confined to uttering disrespectful verse about the royal family. While Sir Francis Burdett was fighting the Westminster election in May 1807, Southey praised him as one 'who hitteth hard, and as it seemeth unto me hitteth the right nail upon the head'.[2] At this time Cobbett was calling upon the electors of Westminster to reject with equal scorn all the traditional party labels, and to insist upon a constitutional reform of abuses. There is no doubt that Southey agreed with this. The people were beginning to despise their rulers, he told Henry Koster in August 1807; 'every day they become more and more convinced of the extent of their prodigality and peculation'. The state wagon was almost sure to overturn, driven so unskilfully down such a steep slope. Even Sir Francis Burdett lacked the necessary talent, though he had integrity and was popular. 'But were there an able man in his place, he might be the political Martin Luther of England.'[3]

In some matters, however, Southey's pension encouraged

---

[1] De Quincey, *Collected Writings*, ed. D. Masson (Edinburgh, 1889), ii. 323.
[2] BL, c. 24, f. 46, 5 May 1807.
[3] 20 Aug. 1807. See *Revista do Instituto Histórico e Geográfico Brasileiro* (1943), clxxviii. 39.

him to be more discreet than before. When he visited London
in the spring of 1808, he had thought of going to see the
celebrated radical Horne Tooke. Wynn strongly urged him
not to go. Tooke was closely associated with Burdett, and
therefore regarded as an active enemy to all orthodox party
men. Wynn was afraid that Southey ran some risk of losing
his pension if he became known as one of the Horne Tooke
circle. Southey so far followed his advice as to keep out of the
way of the person who might have introduced him to Horne
Tooke, but he insisted that he could not bear to have it supposed that he was 'bound with a Treasury chain'. Besides,
he could not really believe that any person in power would
wish to take away his pension. 'I think nothing about them,
and have literally more to do with any times than my own.'[1]
The fact remains that Southey wanted to meet Horne Tooke,
and did not do so.

Southey's feeling that other times and other lands were
more interesting than *tantara-rara* politics accords with a
widely diffused sentiment that party politics were futile,
meaningless. Walter Scott was writing his *Marmion* at this
time, and the famous lines on Pitt and Fox in the introduction
to the first canto illustrate the sense of anticlimax produced
by the death of these men in 1806—men who were in their day
the object of so much passionate loyalty, so much bitter
hatred.

> Theirs was no common party race,
> Jostling by dark intrigue for place—

and the political strife of 1807 so obviously was a 'dark
intrigue'. Hence Scott's sad reflection that 'the wine of life is
on the lees'. From a very different point of view, Leigh Hunt's
Examiner began in 1808 with the express intention of
strengthening this new freedom from party spirit. 'Party',
it said, quoting Swift, 'is the madness of many for the gain of
a few.'

[1] *SL*, i. 373–4, 6 May 1808. Incorrectly dated by J. W. Warter.

With the outbreak of the Peninsular War, however, politics again became a serious matter. Southey could once more feel that the struggle between France and Britain was a contest between the Evil Power and the Good. For him, the all-important division in domestic politics became that between those who were zealous in their support of the war, and those who were only tepid.

4. THE SPANISH INSURRECTION

In the summer of 1808 there was a general rising in Spain against the government imposed by the French. The news aroused immense enthusiasm in England, and Southey joined in it most heartily. He was well acquainted with the Peninsula and its literature, and few things could have given him more pleasure than that successful resistance to Napoleon should have begun there. He did not go as far as his friend Walter Savage Landor, who went to Spain as a volunteer. (Southey was after all a family man, with burdensome domestic responsibilities.) But, as the letter which he wrote to Tom Southey in August 1808 shows, he followed Landor in spirit.

Landor is gone to Spain! to fight as a private in the Spanish army, and he has found two Englishmen to go with him. A noble fellow! this is something like the days of old as we poets and romancers represent them,—something like the best part of chivalry,—old honours, old generosity, old heroism are reviving,—and the career of that cursed monkey nation is stopt, I believe and fully trust, now and for ever.[1]

Charles Wynn was equally carried away, though again only in spirit. 'I am more surprised', he told Southey, 'at those who stay at home than those who volunteer for Spain. So glorious an insurrection is I believe unparalleled in history. . . .'[2]

[1] BM MSS. Adds. 30,927, f. 135, 16 Aug. 1808. Cf. *LC*, iii. 162.
[2] NLW, 4814 D 36, 23 Aug. 1808.

Wordsworth was not exaggerating when, in an eloquent passage in his *Tract on the Convention of Cintra*, he described the 'mighty change' in popular feeling towards the war produced by the Spanish rising. The war took on a new dignity; this corruptible put on incorruption, and this mortal put on immortality.[1] The extent of the sympathy for the Spanish cause in the summer of 1808 is shown by the fact that even Leigh Hunt's *Examiner* felt constrained to join in it for a period, and this in spite of the paper's sharing the radical-Whig sentiment that the war with France was neither just nor necessary. Its immediate reaction was, indeed, unfavourable. When it was decided to send British troops to Spain to assist the rising, the *Examiner* of 19 June censured the 'Impolicy of British Interference in Spain'. Spain was in a miserable condition. 'The poison of despotism' tainted the gifts of an exuberant Nature. Spaniards could not exert themselves to fight for such a government because they could not be worse off under the French. Reports of Spanish successes, it was explained in the same issue, came from stock-jobbers and newspaper editors. There was no authentic information. By 10 July, however, the paper had worked itself up into a qualified ardour, and by 24 July even the qualifications had been discarded.

This unanimous exhilaration was upset in September by news of the Convention of Cintra. By its terms the British generals in Portugal (including Sir Arthur Wellesley) allowed a defeated French army to be evacuated from Portugal to France. The news of the Convention aroused great indignation in Britain. Never in his recollection, Southey told Landor, had any feeling been so general. Everyone he met was boiling over with shame and rage.

My cry was break the terms, and deliver up the wretch who signed them to the French, with a rope round his neck. This is what Oliver Cromwell would have done. Oh Christ—this England, this noble country—that hands so mighty and a heart so sound should

[1] *Prose Works of W. Wordsworth*, ed. W. Knight (1896), i. 118.

have a face all leprosy, and a head fit for nothing but the vermin that burrow in it![1]

It was in a mood like this that many county meetings were held to condemn the Convention. At the Hampshire one (reported in the *Examiner* for 6 November) Cobbett attacked the Wellesley family. He said they were being protected by ministers. The unpopularity of the Convention, in fact, was extremely useful to the opposition. The *Courier* was not arguing unfairly when it claimed (on 14 January 1809) that *The Times* and the *Morning Chronicle* held up Sir Arthur Wellesley as the chief culprit among the generals because this would weaken the political position of his brother the Marquis Wellesley, and prepare the way for a return to power of Lord Grenville and Lord Sidmouth (formerly Henry Addington, and a member of the ministry of 'All the Talents'). The fact that the agitation against the Convention was anti-ministerial explains why Lord Lonsdale refused to allow a Westmorland county meeting to consider the issue. His refusal is of some importance for the student of English literature, as it moved Wordsworth to write his celebrated *Tract*.

Wordsworth's objection is to the gentlemanliness of the Convention. He deplores the acceptance in it of Napoleon's imperial title (unrecognized by the British government). He censures the generals' readiness to treat with the French rather than beat them into submission. The British Command, he says, did not assume the 'lofty deportment' which the strength of their armies and the nature of their mission entitled them to. Wordsworth's own view of the nature of their mission is somewhat extravagant. They were supporting a renovation of human nature—*redeunt Saturnia regna*. The moral and physical energies of the Spaniards had 'put forth their strength as in a flood; and, without being sullied or polluted, pursue—exultingly and with song—a course

[1] Forster Collection, Victoria and Albert Mus. 481, f. 5, 26 Nov. 1808. Cf. J. Forster, *Walter Savage Landor* (1869), i. 236.

which leads the contemplative reason to the ocean of eternal
love'.[1] This lyrical outburst leads even Wordsworth to
realize that what he says must seem remote from and difficult to harmonize with 'the petty irritations, the doubts and
fears, and the familiar (and therefore frequently undignified)
exterior of present and passing events'.[2] He knows that the
true sorrow of humanity consists in the failure of ordinary
life to 'correspond with the dignity and intensity of human
desires'.[3] But he refuses to believe that the Spanish insurrection was not an adequate outlet for that dignity and intensity.

He was able to maintain this belief only by keeping aloof
from the more sordid and commonplace particulars of the
insurrection. As he put it in one of the sonnets composed
while he was writing the *Tract*, he did not 'weigh the hopes
and fears of suffering Spain' in surroundings that suggested
the intrigues and factions of the World;

> Not there; but in dark wood and rocky cave,
> And hollow vale which foaming torrents fill
> With omnipresent murmur as they rave
> Down their steep beds, that never shall be still.

In this setting he explores the human heart and gathers
'triumph, and thoughts no bondage can restrain'. The kind
of 'bondage' that Wordsworth resents is that of the awkward
objections which John Rickman made to the *Tract*. Long
before the *Tract* was published, he told Southey, it had been
avowed ('though with decent Reserve') that the Convention
was caused by the uncertain loyalty of the Portuguese, and the
necessity of destroying Lisbon should the French have
defended themselves in it.[4] Wordsworth was elated by the
uncomplicated enthusiasm aroused by the insurrection, and
the uncomplicated indignation aroused by the Convention,
and the *Tract* is an attempt to vindicate the refusal to have
these emotions damped by the littleness of political detail.
The Convention of Cintra was denounced by the universal

---

[1] *Prose Works of W. Wordsworth*, ed. W. Knight (1896), i. 212.
[2] Ibid., p. 213.   [3] Ibid., p. 272.   [4] HM, 8 Oct. 1810.

voice of the people—denounced 'with that unanimity which
nothing but the light of truth spread over the inmost concerns
of human nature can create'.[1] Therefore the voice of the
people is the voice of God, and can only be ignored by
politicians at their peril. One of the most striking things about
the *Tract*, indeed, is the sense of power with which it is
impregnated, a feeling engendered by participation in a universal emotion. The first paragraph is a fine description of a
moment when 'public opinion' is shocked. The news of the
Convention, he said, 'did not spread with the commotion of
a storm which sweeps visibly over our heads, but like an
earthquake which rocks the ground under our feet'.[2]

The agitation over the Convention of Cintra was only
the first shock of the earthquake. Its immediate effect was
to leave public feeling confused and disappointed over the
Spanish war, so that even Southey's ardour was somewhat
cooled; although he never doubted that the Spaniards would
ultimately succeed. By February 1809 Landor had returned
from Spain, and in a letter to him Southey expressed the hope
that he would not return there. Swift, decisive action by the
British might have brought the Peninsular campaign to a
spectacular close. 'But we are palsied at home. There is not
one statesman among us who has either wisdom or virtue.'[3]
Writing on 9 February 1809 these words have a more specific
meaning than Southey's earlier charges of roguery among all
parties. It was just at this time that the House of Commons
was investigating charges of corruption brought against the
Duke of York. He was accused, and, as the event showed,
not without reason, of allowing a former mistress of his, Mrs.
Clarke, to secure promotions in the army through her bed-
room influence. Wilberforce was shocked by the moral in-
sensibility which the House showed in the course of the
inquiry—every *double entendre* was fully appreciated by
members. The whole affair, he thought, would do 'irrepar-

---

[1] *Prose Works of W. Wordsworth*, ed. W. Knight (1896), i. 145.
[2] Ibid., p. 114.   [3] *SL*, ii. 127–8, 9 Feb. 1809.

able mischief to public morals, by accustoming the public to
hear without emotion of shameless violations of decency'.
Sydney Smith tried, though in vain, to give conversation 'a
little tinge of chastity and propriety', but was embarrassed by
a temptation 'to pretend to a knowledge of the irregular
passions which I am the farthest from any man in the world
from possessing'. The love letters of the Duke and his
'darling' were a great popular success. Never before had there
been such a thorough exposure of royal licentiousness; never
had prurient curiosity been so amply satisfied. Mrs. Clarke
herself was 'elegantly dressed, consummately impudent, and
very clever'. It was curious, said Wilberforce, 'to see how
strongly she has won upon people'.[1] Curious and ominous.
John Rickman, who as secretary to the Speaker of the House
of Commons sat through the whole inquiry, was not as concerned as Wilberforce about the state of public morals. But,
as he told Southey, it was good that while Government lasted
it should remain decently respectable. 'Now this investiga-
tion stirs up the Swinish Multitude to Blasphemy.' Southey
replied that he rather liked the inquiry—'being swinishly
inclined'.[2] Perhaps Wordsworth rather liked it too. This would
explain why in 1809 Sir George Beaumont found it necessary
to warn Haydon about Wordsworth's 'terrific democratic
notions'.[3]

The strong feelings that had been aroused by the Convention of Cintra were given a new direction by this scandal. It
was the second shock of the earthquake. Even the *Courier*,
though the newspaper was no friend to Whigs and reformers
who stood to profit by the revelations of corruption and
demoralization, joined in the cry against the Duke. It was
scornful of the idea put about by the Duke's apologists that
the charges against him were part of a jacobin plot. The

[1] R. I. and S. Wilberforce, *Life of W. Wilberforce* (1838), iii. 402–3;
S. Smith, *Letters*, ed. N. C. Smith (Oxford, 1953), i. 155–6.
[2] HM, Rickman to Southey, 15 Feb. 1809; Southey to Rickman, 18 Feb.
1809.
[3] B. R. Haydon, *Autobiography*, ed. T. Taylor (1926), p. 97.

loyalty of the public must inevitably be weakened, the *Courier* asserted, 'if they perceive the cry of "the state is in danger" set up to screen the most degrading private vices, such as a double adultery'.[1] The language which the *Courier* allowed itself at this time indicates the ferocity of public feeling. Thus, on 13 February it observed that the Duke's defenders had exposed themselves to the charge of being 'the panders of the basest passions, the very pimps to the man of the greatest power'. Two days later the paper quoted one of the many sermons which alluded to the Duke of York's case. 'Towards the conclusion the Clergyman said, "whosoever lays his head in DALILA's lap shall be shorn of his power". The congregation instantly made the application, and it has been since the subject of earnest remark.'[2] On 25 February the *Courier* strongly censured the Duke's letter to the House of Commons, in the course of which he asked them not to condemn him without trial. Bearing in mind the evidence that had already been given, the *Courier* could hardly find words to express its indignation. 'Does he dread that a majority of the House of Commons is in the reported conspiracy against the House of Brunswick, or that the Jacobinical Plot is hatching in St. Stephen's Chapel?'

In fact the Duke was acquitted, although about 150 members voted against him. The minority was so influential (it included Wilberforce) that the Duke was in fact severely censured, and he resigned. The *Courier* commented in these terms:

It was to no purpose that a nominal Majority voted one way; the Minority was so large and so respectable, that its weight prevailed, a circumstance which cannot fail of inspiring confidence in the general body, notwithstanding any well-grounded unalterable opinions of the defects in the way of electing its Members, and the necessity of gradual, gentle reformation. For surely the structure of a Body which has acted so virtuously, should be touched with gentleness and apprehension![3]

[1] *Courier*, 9 Feb. 1809.   [2] Ibid., 15 Feb. 1809.
[3] Ibid., 22 Mar. 1809.

The *Courier*'s logic may be questioned, since there was no denying that a majority of the House of Commons had voted for acquittal in the face of damning evidence. There was a cry set up for a reform of Parliament which should cut away the influence of men in power. The *Courier*'s belief in 'gradual, gentle reformation' was very moderate indeed. More people at this time were inclined to echo Burdett's demand for a radical cure for abuses. On 29 March 1809, at a meeting in Westminster, Burdett said that 'a Parliamentary reform is now absolutely necessary'. Southey uses the same language, for example, in letters to Grosvenor Bedford and William Taylor on 21 April and 24 May respectively. To quote the letter to Taylor:

Being myself for thorough reform—for Forsyth-ing the rotten tree of the constitution, and, if that did not do, for planting a new one in its place,—I care not about the struggle of parties, and grow to perceive that there is the same utter lack of common honesty and common talent in both. Of the two, I believe I hate the Whigs the worst, for their rascally feelings towards Spain; and of the Whigs, Whitbread, for the way in which he always speaks of Bonaparte.[1]

'The rotten tree of the constitution' has the genuine Burdettite ring; and a tendency to regard the Whigs as rather worse than the Tories was very prevalent among radical reformers at the time. Thus, at a Hampshire county meeting on 27 April 1809, Cobbett denounced the Whigs in terms as strong as the *Courier* itself could wish. On 1 May, at a reform meeting at the 'Crown and Anchor', William Smith, M.P. for Norwich, had great difficulty in obtaining a hearing simply because he was a regular Whig. Robert Waithman, probably the most active of the radicals in the City of London, charged the Whigs with having gone back on every promise of reform, and 'thanked the present Administration for

---

[1] J. W. Robberds, *Memoir of William Taylor* (1843), ii. 276. William Forsyth was a celebrated eighteenth-century gardener who specialized in the diseases of trees. For the letter to Grosvenor Bedford, see BL, c. 24, f. 106.

opening the eyes of the people by openly abetting Corruption'.[1] Southey had no great admiration for these reformers. There are signs, indeed, that he was looking for a political Messiah to lead the country out of its sterile party politics. 'Never was there a time', he told his brother Tom, 'when one truly great man could be ot such service to his country as now. . . .'[2] Still, in the absence of the truly great man, it was possible that the radicals' limited and sordid concern with 'economical reform' might grow into something more valuable. In a letter to Rickman written some time in the spring of 1809, he argues that the issue of the constitutional conflict must either be liberty or despotism.

In the one case England will be what I would willingly part with a few limbs to make it,—in the other,—thank God there is a good climate in Brazil and I can speak Portugueze, for by God's blessing if I am to live under a Despotism it shall not be at home. But I have no heart for the ultimate result. . . .[3]

In the light of the later development of Southey's views, it is the last comment which is the most significant. It is curious to see yet another of Southey's half-serious emigration projects mentioned in this context.

The public demand for reform was now very strong. Wordsworth, who considered himself a temperate reformer, told Daniel Stuart that 'if there be not a reform, the destruction of the Liberties of the Country is inevitable'.[4] Even ministers had to put on an appearance of reforming zeal. Early in May 1809, Curwen, one of the members for Cumberland, and a Whig, introduced a Bill for preventing bribery in elections. In a modified form it was supported by the ministry. Southey himself had no time for the Bill. It would do nothing but mischief, he told his brother Tom, because it left the influence of the Treasury untouched (ministers can reward by

[1] *Courier*, 2 May 1809.
[2] BM MSS. Adds. 30,927, f. 149, 12 Dec. 1808.
[3] HM.
[4] W. Wordsworth, *Letters, The Middle Years*, ed. E. de Selincourt (Oxford, 1937), i. 315, 25 May 1809.

methods less tangible than the payment of cash) while it
destroyed influence everywhere else. Southey was personally
acquainted with Curwen, and described him as a mere hunter
after popularity.[1]

Such condemnations of Curwen's Bill were common among
radicals, and led the *Courier* to reflect that bad as the Whigs
were, they still played the constitutional game, and were
therefore less dangerous than people who were aiming at universal suffrage—the most vain of all systems of government,
and the most horrible of all tyrannies.[2] On 5 May, when the
Courier reported the introduction of Curwen's Bill, the paper
included a long article on Parliamentary Reform. This article
censured Burdett for his refusal to co-operate with other
public men.

He and his partisans have long branded the Opposition as more
servile, perfidious, and corrupt than Ministers, for no other purpose than to destroy their credit with the People, that he, Sir
Francis, may unite under him all sorts of tempers out of humour
with our system of Government, the moderate Reformer, as well
as the violent Revolutionist.

The Whigs were black, but the radicals were double-black,
and the *Courier* found itself in an awkward position, for this
distinction is difficult to maintain.

Thus, when on 10 September 1809 Southey wrote to
Daniel Stuart (the editor of the *Courier*) that his view of
politics differed from Stuart's in only two respects—in dis-
approving of the raid on Copenhagen and in giving Sir
Francis Burdett credit for good intentions[3]—the difference
was in fact a very considerable one. Southey was writing to
Stuart about the proposal made to him during the summer of
1809 by the Scottish publisher Ballantyne to write the history
of the year 1808 for a new *Edinburgh Annual Register*. Southey
was at work on this till the following April. The part which
was of greatest interest to him was the account of the Spanish

[1] *SL*, ii. 147–8, 6 July 1809.   [2] *Courier*, 4 May 1809.
[3] BM MSS. Adds. 34,046, f. 247.

insurrection, but he was compelled to say a good deal about domestic politics too. He felt very much in sympathy with those 'parliamentary Ishmaelites' the radical reformers because their hand *was* against every man's. Burdett supported ministers after 1807 'not because he liked them, but because, he said, there were no better to supply their place'. This, said Southey, was the feeling of the people in general. 'They rejoiced in the fall of the last ministry, but it was with the joy of a vindictive temper, not of hope. . . .'[1] In later pages Southey often finds fault with the intemperance of Burdett's speeches, even though he approves of their substance. Southey fully concurred, for example, in Burdett's attack on Castlereagh's modifications of Windham's limited service army law. But the speech, though eloquent, and excellent in purport and principle, was injudicious in temper, because it was calculated to exasperate his opponents, not conciliate them.[2] Or again, Southey had no patience with ministerial opposition to the Bill to abolish offices in reversion, and agreed that on this matter ministers showed themselves to be rather the King's menials than his servants. But Burdett's intemperate language, 'by continually supplying censure with fresh materials, and giving indeed too good reason for alarm and disgust to the best disposed, lessens the effect which his talents and undaunted spirit might produce, were they but more wisely directed'.[3] Southey thus had definite reservations about Burdett. But he did not agree with the systematic attacks which the *Courier* was making on him, twisting his language so unscrupulously that on one occasion Coleridge was moved to protest.[4]

Cobbett was regarded by Southey with less favour. 'Cobbett may by possibility not be a rascal', he told Wynn in July 1809, 'because he set out with the worst opinions in the world, and has ever since been getting farther and farther

---

[1] *Edinburgh Annual Register for 1808*, part i, p. 13.
[2] Ibid., p. 88.   [3] Ibid., p. 167.
[4] BM MSS. Adds. 34,046, f. 100, 8 May 1809.

from them.'[1] There was at least one article in *Cobbett's Register* of which Southey fully approved. This was contributed by a writer who signed himself 'Vindex', and dealt with the question of tithes in Ireland, showing how the issue was exacerbated by the 'hopeless poverty and grinding oppression' to which the Irish were subjected.[2] Southey's considered opinion of Cobbett is given when discussing his championship of the theory that England's wealth was not dependent on manufactures. 'This demagogue, who, treating all subjects with the same confidence, whether he understands them or not, dashes forward, right or wrong, seldom failing, even when most erroneous, to exhibit proofs of a vigorous and fearless mind. . . .'[3] Southey forgave Cobbett much because he strongly supported the war. He was the most effective defender of the Orders in Council, by which Britain retaliated against French decrees aimed at strangling British trade. Whitbread, on the other hand, comes in for some very severe criticism mainly because he was the leading spokesman of the peace party. His arguments are dismissed as insane; he 'insulted the common sense of the country'. He was on occasion supported by Burdett, and Southey commented that the latter's zeal for reform, 'sincere as it is, would be less liable to calumny if he discovered more regard for the honour of England, and more feeling for the liberty of Europe'.[4]

Southey was probably always a little uneasy about the pacifist tendencies of reformers. He tried to persuade himself that it was the true and consistent lovers of liberty who were most convinced that 'this war has long been a business of national life and death'.[5] But to sustain this point of view, there were far too few people like that dashing sailor and notable democrat Lord Cochrane. Southey's difficulty is illustrated by his feelings when invited to become a contributor to the new *Quarterly Review* in the autumn of 1808.

---

[1] NLW, 4812 D 215, 6 July 1809.
[2] *Edinburgh Annual Register for 1808*, part i, pp. 105, 129–30.
[3] Ibid., p. 26.   [4] Ibid., p. 64.   [5] *SL*, ii. 125, 20 Jan. 1809.

This journal was founded in order to combat the pernicious politics of the *Edinburgh Review*, which had given great offence by publishing the notorious 'Don Cevallos' article on affairs in Spain. The main cause of offence was the article's open 'jacobinism'. The revolt in Spain, it argued, had been that of a whole people rising against a corrupt government, and the people of England, by identifying themselves with that revolt, had shown their support of democratic principles. Who now, the writer inquired, would ever more 'presume to cry down popular rights, or tell us that the people have nothing to do with the laws, but to obey them,—with the taxes but to pay them,—and with the blunders of their rulers, but to suffer from them?'[1] Once more the words *liberty* and *people* could be uttered freely. Feelings of liberty and patriotism (in the older, subversive sense), which since 1793 seemed to have been completely extinguished, were reawakened.

Presumably it was this part of the article that impelled the Earl of Buchan to open his front door and kick the offending number of the *Edinburgh Review* out into the street. Walter Scott was so indignant at its tone that he wrote immediately to have his subscription stopped. Others, if we may believe Sydney Smith, cleared their libraries of every number of the abominable journal, and then fumigated the shelves. But such people were anti-jacobins who were alarmed at the dangerous turn taken by public feeling after the Convention of Cintra. Robert Southey would not have been offended in the least by the article's jacobinism. Coleridge himself argued in a similar way in *The Friend*. 'It was not', he said, 'till the Spanish insurrection that Englishmen of all parties recurred, *in toto*, to the old English principles, and spoke of their Hampdens, Sidneys, and Miltons, with the old enthusiasm.'[2] But with the democratic sentiments in the 'Don Cevallos' article were mingled doubts about the ability of the Spaniards to sustain a long war with France, and to Southey this was shameful

---

[1] *Edinburgh Review*, xiii. 222. The article was by Jeffrey and Brougham.
[2] *The Friend*, sect. 1, essay 5 (Bohn ed. 1899, p. 137).

defeatism. He therefore agreed to support the new rival to
the *Edinburgh* in order to keep up the spirit and honour of
the nation. But he was concerned about the Tory bias of the
Quarterly, and made it quite clear that his support implied no
change in his opinions on constitutional reform. Though a
supporter of the Church Establishment, he was no churchman,
and he insisted on freedom of opinion in his contributions to
the review. Still he had serious misgivings. He told Grosvenor
Bedford that he feared its subservience to ministers, and that
he would have to write for it with his gloves on, for it would
be a dirty business. 'The principle which justifies me is this,
that their influence will give currency and weight to my
opinions upon other subjects.—And tho my opinions all hang
together, *all the hanging* which they imply will not be per-
ceivd.'[1] He proposed to find out how much free and fearless
thinking the review would tolerate by writing an article on
the Baptist mission in India. He evidently wrote this article
on the lines he had followed in the *Annual Review*, making
clear that it seemed to him important to propagate Christianity on account of its moral institutes, not because he believed
in or attached any importance to the doctrines of the Trinity
or the Incarnation or Eternal Punishment. He considered that
he had written with considerable restraint. If he had written
in his own person he could have spoken out more emphatically
concerning the corruptions of Christianity. Even so, he was
aware that he would offend the high orthodox men in Church
and State. And why not? They would always think as they were
told anyhow, and the *Anti-Jacobin* and *British Critic* were
'good enough for their faces of brass, brains of lead, and
tongues of bell-metal'.[2] The *Quarterly* should aim to interest
people with minds of their own.

So Southey might think, but not the editor, William
Gifford. When Southey saw the 'cruel mutilation' to which
his article had been subjected, and how 'dexterously' Gifford

---

[1] BL, c. 24, f. 86, 18 Nov. 1808.
[2] Ibid., f. 89, 24 Nov. 1808; *LC*, iii. 199, 20 Dec. 1808.

had cut it down to the standard of orthodoxy, he almost
vowed never to write for the *Quarterly* again. He restrained his
feelings when he received the payment—£21. 13*s.*; but the
'gelding' which some of his articles suffered in the *Quarterly*
was to be a constant source of complaint.[1]

The article on the Baptist mission was an indirect reply to
the malicious and entertaining attack on these missionaries
by Sydney Smith in the *Edinburgh Review*. There can be
little doubt that one quite important reason for Southey's
willingness to help the *Quarterly* was a desire to be even with
the *Edinburgh*. In the very first number of that review Jeffrey
wrote a rather severe critique on the Lake Poets by way of an
article on *Thalaba*. Later on, *Madoc* had likewise received an
unfavourable notice. Southey was not the man to endure
unfriendly criticism without retaliation, and Jeffrey was only
the chief of the critics whom he attacked. A minor poet
called Peter Bayley had abused *Joan of Arc*, describing it as
'a mis-shapen mass, half verse, half prose', and censuring its
anti-national spirit. Southey had his revenge in the *Annual
Review for 1804*. He explained his motives to Miss Barker
with characteristic exuberance. Bayley, he said, had

committed high treason against me in the first place; but what he is
to be damned for is, first, having stolen by wholesale from the
'Lyrical Ballads', and then abusing Wordsworth by name. I will
break him upon the wheel, and then hook him up alive, *in terrorem*,
and make his memory stink in the noses of all readers of English,
present and to come.[2]

Or again, in 1807 he asked Grosvenor Bedford whether he
could find out from Gifford who reviewed *Thalaba* in the
British Critic, and *Madoc* in the *Monthly Review*. This information would give him an opportunity of 'showing both
gentlemen what a very different thing the sting of a dragon is

---

[1] BL, c. 24, f. 99, 7 Mar. 1809.
[2] *SL*, i. 254. See *Poems*, by Peter Bayley, jun. (1803), pp. 3–4. This
volume contains a ludicrous imitation of a Lyrical Ballad, 'The Fisherman's
Wife', and the offensive reference to Wordsworth may be found on p. 201.

from the bite of a sucking-flea'.[1] So far as the *Edinburgh* was concerned, he disclaimed any desire for retaliation when writing to Walter Scott, but admitted it in the intimacy of a letter to Rickman. 'In my hatred to the Scotchmen', he wrote to him on 18 February 1809, '(a little revenge being mingled therewith) I wish this Quarterly to succeed.'[2] That Southey bitterly resented Jeffrey's impudent critiques is clear from every reference to him in his letters. When he met Jeffrey in Edinburgh in October 1805, he got much satisfaction out of observing that Jeffrey was only five foot one inch high. (Southey himself was nearly six foot.) It was impossible, he said to Wynn, to feel angry with anything so diminutive. As for taste and learning, he wrote to Danvers, 'the whole corps of Edinburgh reviewers appear miserably puny to me, who have been accustomed to live with strong men'.[3]

Southey would naturally tend to disagree with any point of view held by *Edinburgh* reviewers, and to sympathize with any point of view or person attacked by it. (One reason for the consistent warmth of feeling that Southey always expressed towards John Thelwall was that early in its career the *Edinburgh* had a quarrel with him.) Inevitably this would tend to be a conservative influence on the whole. Southey's conversion to Toryism, however, was precipitated by the course of public events in the year 1810.

[1] BL, c. 24, f. 59, 5 Dec. 1807.   [2] HM.   [3] *SL*, i. 342, 346.

III ∾ TORY

1. 1810

It was easy for Southey to be a democrat in 1808 because
there had been so much popular enthusiasm for the war.
By 1810 things were different, and Southey had to face the
fact that parliamentary reform might give power to 'peace-
mongers'. His difficulty was pressed home to him by the
Walcheren debates in the Commons in the spring of 1810.
A military expedition to take the island of Walcheren in the
Netherlands, and in particular to seize the town of Flushing,
failed completely. This exposed the ministry to damaging
criticism, and on 26 January the opposition managed to
secure a majority in favour of an inquiry into the causes of
the disaster. Rickman told Southey that the ministry under
Spencer Perceval was unlikely to last long, and would probably be succeeded by a coalition including the Grenville
section of the Whigs. Southey replied that this would be
against the national interest. 'These people have all been
tried and found wanting. Look where I will, I can see no good.'[1]
On 2 February Southey told Wynn that he would have con-
gratulated him on the opposition victory in the Commons if
some of the opposition had not been worse than the ministry
—worse because of their spineless attitude to the war. 'I
would rather see any set of men in power than those who
so basely calumniate the Spaniards,—rather have a Cabinet
composed of the Devil and his Angels if they would carry on
the war, than of men who are ready to bow the knee to
Buonaparte.'[2] As it turned out, however, the Whigs failed to

[1] HM, 17 Jan. 1810.   [2] NLW, 4812 D 221.

secure majorities when the decisive votes were taken on
30 March; and if, as was commonly said, this showed the
stranglehold of corrupt influence on the House of Commons,
Southey had reason to be grateful for corruption. It might
shield the vices of the Duke of York, but it also saved Britain
from betraying the Spaniards. That Southey still leaned to
the popular side in politics, however, is shown by his comments on the Gale Jones case.[1]

This arose directly out of the inquiry into the Walcheren
expedition. Among the most determined partisans of the
ministry was Charles Yorke, one of the members for Cam-
bridgeshire. He moved the exclusion of the public from the
Walcheren inquiry, with the result that the press was unable
to report, and the official minutes alone were published.
John Gale Jones, the proprietor of a debating society called
the British Forum, advertised a motion for debate on the
freedom of the press in which Yorke's name was given unfavourable prominence: 'Which was a greater outrage upon
the public feeling, Mr. Yorke's enforcement of the Standing
Order to exclude strangers from the House of Commons, or
Mr. Windham's recent attack upon the liberty of the press?'
Yorke brought this before the House of Commons as a
breach of privilege, and his plea was upheld. Gale Jones was
not merely reprimanded but consigned to Newgate prison for
the remainder of that sitting of Parliament.

When Gale Jones's case was being heard, Burdett was
not in the House. Some days later, however, he came down
to lodge his protest against these proceedings. Moreover,
he printed the speech, with violent additions, in *Cobbett's
Register*. This was in turn taken up as a breach of privilege,
and Burdett was ordered to be committed to the Tower. He
challenged the authority of the Speaker's warrant to deprive
him of his liberty, and effectively resisted arrest for three days,
thus making himself the centre of serious disturbances in

---

[1] After his conversion to Toryism, Southey changed his view of the case.
See *SL*, ii. 251. Letter to Charles Wynn, 4 Feb. 1812.

London which may well have seemed like the first convulsions
of a violent revolution.

The attitude of the *Courier* to these events will serve as a
useful introduction to Southey's comments on them. Speaking
summarily, it was hostile to the interpretation of parliamentary privilege put forward by Yorke and endorsed by a
majority of the House of Commons; and this attitude over-
bore, to a surprising extent, the almost malicious hostility of
the *Courier* to Burdett himself. On 2 April the *Courier* said
that Gale Jones was the victim of a dangerous practice,
amounting to a denial of trial by one's peers. Moreover, if the
precedent were established, the House of Commons would
virtually have the power of stifling comment on its conduct.
This would hardly appeal to newspapers of any party.

On Saturday, 7 April, the *Courier* described the attempts
made on the previous day to arrest Burdett, and the concur-
rent window-smashing of the mob. In spite of the alarming
spirit thus manifested, the *Courier* persisted in its claim that
the House of Commons had proceeded on very weak ground
in dealing in this manner with Jones and Burdett. It did not
falter the following week, and regretted that members of
Parliament had allowed themselves to be frightened out of
pressing the constitutional issue. (Both Curwen and Sir
Samuel Romilly had made the disturbed state of the country
a reason for not proceeding with the case immediately; the
whole House seemed to have become virtual 'champions of
unlimited privilege and power'.[1]) On 11 April the *Courier*
observed that the behaviour of the mob at the time of Burdett's arrest was not apparently inspired by disaffection to the
government. There were no secret committees, no revolutionary placards. 'There was none of that dark and dangerous
spirit that was developed at different periods of the last war'
—that is, during the seventeen-nineties. On Friday, 13 April,
however, the *Courier* withdrew a little from this position.
The odium with which Burdett and his partisans had covered

[1] *Courier*, 12 Apr. 1810.

the opposition to the excessive claims of the House of Commons made it 'useless and imprudent' to press the claims of the liberty of the subject, for the time at least. But it insisted on the rightness of its case, and developed and reinforced its arguments in articles published on Saturday and Monday. On Tuesday, 17 April, it reported the debate in the Commons on Romilly's motion for the release of Gale Jones. (The motion was lost by 112 votes to 160.) The *Courier* warmly approved of Romilly's conduct, and expressed the hope that Gale Jones would not submit by petition, in order that the question of imprisoning for libel without trial might be legally settled.

In the discussions on the Gale Jones case, Southey's friend Wynn had supported the privilege of the House of Commons, although he was opposed to the severe measures against Jones himself. He prepared and published an *Argument* in favour of the Commons' power to imprison for breach of privilege, and sent a copy to Southey. On 28 May, Southey wrote back expressing his disagreement. If the Commons possessed the power of detention then it was time it was taken from them, 'for while it exists all discussion upon political affairs is matter of sufferance and not of right. Once establish the case of Gale Jones as a precedent, and we have no other security against an actual despotism than what may be found in the fears of the Ruling Powers.'[1] It is likely that Southey had been strongly influenced by the arguments of the *Courier*. The reports in the *Courier* of the behaviour of Burdett and his supporters must, on the other hand, have strengthened his doubts about the good intentions of the radicals. Burdett's attempt to resist arrest, there seems little doubt, was a trial of strength between himself and the Government. As his modern biographer triumphantly exclaims: 'To put Burdett in the Tower an army of 50,000 men had been necessary. This bare circumstance spoke more than whole volumes.'[2] Evidently it did. Francis Place and Henry Hunt

[1] NLW, 4812 D 223.
[2] M. W. Patterson, *Francis Burdett and his Times* (1931), i. 277.

both bear witness that the gallant Lord Cochrane contemplated full-scale measures of armed defence.[1] And on 24 April (a fortnight after the arrest and the riots) the *Courier* remarked that 'the late boastings and audacity of some of the partizans of Sir Francis Burdett countenance the rumour, that they have been weak enough to suppose a revolution actually at hand'.

On 1 May 1810 the *Courier* had one of its pangs of conscience about the support it might in the past have unthinkingly given to the Burdettite contempt for the Whigs, the 'general anathemas' of those who wished to undermine the whole Constitution. The writer even went so far as to say that there was nothing disgraceful in wanting to wrest office from the party in power. This was a strange contrast to its attitude six weeks before, when the *Courier* had triumphed in the embarrassment felt by the Whigs whenever the accusation was made that they were Outs who wanted to be In. No doubt this change was a reaction to the common danger brought to light by the Burdett riots.

The article (of 14 March) which spoke so contemptuously of the Whigs was prompted by another article which deserves some consideration here. In the number of the *Edinburgh Review* which appeared some time at the end of February 1810, though it was dated December 1809, Jeffrey had contributed a discussion of the state of the parties. He asserted that the country was divided between the partisans of democracy and arbitrary power, and that unless something were done they would clash violently. Only the Whigs stood between the intending combatants. Jeffrey's advice to the Whigs was that they should take the side of the democrats, and, while leading the people in the struggle for their just claims, moderate the fury of that struggle.

Nobody seems to have taken this article very seriously. Leigh Hunt, in three articles in the *Examiner*, poured scorn on the idea that the Whigs were the Sabine Women of the

[1] G. Wallas, *Life of Francis Place* (1918), p. 51.

Constitution. Supporters of the ministry, for their part, affected amusement at the contortions with which the desperate Whigs sought popularity. As for the Whigs themselves, by 30 May the *Courier* was able to congratulate them on the way they had seen the folly of the *Edinburgh Review*'s advice. They were even outrunning ministers in their condemnation of the Burdettites.

This would not have made Southey think any worse of the Burdettites. It was a union of Burdettites and Whigs that would have alarmed him. On the other hand, the Burdett riots had shown that the fears of revolution expressed by both Southey and Jeffrey were not without foundation. Perhaps Southey took what consolation he could from the *Courier*'s comment on 4 May: 'This state of affairs seems to give a considerable degree of uneasiness to many persons— they see danger to the Constitution; they are visited by the most dismal apprehensions of a revolution. This fear is exactly what the Democrats wish to encourage—But it is an idle one.' The machinery of government had dealt with Despard's conspiracy, and would be competent to deal with any conspiracy among Despard's successors. Southey could none the less hardly fail to be alarmed. He had been reading Middleton's *Life of Cicero*, he told Rickman on 9 March 1810, and noted that 'the Signs of the Times are almost as bad now as they were then'. One of the disasters in Cicero's time of which Southey feared a recurrence was the *bellum servile*, a war of slaves against their masters. Rickman was inclined to be less concerned, though for reasons that would not have given Southey much comfort. It is the calm of the eighty years before the French Revolution that is exceptional, he said, not the bloody horror which has been usual throughout human history. The French have merely returned to normal. 'I hope still', Rickman concluded, 'that in our time Common Sense aided by Increasing Science may cause her still small Voice to be heard.—But this is perhaps *Hope* without *Expectation*.'[1]

---

[1] HM, Rickman to Southey, 12 Mar. 1810.

During the summer of 1810 the danger of an economic breakdown was added to the danger of mob-violence. There was an unprecedented number of bankruptcies, and a corresponding amount of unemployment. The trouble was caused partly by the closing of continental markets to British goods as a result of French economic warfare, partly by the failure of over-sanguine attempts to exploit new South American markets. A number of private bankers failed, and this affected many more people than those directly connected with manufacturing trades. Moreover, since a great deal of the currency in circulation was issued by local banks, and the failure of a bank made its notes worthless, people were impoverished who had no direct connexion with the bank at all. A Whitehaven newspaper, the *Cumberland Pacquet*, had in its issue for 31 July a report of the failure of twelve banks in the west of England. The *Monthly Magazine*, in its commercial report for July, noted the failure of a London banking house,[1] together with the banks connected with it in the provinces. Five Manchester banks had also stopped payment. 'Speculative exports to South America are the rock upon which these houses have split. In consequence of these unexpected events, public credit is at the present moment as low as ever it has been in the memory of man.'[2] In addition to the succession of bankruptcies, which continued through August and September, confidence was shaken in the currency itself. Earlier in the summer a parliamentary committee, set up to inquire into the causes of the high price of bullion, came to the conclusion that there was an excessive issue of bank-notes, and recommended that cash payments by the Bank of England (suspended in 1797) should be resumed within two years. This report contributed to the general decline in commercial confidence, and even sober observers were being disturbed by apprehensions of national ruin. Towards the end of

---

[1] Presumably Brickwood & Co. See L. S. Pressnell, *Country Banking in the Industrial Revolution* (1956), p. 466.

[2] *Monthly Magazine*, Aug. 1810, p. 95.

September William Wilberforce expressed himself with
uneasy indirectness to Lord Muncaster about Britain's prospects. He admired the 'conveniences of a highly civilized state
of society', such as the rapidity with which mail was carried.
But people were not grateful enough for them.

> I cannot help at times, giving way I will not say, but, at least,
> lending an ear to suggestions which arise in my mind, that our
> comforts will be abridged, and our pride be humbled. But I will
> abstain from striking this string, at least at present. Let me not
> excite melancholy ideas in your mind.[1]

Wilberforce was probably afflicted with profound melancholy three days after writing this letter. On 28 September
the *Courier* (an evening paper) published the news that
Abraham Goldsmid had committed suicide early that morning.
Goldsmid was one of the leading bankers of London, and for
that year contractor for the government loan. The Funds had
already been at a discount, and Goldsmid's suicide depressed
the value of stock catastrophically. As the *Courier* wrote:
'Words would be inadequate to express the surprise, the
alarm, and the dismay that was visible. . . . We question
whether peace or war suddenly made ever created such a
bustle as the death of Mr. Goldsmid.'[2] It turned out that
Goldsmid's business was not in such serious difficulties as he
thought. But the shock to credit was profound.

In all these commotions it must be allowed that the professional economists do not seem to have been unduly
alarmed. Most of their comment is concerned with the technicalities of the Bullion Committee's report. To understand
the kind of dismal suggestions to which Wilberforce found
himself lending an ear one must turn to lay observers. Thus,
a pamphlet by a 'British Merchant' is of some psychological
interest. It is called *An Exposé of the present ruinous system
of Town and Country Banks*, and was published in September

---

[1] R. I. and S. Wilberforce, *Life of W. Wilberforce* (1838), iii. 465–6, 25
Sept. 1810.
[2] *Courier*, 28 Sept. 1810.

1810. The author was no revolutionist, as is shown by his
earnest dedication to George Canning, and by the nature of
his proposal to establish district banks guaranteed by the
local nobility, gentry, tradesmen, and farmers, which would
not be allowed to engage in speculation of any kind. Near
the beginning of the pamphlet, the 'British Merchant' expresses astonishment at the apathy of people in the face of the
present crisis.

I behold extravagance and unconcern continue their destructive
course, without exciting a terror, or even the slightest wish for a
better management of its affairs! . . . Like infatuated Mariners, we
are in the midst of shoals and quicksands, and suffer ourselves to be
lulled into sleep, and to be ingulphed in the waves that heave around
us.[1]

A little later, however, when he describes the effects of bank
failures and a fall in the stocks, his opinion changes. 'We
stand aghast with terror; we overwhelm the public credit by
fear, and shake the palladium of the Country with clamour
and cries!'[2] The contradiction is not as great as it appears,
for even an infatuated mariner might be aghast with terror
when faced with the immediate prospect of being 'ingulphed'.
Terror, apathy, elation—these are all possible reactions to
the vast increase of business activity which we call the Industrial Revolution. The 'British Merchant' was alarmed by the
insecurity which was a necessary consequence of that vast
increase. The great enemy, he says, is speculation. Commerce
itself is good. It creates wealth gradually and surely. Speculation is sudden and uncertain. He instances the evil effects of
the wealth of America on the Spaniards in the sixteenth
century.

NO SOONER DID THEY OBTAIN WEALTH WITHOUT LABOR, than
unbridled passions began to predominate, and a love of immoderate
enjoyments stamped the Nation with the horrible character of
treachery and licentiousness! Woe to the people who obtain wealth
without labor! Woe to the man, and to the million who can draw

[1] *An Exposé* (1810), pp. 4–5.   [2] Ibid., p. 9.

thousands from out of the mine, or from out of the TOWN and COUNTRY BANKS without inheritance, property, or labor. Woe to the man and to the million who are enabled by such means to embark in flagitious speculations, and thereby to abandon an honorable and an industrious trade.[1]

Now, he goes on, even the accumulations of the industrious are jeopardized by the speculative system, and all are liable to be involved in a common ruin. The mentality of speculation, too, is spreading, so that honest traders are corrupted, and 'the flagrant appetites, the uncontrouled avarice, the intemperate passions of individuals of almost every rank, dispose them to take advantage of other men's wants . . .'.[2] As Burke might have put it, the spirit of the Industrial Revolution lies deep in the corruption of our common nature.

Those who are tempted to dismiss the 'British Merchant' as simply the kind of Jeremiah with which every generation is afflicted should turn to the *New Annual Register*. This was an anti-ministerial publication, and therefore disposed to take a gloomy view of the country's prospects while under Tory rule. But its tone is temperate, and it is not in the least eccentric. In 1810 it drew attention to the insecurity of wealth which depended on bills that might or might not hold. It compared the merchant of modern times with his counterpart in 1760, noting that the modern merchant 'draws much of his gain from speculating in the funds, and in the loans which government annually need'. Fortunes are built up by methods which demand 'good fortune, chicanery, and the arts of gambling', not 'perseverance in more slow but more honourable methods'.[3] The writer concluded with the hope that trade would recover as it had recovered from less serious blows. But the final sentence was desponding. In view of the war and the inflated currency 'there is much reason to dread that the commerce of Britain has seen its best days'.[4]

---

[1] *An Exposé* (1810), p. 11. [2] Ibid., p. 19.
[3] *New Annual Register for 1810*, chap. 13, p. 265.
[4] Ibid., p. 266.

Other writers at this time, perhaps recalling Volney brooding over the ruins of Palmyra, but without the optimistic conclusion inspired by the hopes of the French Revolution, saw Britain going the way of other great empires in the past. Thus, in the *Monthly Magazine* for February 1811, Sir Richard Phillips (under the signature of 'Common Sense') discussed the increasing size of London, and remarked that 'great cities contain in their very greatness, the seeds of premature and rapid decay'. He foresaw the time when the uncontrollable forces which had stimulated the growth of London should have ceased to work; then the houses would become too many for the inhabitants, and some areas would become dilapidated, others depopulated altogether. 'This disease will spread like an atrophy in the human body, and ruin will follow ruin, till the entire city is disgusting to the remnant of the inhabitants, they flee one after another to a more thriving spot; and at length the whole becomes a heap of ruins!' This had been the fate of Nineveh, Babylon, Antioch, and Thebes; and Rome, Delhi, and Alexandria were following the same path. London's turn would surely come.[1] In October the same magazine published an 'anticipation of the year 3000', which begins thus:

If Great Britain be doomed, a second Rome, to fall under the attack of the modern Franks, if our fleets be destined to ruin, or our colonies to extinction, if our population be fated to be dispersed into foreign countries, or to be employed in a state of servitude in foreign mines, the remarks of foreign historians on our national character and our imperial works, in a future age, will be singular and, perhaps, fastidious. . . .[2]

The events of 1810 brought to the surface a current of thought of which there are many traces in earlier years. Goldsmith had been concerned about the consequences of the accumulation of wealth and the decay of men, including the decay of their villages and cities. And this was more than a

---

[1] *Monthly Magazine*, Feb. 1811, pp. 3–4.
[2] Ibid., Oct. 1811, p. 228.

repetition of the old theme of the transience of earthly glory. There is a sense of something aberrant, something monstrous at work in the devastation of the Deserted Village. In a very different mood from Goldsmith's, Lady Holland made a similar point in her journal in March 1800. Reading an account of the ruins of Persepolis, she reflected how lacking in grandeur the ruins of London would be—mere brick-dust, except for St. Paul's and the bridges.

> In future times when this little island shall have fallen into its natural insignificancy, by being no longer possessed of a fictitious power founded upon commerce, distant colonies, and other artificial sources of wealth, how puzzled will the curious antiquary be when seeking amidst the ruins of London vestiges of its past grandeur.[1]

'Fictitious power founded upon commerce', 'wealth without labor'—that was a principal source of anxiety. No one likes to be gnawed by the suspicion that he is getting something for nothing. Such gain is always felt to be impermanent, and the idlest of aristocracies will attribute to itself social usefulness, if pressed. Perhaps the most striking expression of this insecurity is Mrs. Barbauld's poem 'Eighteen Hundred and Eleven'. She prophesies the abandonment and decay of London, and the lapse of England into an agricultural and primitive condition; visited (a pleasant touch) by American tourists.

> Oft shall they seek some peasant's homely shed,
> Who toils, unconscious of the mighty dead,
> To ask where Avon's winding waters stray,
> And thence a knot of wild flowers bear away.[2]

The seeds of the decay of the social order lie in the methods of expanding commerce.

> Arts, arms, and wealth destroy the fruit they bring;
> Commerce, like beauty, knows no second spring.
> Crime walks thy streets, Fraud earns her unblest bread,
> O'er want and woe thy gorgeous robe is spread,

[1] Elizabeth, Lady Holland, *Journal* (1908), ii. 54.
[2] A. L. Barbauld, *Eighteen Hundred and Eleven* (1812), p. 11.

And angel charities in vain oppose:
With grandeur's growth the mass of misery grows.[1]

This idea persisted well into the nineteenth century, notably
in the later writings of Cobbett, who rejoiced at the impending collapse of the paper-money system and the return of
small farms and a cottage economy. Robert Owen looked
forward to the time when 'grass would be growing in Fleet
Street and Cheapside, and the happier human race would be
living in parallelograms upon co-operative principles'.[2] It
served as a gloomy speculation, inserted only to be dismissed,
in Humphry Davy's *Consolations in Travel*, published in 1830,
and provided Macaulay with a famous rhetorical flourish.
The Catholic Church, he wrote in 1840, 'may still exist in
undiminished vigour when some traveller from New Zealand shall, in the midst of a vast solitude, take his stand on
a broken arch of London Bridge to sketch the ruins of St.
Paul's'.[3]

At this point the reader may object that Macaulay was
obviously not in the least disturbed by his prophecy of the
final ruin of London, and probably Mrs. Barbauld was quite
easy in her mind too. Owen and Cobbett no doubt believed in
their prophecies, and so did many of their proletarian disciples; but it is questionable whether many informed readers
did. The *New Annual Register* wanted to make a point against
the war, and the 'British Merchant' was an old fool in a panic.
At no time did a large section of the public seriously think
that Britain's commercial economy was going to collapse.
Something was bound to turn up, and of course it did. All
this is true. But it does not alter the fact that extreme
apprehension existed below the surface, no less real because
only fitfully expressed. The apprehension emerges in Wilberforce's dismal suggestions, in Josiah Wedgwood's regret that
he was a father because 'he feared he might be leaving his

---

[1] Ibid., p. 24.
[2] Charles Knight, *Passages of a Working Life* (1864), ii. 109.
[3] T. B. Macaulay, *Works*, ed. Lady Trevelyan (1866), vi. 455.

children to evil days', and in Southey's own wish that the next
hundred years were over.[1] The collapse of the British economy
was possible, but like nuclear war it was virtually unimagin-
able. One could not plan for it, except in terms of the eccentric
policies of Cobbett and Owen. As Southey remarked in 1819,
when he believed that revolution was at hand, he behaved as
the people did before the Flood: he ate, drank, and went on
with his usual employments as if things were to last his
time.[2] The surface optimism should not make one forget the
uneasiness beneath.

Micawberish optimism was vindicated by the recovery of
the British economy from the great crisis of 1810–11. In
spite of the American Non-Intercourse Act, trade and credit
showed signs of improvement in the summer of 1811, partly
because the war in Spain and Portugal was going more
favourably. In a comparatively short time the widespread
uneasiness was forgotten. When Thomas Tooke came to
describe the crisis of 1810 in his *Thoughts and Details on the
High and Low Prices of the Last Thirty Years* (1823), he
writes as though he were discussing the events of the previous century. He finds it necessary to prove with careful
documentation that he is not exaggerating the distress
attending the 'tremendous fluctuations' in which so large a
number of commercial establishments were swept away,
without leaving a trace of their existence. People had come
to think that nothing more than 'a high range of prices
prevailed about the time referred to'.[3] How quickly the
atmosphere changed is illustrated by the kind of review that
Croker was able to give Mrs. Barbauld's poem in the *Quarterly*
of June 1812. After quoting a passage which describes how

> No more in crowded mart or busy street,
> Friends greeting friends with cheerful hurry greet—

[1] Mrs. Henry Sandford, *Thomas Poole* (1888), ii. 187 (This Josiah Wedgwood was the son of the founder of the pottery firm); *SL*, i. 293, 7 Dec. 1804;
BL, c. 24, f. 107, 30 Apr. 1809.
[2] BL, d. 47, f. 174, 5 Nov. 1819.
[3] T. Tooke, *High and Low Prices* (1823) i. 118–19.

Croker is moved to ask where Mrs. Barbauld can live, 'for the description just quoted is no more like the scene that is really before *our* eyes, than Mrs. Barbauld's satire is like her "Lessons for Children", or her "Hymns in Prose"'.[1] No doubt this joke was well received in the summer of 1812. It might not have been so amusing in the early months of 1811.

Crabb Robinson complained that Mrs. Barbauld's poem was disheartening and dastardly,[2] and this would not commend it to Southey. Yet there is a disconcerting sympathy between the anti-commercial spirit of 'Eighteen Hundred and Eleven' and that of *Letters from England*. Judging from the review of Pasley's *Military Policy*, which will be discussed in the next section, Southey attempted for a time to push these anti-commercial sentiments out of his mind. His few comments on the bullion question show that he was mainly interested in supporting the view that there was no serious economic crisis. To have taken any other view would have been to support the critics of the war, and worse still to reinforce the power of William Cobbett. In the winter of 1810–11 Cobbett's views were becoming increasingly popular. Week by week in his *Political Register* he was attacking the paper-money system. Southey recalled to Bedford how people who lost by the failure of country banks immediately became converts to Cobbett. 'We had a specimen of this at Keswick as you may remember.'[3] Southey is almost certainly referring to the failure of one of the Workington banks in December 1810. Workington money was in general use around Keswick, and the town was consequently in a great ferment. 'Luckily', Southey told Bedford, 'all that we had was of the other Bank.'[4] Thus, Southey could witness at first hand the powerful and disruptive influence of Cobbett

[1] *QR*, vii. 310.

[2] E. J. Morley, *H. C. Robinson on Books and their Writers* (1938), i. 64.

[3] BL, c. 24, f. 164, 10 May 1811.

[4] Ibid., f. 141, 14 Dec. 1810. He was not so fortunate when the other Workington bank failed in July 1812. See HM, Southey to Rickman, 28 July 1812.

at work. That Cobbett should win converts was a circumstance most unwelcome to lovers of tranquillity and order,
and still more unwelcome to supporters of the war. Cobbett
was now more interested in denouncing corruption at home
than the enemy abroad. On 9 July 1810 he was sentenced to
two years' imprisonment for printing an attack on German
troops who had carried out a flogging of British soldiers at
Ely. This article was only one offence out of many. Cobbett's
style was an offence in itself. Its tough irreverence fitly
expressed the temper which Southey feared in the populace.
The government that founds its prosperity on manufactures
sleeps on gunpowder. It looked now as though the gunpowder
might be ignited. Southey's fears are plainly expressed in his
history of the year in the *Edinburgh Annual Register for 1809*.
He began writing this in the September of 1810, the earliest
reference to it being in a letter to Walter Scott written on 17
September, eleven days before Goldsmid's suicide. It occupied
him throughout the winter. In this he had to report the inquiry
into the conduct of the Duke of York and Mrs. Clarke, and
by now he regarded the business in a different light from
that which he had seen it in at the time. He was no longer
'swinishly inclined'. He still strongly disapproved of the
acquittal of the Duke by the House of Commons, and added
that ministers, who had earned the confidence of the country
by their spirited conduct of the war, largely forfeited that
confidence by 'their obsequiousness to the royal family in
this unhappy transaction'. The 'enemies of government'—
Southey means the revolutionaries, not the constitutional
opposition—did not fail to profit to the utmost from this loss
of confidence. 'As if some political Saturnalia had been
proclaimed, they gave free scope to all the insolence and
brutality of vulgar exultation.'[1] At this point Southey
developed a comparison between the jacobinism of 1794 and
that of the present day. Then it had been a movement of
intellectuals. Now it had sunk to the populace. No longer was

---

[1] *Edinburgh Annual Register for 1809*, part i, pp. 228, 230.

the appeal to the Rights of Man, to the generous feelings.
It was to the sordid motives of envy and parsimony.

Southey had come round to the *Courier's* view of Sir
Francis Burdett. He was especially alarmed at Burdett's
disrespect for the House of Commons, and his tactical flattery
of the royal family.[1] (The *Courier* had remarked of a speech
by Burdett at the 'Crown and Anchor' on 1 May 1809 that
'if the Royal Dukes will but unite with the Jacobins, each
may have his Gloucester-place Establishment'.[2]) Southey
was still able, however, to approve of Burdett's exposure of
a 'job' by which Chelsea pensioners were deprived of land
which had been assigned to them. The land was four and a
quarter acres in extent, of which 'the quarter had been
assigned to the hospital,—the four acres to Colonel Gordon'.
Perceval, the Prime Minister, had attempted to be sarcastic at
Burdett's expense, but Southey concluded that the grant to
Colonel Gordon was 'exceedingly improper, and not less
imprudent'.[3] In September 1810 he apparently still thought
of himself as a 'democrat', if one may judge from a letter he
wrote to James Ballantyne about objections which had been
made to the *Register* for 1808. A 'democratical colouring', he
said, 'must needs be the sunshine and life of whatever pro-
ceeds from me'. But his democracy was unconnected with
faction or party, 'true to the interest and honour of England
and going head and heart with the King and with the Government'. The *Register* would mainly offend Cobbett's disciples,
the Emancipators, and the peace-mongers.[4] As late as October Southey could not be classified as a regular supporter
of the Tory ministry. In that month he was visited by a
French-born traveller from America, Louis Simond. Simond
noted that the youthful democratic feeling of Southey,
Coleridge, and Wordsworth had come down to what he
called Whiggism, and, Simond added, 'may not even stop

[1] Ibid., pp. 241 et seq.
[2] *Courier*, 3 May 1809. Mrs. Clarke's house was in Gloucester Place.
[3] *Edinburgh Annual Register for 1809*, part i, pp. 232–4.
[4] 19 Sept. 1810. National Library of Scotland MS. 1817, pp. 19–20.

there'. He was surprised by Southey's hostility to Malthus, remarking that such hostility was usually a sign of the 'thorough reformer'. But Whigs and radicals, he explains, have many points of contact, and it is easy to slide out of one party into the other. 'When the metamorphosis takes place, it happens frequently that the new insect, fresh out of his old skin, drags still some fragments of it after him,—just enough to indicate what he was before.'[1]

By November the metamorphosis was becoming complete. It may have been advanced in the course of a short visit by Rickman to Keswick at the end of October. As a result of this visit Rickman started to send Southey scraps of news and parliamentary papers. He was glad, he said, to see the poet turning his talents, 'which in lustre surpass any extant, to rational Politics, the most worthy study, as the most beneficial to Mankind'.[2] Evidently the two men discussed politics at some length, and it is likely that Rickman strongly pressed his own Toryism upon Southey. He had a forceful character, and must have been a difficult man to disagree with. In a letter dated 10 November Southey acknowledged the receipt of a bundle of parliamentary papers, and added: 'I shall be very much the better for your comments on passing events,— and you will see by the 1809 volume that many things which I learnt from you here have not been forgotten.'[3]

The effect of Rickman's comments may be more conveniently discussed in the next section. As was noted earlier, the Workington bank failure in December would have tended to alarm Southey into opposition to reform. But probably the decisive influence in making a Tory of him was the Regency issue, which filled the newspapers from November onwards. George III had become insane, and as the Prince of Wales was supposed to favour them, the Whigs pressed for an unrestricted Regency. Ministers, on the other hand, wanted

---

[1] L. Simond, *Journal of a Tour . . . in Great Britain* (Edinburgh, 1815), i. 350-3.
[2] HM, 31 Dec. 1810.   [3] HM.

first to delay the setting up of a Regency, and then only to appoint a Regent under restrictions. They argued that the King's insanity might prove as temporary as his first attack in 1788. It was generally believed that the Whigs would come into power, and the Burdettites fully supported them in their efforts to secure an unrestricted Regency. On 1 November, for example, it was on Burdett's initiative that a division was taken on a ministerial proposal to adjourn the House of Commons for a fortnight, thus moving the *Courier* to horrified comment on his indecent haste in assuming that the King was permanently insane. Meantime the Whigs continued to speak in desponding terms of the war in Portugal, and it was believed that a new ministry would certainly enter into a negotiation with France over affairs in the Peninsula. This would be more than enough to make Southey completely antagonistic to all reformers. It is true that as late as 22 January 1811, he told William Taylor of Norwich that Lord Holland, if he came into power, might do more for the Spaniards than the present ministry, 'unless he be as much crippled by his colleagues as Canning was'.[1] This was at a time when rumours were circulating that the Prince Regent might appoint a ministry of 'Foxites' and 'Prince's Friends'. Lord Holland was named by the *Courier* as the possible Prime Minister, and Sir Francis Burdett (odd thought) as Home Secretary.[2] Lord Holland was a Whig who was as enthusiastic as Southey about the Spanish war, so that there was some reason in Southey's hope. But as Whitbread would have to be a member of any Foxite cabinet, it looks as though Southey was clutching at a straw. Besides, in a letter to William Taylor, he would be inclined to appear as liberal as possible; just as, in writing to Walter Scott in the previous September, he sounds as though he were already a Tory.[3]

[1] J. W. Robberds, *Memoir of William Taylor* (1843), ii. 340.
[2] *Courier*, 25 Jan. 1811.
[3] *LC*, iii. 292, 17 Sept. 1810. 'Upon almost all points of present politics I believe there is little difference of opinion between us. . . .' Southey is probably referring primarily to their common opinion that the war should be

In the event, the Regent kept the Tories in power. But
Southey was not now in a mood to revise his opinions.
Henceforth he strongly supported the ministers.

2. STRONG GOVERNMENT

'Of home politics I was very ignorant', Southey told Grosvenor Bedford on 16 February 1811, 'never liking them well
enough to feel any interest beyond that of an election feeling.'
As the annalist of the *Edinburgh Annual Register*, it was now
his business to be better informed, and he had spared no pains
to become so.

> Of three points I have now convinced myself, that the great
> desideratum in our own government is a Premier instead of a
> Cabinet,—that a regular opposition is an absurdity which could not
> exist anywhere but in an island, without destroying the govern-
> ment,—and that parliamentary reform is the shortest road to
> anarchy.

Southey thus dismissed his earlier reforming opinions as the
product of ignorance. He had not really changed his mind;
he had merely begun to think about the subject. The previous
November Rickman had sent him some parliamentary papers
concerning the Reform Bills which Curwen and Burdett had
introduced in 1809, and had added his own comments.
Southey acknowledged receipt of them on 1 December 1810,
and said that he had observed that some of the arguments for
reform were rather 'staggering'. 'I will when occasion
offers, as it will shortly do, state them fully, and give them
their fair weight, whether they turn the balance in my own
mind or not.'[2] The occasion offered when he came to con-

carried on with the utmost vigour. Cf. a letter to the Rev. Herbert Hill, 28 Dec.
1810. Longman's were proposing to start a new review, totally independent in
politics, and asked Southey to co-operate. 'I suppose they thought their politics
would tempt me,—but I am not intolerant in these matters, and the Pitt-
idolatry of Gifford and Canning is of no consequence to me. I care little for
any temporary politics except the point of standing by the Spaniards, and carrying on the war with Buonaparte. . . .' Keswick MSS., Hill letters 1807–19, f. 72.

[1] *LC*, iii. 302–3.   [2] HM.

sider the two Bills of 1809 in the *Register*. In the earlier part
of the history of the year he had made one or two comments
which might have been made by a man who was sympathetic
to reform. Thus, in a debate on the corrupt disposal of a seat,
Windham had pointed out the danger of any degree of reform. The removal of a single brick might lead to the collapse
of the whole building. '"Such reform would inevitably ter-
minate in revolution." In reply to this, Mr. Whitbread reminded him, that the pertinacious resistance to all reform
had been the principal cause of the ruin of the continent.'[1]
Southey rarely agreed with Whitbread, but it is evident that
he did so here. However, the very full discussion of the
Reform Bills which begins on page 249 of the *Register* shows
a decided hostility to reform. Up till this time Southey had
assumed that the influence of the ministry in the House of
Commons was too great. When Curwen's Bill was being
discussed, his main objection to it was that it would leave
Treasury patronage untouched, and destroy patronage
everywhere else. But now he was persuaded that the odds
against ministers were frighteningly great. There were four
parties in the Commons (the Ins, the Outs, the Sidmouth
group, and the radicals), three of whom were always potenti-
ally hostile to the ministry. Without additional influence to
counteract this opposition, no ministry could stand three
months, and the government of Britain would be virtually
dissolved. Burdett's reform aimed at making all elections
popular, like those in Westminster, which meant that all
members would be anti-ministerial. The inevitable result
would be anarchy. Public opinion, Southey continued, had
reached the utmost influence proper to it. Any extension of
its power would put the country at the mercy of demagogues.

Southey proposed that the electorate should be restricted
to those who had the education necessary to choose wisely
and thus preserve political stability. This could be done by
having indirect elections, as was the custom in Spain, or by

[1] *Edinburgh Annual Register for 1809*, part i, p. 240.

raising the value of the freehold qualification for voting. On consideration, however, Southey decided that it would be undesirable to reduce the number of freeholders, because the large county electorates served as a countercheck to the influence of the great landlords. Such influence was bad because it weakened the ministry and strengthened the forces of the peace-mongers. Another countercheck of which Southey approved was a graduated income-tax which should prevent great accumulations of property.

The influence of Rickman appears most clearly in Southey's belief in the need for 'strong government'. Cabinet government encouraged compromise and vacillation. 'We want', said Southey, 'a responsible prime minister, to whom all the departments of state should be subordinate.' Opposition was well enough in time of peace, but in war the deliberate obstruction of the measures proposed by the government was half-way to treason.

Southey concluded by pointing out that there was plenty of scope for the philanthropic reformer within the existing constitution. The condition of the poor must be improved, plans for national education carried out, Christian missions abroad supported. The poor laws and the penal code needed revision, and there was room for reform in the navy. The supreme need, however, was to carry on the war against France. Political freedom was secure in Britain as it had not been in the days of the Pitt and Grenville administration in the seventeen-nineties. It had not been secure then because public opinion supported persecution, and the demagogues were for Church and King. The mob outdid the government in intolerance, as the Birmingham riots showed in 1791. 'Whether the fiend who bestrides it and spurs it on, have jacobin or anti-jacobin written on his forehead, the many-headed beast is the same.'[1] That sentence reveals the real continuity between Southey's earlier and later political opinions. He was always haunted by a fear of the mob,

[1] *Edinburgh Annual Register for 1809*, part i, p. 294.

which in its turn represented forces which human wisdom and human institutions were unable to control. Much of the urgency with which he called for aggressive war seems to have come from his need to grapple with a palpable monster. It happened that just at the time of his conversion to Toryism a book was published which strongly urged the necessity of an aggressive policy in the conduct of the war against France, and naturally enough Southey welcomed it. It was written by Captain C. W. Pasley of the Royal Engineers: *An Essay on the Military Policy and Institutions of the British Empire.*

Pasley's book was widely read and commended from its first appearance. Jane Austen praised it. She protested against reading it at first, but on inspection found it 'delightfully written and highly entertaining'. Pasley, she remarked to her sister Cassandra, was the first soldier she had ever sighed for.[1] Jane Austen is not very explicit about what appealed to her in Pasley's book. But there is a cavalier assurance, a certain easy ruthlessness in the handling of his arguments, which *is* rather fetching. 'War', he said, 'we cannot avoid; and in war we cannot succeed by merely displaying the valour, unless we also assume the ardour, and the ambition of conquerors.'[2] Hence he argued that, for example, instead of acting as the ally of the Sicilian government, Britain should make Sicily into a British territory. Sweden, he thought, might welcome a federal union with Great Britain. Hitherto Britain had been frightened of great conquests, because 'Great conquests excite great jealousy, and give rise to loud and continued clamours; but the warlike spirit, by which alone they can be effected, commands respect; and increasing power gradually changes the respect of other states into submission'.[3] A characteristic piece of Pasleyan logic occurs in the discussion of Britain's relations with the United States of America. He

[1] Jane Austen, *Letters*, ed. R. W. Chapman (1932), ii. 292.
[2] C. W. Pasley, *Military Policy* (1810), p. 448.
[3] Ibid., p. 177.

points out that Britain would have great difficulty in conquering America, and that therefore it is prudent to pursue
a policy of conciliation. But this ought not to descend into
weakness, and if war should break out it would be wisest to
prosecute it with the utmost vigour.

In short, according to the maxim, which I have already so often
repeated, but which cannot be too deeply impressed in our minds,
we ought not to make war against them by halves, but to do them
all the mischief possible. By so doing, instead of adding to the
present absurd and groundless hatred, which the populace of many
parts of America now seem to feel against us, (although I admit
that whether they hate us or not is of little importance), we shall
only make them respect us; and as we ought always to hold out,
that we fight unwillingly, that we have no views of conquest (for
this, as was observed, is not our policy), but that we are ready, at a
moment's warning, to renew a friendly intercourse, . . . the stream
of popularity may even, in course of time, run in our favour
throughout the Union.[1]

The parenthetic refusal to allow any importance to the good
or bad opinion of the American people is typical of Pasley's
gentlemanly bravado. His recommendation of raiding the
American coast evidently appealed to Southey, who, at the
beginning of 1813, told Walter Scott how he thought the war
with the United States ought to be conducted. He would,
he said, send out a British fleet to threaten the coastal cities
with Congreve rockets. Peace would be offered on condition
that America accepted British terms and paid the expenses of
the expedition. If the terms were not accepted, 'I would run
down the coast, and treat the great towns with an exhibition
of rockets', all expenses being charged to the U.S.A., until
'they chose to put a stop to the illuminations by submission,—
or till Philadelphia, Baltimore, New York &c—were laid in
ashes'.[2] It was in this spirit that the famous raid on Washington was later carried out.

Pasley's argument, and his confident tone, were well

---

[1] C. W. Pasley, *Military Policy* (1810), pp. 443–4.
[2] 13 Jan. 1813. National Library of Scotland MS. 3884, f. 19.

calculated to appeal to a war-time public. Some readers may
have felt reservations—for example Crabb Robinson. He
called it 'a fearful work', referring partly, no doubt, to the
emphasis laid (in the early chapters) on the great and
increasing power of France; but also expressing his distaste
for Pasley's power politics. 'The necessity', he wrote, 'of
throwing aside scruples as to the means of carrying on a
defensive war is to me satisfactorily urged.'[1] This is not
an enthusiastic acceptance of Pasley's point of view. What
Crabb Robinson conceded with reluctance, however, John
Rickman welcomed with his whole heart. 'I have not felt my
English heart so warmed and dilated for Years', he remarked
to Southey. He was confident that the British form of government was itself a sufficient guarantee against the abuse of
conquests.

We are indeed slandered about the East Indies—But can any
body think the people there not infinitely benefited by our pre-
ponderance. I believe nearly as much as their habits allow.—I know
that by intermixture and colonization much more might be done;
but the good is great already, and nearer home and among Europeans
I see no chance of abuse of our power—when it is established.[2]

Southey concurred. He hoped that he would be able to review
Pasley for the *Quarterly*. 'I am as ardent for making the world
English as he can be.'[3] His ardour was confirmed when he
read the book for himself. Pasley believed in 'a sort of
political *Islam*,—which teaches us to propagate freedom and
good laws by the sword'.[4] Gifford might not like it much, for
Pasley's whole argument was directed against the system of
alliances and subsidies with which Pitt was identified—and
no ill must be spoken of Pitt in the *Quarterly Review*. As it
turned out, however, Gifford was willing to let Southey
review the book, and Rickman in particular received this
news with joy. He looked upon it as a great event, an oppor-

[1] E. J. Morley, *H. C. Robinson on Books and their Writers* (1938), i. 21,
28 Jan. 1811.

[2] HM, Rickman to Southey, 31 Dec. 1810.

[3] HM, Southey to Rickman, 5 Jan. 1811.   [4] Ibid., 11 Jan. 1811.

tunity to establish 'a new general habit of thinking' which would put an end to the influence of the 'White-livered, abject favourers of Bonaparte'. He promised to let Southey have notes and observations on Pasley which could be interwoven into the review, especially concerning political economy, which was Pasley's weakest side.[1] A week later Rickman sent two 'dissertations', one on the army and another on population, and promised more. 'I have about 100 Marginal Notes on which to say something', he said, and added, in irrepressible high spirits, 'Have I not worked well in the last 48 Hours?'[2] The following day he sent him a sheet of political economy. 'I hope', he observed, 'you will rewrite all my Notes that you think worth retaining, both because my Handwriting ought not to be seen, and because you will involuntary improve it in the Manufacture, especially the Jokes, which are well meant, but badly executed.'[3] Three days later, 'I send you the Commercial Diatribe; next you will have the Finance, rather more striking'.[4] Nine days later—

I send another Supply, which goes through the Book, but I have several detached Observations—arising from it, which will fit about 3 sheets of my Half Column writing—Then I shall begin upon the Sequela; to exterminate Anarchists, Bonaparteans, and Croakers— I will send a Pacquet on Monday, and probably the last on Wednesday next. . . .

In addition to this factual material, Rickman also gave Southey advice on the tone of the review. At first he favoured an aggressive method, and told Southey a discreditable story about Whitbread which might be alluded to in an underhand way. Later, however, he decided that in order to do solid good, the review should be written in a 'gentle and persuasive' manner. Southey could always use the Whitbread scandals in the *Edinburgh Annual Register*.[6]

Unfortunately the 'dissertations' which Rickman sent to

---

[1] HM, Rickman to Southey, 26 Jan. 1811.   [2] Ibid., 2 Feb. 1811.
[3] Ibid., 3 Feb. 1811.   [4] Ibid., 6 Feb. 1811.   [5] Ibid., 15 Feb. 1811.
[6] Ibid., 3, 6, 9, and 24 Feb. 1811.

Southey do not appear to be extant. It is clear that he sent far more than could be used in one article, and Southey had the notion of putting the material together in a pamphlet, cast in the form of a 'Letter to Perceval'.[1] The review article was in proof by the beginning of March, and the *Quarterly's* publisher, John Murray, sent a copy to Rickman on which he was able to put his final notes and additions. On 12 March 1811 Southey told Rickman that while he was not satisfied with his own share of the article, the material supplied by Rickman made it not unworthy of Pasley. And so the two men eagerly awaited the appearance of the ninth number of the *Quarterly Review*, which, through their article, was to establish a new general habit of thinking in Great Britain.

When the ninth number did appear, the Pasley article was not in it. Southey was informed that what he had written about Sicily would be offensive to the Sicilian government, and that therefore the article would have to be revised. Southey's objections to the Kingdom of the Two Sicilies illustrate the persistence of his jacobin views in European politics after he had become a conservative at home. This appears plainly enough in the *Life of Nelson*, where the so-called jacobins of southern Italy are associated with the English opponents of Charles II and James II, and not with the French regicides. It was therefore very proper that the Pasley article should be toned down on this subject before appearing in the *Quarterly*. J. W. Croker was given the task of rewriting the offensive passages, and it appeared in the tenth number of the review. Southey told Wynn that he did not own it, as the omissions and alterations which had been made in it led the article to contradict some of the opinions which he most wished to enforce. He got what consolation he could from the reflection that he could attack the Sicilian government without interference in the third number of the *Edinburgh Annual Register*.[2]

[1] HM, Southey to Rickman, 4 Mar. 1811.
[2] *SL*, ii. 228, 19 July 1811.

The article, as published, contains a shrewd and witty criticism of Pasley's arguments in favour of Britain's seizing Sicily. Presumably this is Croker's work. Croker, however, is not saying anything very different from the criticism expressed by Wordsworth in a letter to Pasley written at the end of March 1811. He objected to Pasley's belief in a policy of conquest. 'I wish', said Wordsworth, 'to see Spain, Italy, France, Germany, formed into independent nations; nor have I any desire to reduce the power of France further than may be necessary for that end.' In a striking sentence later on in the same letter, Wordsworth sums up a belief which strongly contrasts with Pasley's: 'My prayer, as a patriot, is, that we may always have, somewhere or other, enemies capable of resisting us, and keeping us at arm's length.'[1] Wordsworth did not share Southey's or Rickman's zeal for 'making the world English', and it looks as though he cooled Southey's zeal a little. At any rate, on 2 April Southey wrote a letter to Walter Scott in which he said that Pasley sometimes talked of conquest when he should be talking of emancipation. The Roman Empire showed the unfortunate consequences of unlimited conquest. Southey more modestly limits his demands to Danish Zealand and Holland, together with islands in the Mediterranean. An independent united Italy should be established under British protection.[2]

So far as one can make out, the economic and commercial part of the article was not tampered with, though some of it may have been omitted. And here Southey seems to have changed his mind as radically as he had on the question of constitutional reform. In *Letters from England*, he had said that it would be well for England when her cities decreased and her villages multiplied. The manufacturing system was pernicious because it produced an uprooted populace. In the Pasley article, however, he transcribed Rickman's 'diatribes' on the contribution of the manufacturing system to Britain's

[1] *Prose Works of W. Wordsworth*, ed. W. Knight (1896), i. 315–16.
[2] *LC*, iii. 307.

strength, apparently without modification. Rickman's gruff
manner is unmistakable in the following:

The prosperous application of large capital we have daily
opportunity of seeing. In one place, a large steam engine performs
the manual labour of five hundred able men; in another place, a
cotton mill works with all the delicacy of five hundred skilful
artisans; and a thousand men may then be marched to the army
without national loss.[1]

The well-being of the country is measured in terms of the
quality of housing and dress among the poor, the increase in
the Post Office revenue, and the amount of tea, sugar, malt,
beer, spirits, and soap consumed. Don Manuel would not
have accepted these criteria without question. Nor would he
have much liked Rickman's opinion that the strength of a
nation consisted in 'industry acting on a sufficient capital'.[2]
What induced Southey to change his mind, or at any rate to
suppress reservations which he surely must have felt? Some
words near the end of the article make his attitude clear. He
quoted 'a wild German writer' who cried 'Oh woe to thee
when doubt comes on!' and commented: 'Woe indeed will
be to the statesmen who doubt the strength of their country,
and stand in awe of the enemy with whom it is engaged!'[3]
To doubt the wisdom of the manufacturing system was
necessarily to doubt the strength of Britain. Southey, one
may guess, was a little uneasy about Rickman's 'diatribes',
but quite apart from the deference he would properly feel
towards Rickman's expert knowledge, he had no means of
modifying the enthusiasm for British industrialism without
weakening the force of the arguments against peace-mongers.
The reviewer of *Letters from England* in the *Edinburgh* no
doubt showed himself insensitive to the suffering caused by
the Industrial Revolution when he censured Don Manuel's
objection to the manufacturing system. But he made a reasonable point when he complained that Don Manuel gave not
the least clue how Britain was to escape from the evil system

[1] *QR*, v. 407.   [2] Ibid., p. 414.   [3] Ibid., p. 436.

in which she was involved. 'After having exerted himself to show the darkness of the dungeon which we have dug for ourselves, he very humanely leaves us to grope our way out of it, the best way we can. In short, he seems to have no very clear views on the subject.'[1] Most readers today will agree that Southey did much when he simply realized that the industrial society of his day was intolerable because of the conditions of life which it imposed on so many people. But he had little idea how to make England's cities decrease, and her villages multiply and grow, and was therefore defenceless against the arguments of Rickman. Southey's earlier views were just submerged by Rickman's. One might say that in the Pasley article he wrote, not as Robert Southey, but as a *Quarterly* reviewer.

The *Quarterly* reviewer was already predominant in an article which Southey wrote in the earlier part of October 1810. It was a severe review of *Hints to the Public and the Legislature, on the Nature and Effect of Evangelical Preaching*, by a Barrister. This barrister was James Sedgwick, a unitarian, and his *Hints* express the alarm which had been felt by many people (including Southey himself and Leigh Hunt) at the rapid growth of Methodism. One reason for Southey's severity was Sedgwick's favourable attitude to Sydney Smith's article on the Baptist Mission in India, from which there is a long quotation in the fourth section.[2] Southey's review was thus part of his private campaign against the *Edinburgh*. But he also seems to have been genuinely indignant at Sedgwick's misrepresentation of Methodist teaching. The Methodists did *not* preach the atrocious doctrine that the believer could commit as many sins as he pleased, confident in being washed white by the Blood of the Lamb. Where the reviewer overmasters Robert Southey, however, is in his comments on Sedgwick's interpretation of the doctrinal position of the Church of England. Sedgwick regarded moral duty as all-important, and doctrinal mys-

---

[1] *Edinburgh Review*, xi. 373.   [2] *Hints* (1810), iv. 76–77 n.

teries as of no importance at all. He claimed that this was
the point of view of the Church as well. Southey asked whether
Sedgwick really believed that the bishops and their clergy
had exploded the doctrines of the Trinity, the corruption of
the human will, and redemption by the cross of Christ. 'Do
our clergy solemnly pray to their maker, weekly before God
and man, in the words of a liturgy which they know *cannot be
believed*? Either this is true, or the Barrister is a libeller, a
rank and convicted libeller.'[1]

One might imagine from this that Robert Southey was now
a true believer, angry with the infidels. Nothing of the sort.
He told his brother Tom, some three months after he had
written this article, that although the Establishment had
been an infinite blessing to England, its creed would not
stand the test of sound criticism.

The story of the Fall, the plenary inspiration of the scriptures,
and the miracles must be given up,—abandon these, insist upon a
diseased moral nature, the necessity and all-sufficiency of grace,
effecting a moral redemption,—preach the doctrine of a perpetual
revelation, appeal to the heart of man for the truth of these doctrines,—and Christianity becomes invincible. The nature of the
Fall, and the questions of the Trinity and the super-human nature
of Christ may safely be left undefined, for every person to understand according to his judgement.[2]

It will be seen that, when he is replying to Sedgwick, Southey
is careful to pass over doctrines in which he has no belief at
all, and mentions those which he believes in, although he
privately thinks them better left undefined. The impression
that Southey creates is that he is much more orthodox than
he really is, and he had been very much annoyed when
Gifford had done this for him in the first number of the
Quarterly. Why had he now become anxious to appear
orthodox? Sedgwick's attitude to the Church of England
was practically the same as his own when he was writing for

[1] *QR*, iv. 484.
[2] BM MSS. Adds. 30,927, f. 171, 23 Jan. 1811.

the *Annual Review*. Like Sedgwick he had called upon it to abandon the Thirty-Nine Articles. The reason for his change of opinion can only be guessed at, for I do not know of any really frank discussion of the issue in any of his letters. But it is very probable that the events of 1810, which turned him against reform, prejudiced him also against 'free and fearless' thinking in matters of religion. He maintained his own dissent, but one feels that he would have liked to conform if he honestly could. He is clearly suspicious of the 'masculine mind' which, in Sedgwick's phrase, presumes to snap asunder the cords which bind it to the rock of error. Southey changes the metaphor a little and suggests that Sedgwick cuts knots which he is unable to untie. A temperament like Sedgwick's, while it might find it in its interest to support the Establishment, was inherently disruptive. If Southey maintained his dissent, it was partly in order to work for a theology to which thinking men could assent. That, at least, was the mission which he glimpsed for himself in the letter to Tom Southey from which I have already quoted. Perhaps the only practicable solution of the religious problem in England, he told his brother, was the setting up of an 'Eclectic Church' which should combine all that is good in each denomination, 'yet so philosophically framed, that as the world grew wiser it would be adapted for a Catholick—i.e.—a universal faith'.

If, he said, he had had the slightest crack in the upper story, he would have set to work on his Eclectic Church long ago, and made himself ten times more conspicuous in the world. This is conceivably true; and it is interesting to speculate on what Southey's influence would have been if he could have brought himself to be a prophet of the Modernists. But he does not come to grips with the issue even in this letter to Tom Southey, and he certainly never came nearer to doing so. It was written in an unusually relaxed state of mind, and in spite of the fact that he was at this time making up his mind against parliamentary reform he was able to say that both with religious and political revolutions, when the age for them is come there is no way but the resource of the traveller in the savannahs of America,—when the grass is on fire behind him, to set fire to it before. Kindle the combustible materials yourself and direct them to your own purposes, or you will be consumed by them.[1]

These remarks were occasioned by a scheme for restricting itinerant preachers, which was formulated in a Bill introduced by Lord Sidmouth in 1811. The Bill was extremely unpopular and was withdrawn. It followed, however, the hints dropped by Sedgwick, and in opposing Sidmouth's scheme and Sedgwick's book Southey was perfectly consistent. The curious thing is that the review and the letter to his brother are so completely different in their approach and in their tone. The division between his private and his public opinions was to be debilitating, the more so as he was not fully conscious of what he was doing. *Quarterly* reviewing was an insidious temptation to insincerity, especially as it was a means of securing greater public recognition and social influence. Southey was gratified by the praise which his review of the Barrister's *Hints* got from the Prime Minister himself. It led him to hope that Canning might compare Bonaparte to Kehama in the House of Commons—it would be good for sales.[2]

He resented the criticism of the *Edinburgh Review* mainly because it tended to depress his reputation with the common reader. Perhaps, too, it gave utterance to doubts which even Southey might occasionally feel about the value of his poetry. Jeffrey had touched a sore point in his review of *Kehama* when he pointed out that Southey's long poems had become progressively less popular—that *Thalaba* had won fewer readers than *Joan of Arc*, and *Madoc* fewer than *Thalaba*. The unfavourable verdict of an author's contemporaries, he remarked, was rarely reversed by posterity: an unkind insinuation, with

---

[1] BM MSS. Adds. 30,927, f. 170, 23 Jan. 1811.
[2] *LC*, iii. 303, 16 Feb. 1811.

some truth in it. Unfortunately for Jeffrey's theory in this instance, however, *Kehama* sold much better than its predecessors. As for *Roderick* (1814), it sold so well that it cleared Southey of his debts to Longman the publisher.[1] 'The worst vexation I can inflict upon him', said Southey of Jeffrey, 'is to write on and continue rising in reputation.'[2] The confidence was not misplaced.

Southey none the less felt that the *Kehama* review had left him free to castigate Jeffrey without restraint, and it so happened that in the summer of 1811 he found a means of both attacking the *Edinburgh Review* and furthering the cause of strong government. During the previous four or five years a considerable number of schools for the poor had been established through the initiative of Joseph Lancaster and his associates. Lancaster was a Quaker who had evolved a system of teaching large numbers of children by one master through monitors. Although it is very doubtful whether the children learnt much under this system, it was undeniably cheap, and opened up hopes of general literacy. Lancaster's schools, however, gave no sectarian religious instruction, and this alarmed the friends of the Church Establishment. The prospect of a whole generation growing up not educated in the principles of the State Church seemed equivalent to a prospect of revolution. So in 1811 strong counter-action was taken in the form of a National School Society for the foundation of schools for the poor, making use of the monitorial system as practised by Dr. Andrew Bell. Bell was an Anglican clergyman who had made use of monitors in a school in Madras. He had published a book about this school from which Lancaster had picked up several ideas, and an arid controversy developed about who should have the credit for introducing the system. Southey took a vigorous part in this controversy. He contributed an article to the *Quarterly Review* for November 1811, in which he showed Lancaster's

---

[1] *SL*, ii. 222–3, 17 May 1811; iii. 46, 18 Oct. 1816.
[2] *BL*, c. 24, f. 163. Letter to Grosvenor Bedford, 3 May 1811.

indebtedness to Bell. He had altered Bell's system in some particulars, and altered it for the worse. Southey was especially critical of Lancaster's elaborate system of punishments, and it must be allowed that the encouragement of corporate ridicule is one of the least attractive features of this school discipline. But the real objection remained the absence of Church teaching. The cry against Lancaster as a Quaker was absurd, Southey told Wynn, but the religious neutrality of his schools was tantamount to favouring dissenting principles. The Church Establishment was already in danger, and Lancaster's schools were adding to the danger. The one good thing that Lancaster had done was to frighten the bishops.[1]

Southey had travelled a long way from his earlier opinion of Lancaster's Anglican critics. In the *Annual Review for 1806* he had accused Archdeacon Daubeny and Mrs. Trimmer of a 'papal intolerance', and made light of their concern for the Church of England.[2] The events of 1810 were partly responsible for the change. An article by Sydney Smith in the *Edinburgh Review* for November 1810, praising Lancaster's system somewhat extravagantly, probably confirmed Southey in his hostility to Lancaster.

He enlarged his *Quarterly Review* article on Bell and Lancaster into a pamphlet, called *The Origin, Nature, and Object of the New System of Education*. He intended to dedicate it to the editor of the *Edinburgh*, but neither of the two copies which I have seen contains such a dedication. A draft of a notebook now preserved in the museum at Keswick indicates what Southey intended to say. He begins by insisting on the fact that the pamphlet is a direct attack on the *Edinburgh Review*, an act of defiance. He will not compliment the *Edinburgh* on the ability with which it is written, because the main ability which it exhibits is 'setting at nought the principles of common morality whenever they interfered with your immediate purpose'. The penalty for this critical antinomianism was that it would destroy the journal's credit with

---

[1] *SL*, ii. 250-1, 4 Feb. 1812.   [2] *Annual Review for 1806*, pp. 278-82.

the public. In the controversy between Bell and Lancaster, the *Edinburgh* was clearly in the wrong on grounds that everyone could understand. 'It is not a matter of learning, or feeling, or taste which is in dispute—it depends upon dates and recorded facts.' When a journalist's facts were so questionable, no one could have much faith in his opinions. (Doubtless Southey was thinking of Jeffrey's opinion of *The Curse of Kehama*.)

It is natural to be amused at Southey's fury, but he had a perfectly serious case against the *Edinburgh Review*. It often was more concerned to be entertaining than to be just, and much of its popularity came from its impertinence. Sydney Smith himself suggested that if Jeffrey were to review the solar system he would damn it: 'bad light— planets too distant—pestered with comets—feeble contrivance;—could make a better with great ease'.[1] It is delightful to begin a review of *The Excursion* with 'This will never do!', but such impudence should not be confused with acute critical discrimination. As another of the *Edinburgh*'s victims put it, that journal had no reason to cultivate the favour of literary men. 'It is of little consequence to mercenary scribblers, whether they please or displease the judicious few, provided they please the multitude.'[2] The *Edinburgh Review*, in fact, was yet another manifestation of the uncontrollable mob, the triumphant Philistines. But in the controversy over Dr. Bell, Southey believed that the Philistines were delivered into his hands, and he intended to 'maul them as unmercifully as ever Samson himself did'.[3]

Southey's friends did not co-operate with him any more adequately than Israel did with Samson. The *Quarterly Review* article on Bell and Lancaster was made much quieter by Gifford. 'I am quite afraid', he told John Murray, 'at Southey's violence and must leave out the passages which

---

[1] S. Smith, *Letters*, ed. N. C. Smith (Oxford, 1953), i. 121.

[2] John Ring, *Beauties of the Edinburgh Review, alias the Stinkpot of Literature* (1807), pp. 1–2.

[2] BL, c. 24, f. 173. Letter to Grosvenor Bedford, 5 Nov. 1811.

attack the E R so personally.'[1] Probably Murray himself was
responsible for the omission of the dedication to Jeffrey in
the pamphlet. Southey would perforce have to submit to his
publisher's sense of prudence.

1811 saw the beginning of the Luddite riots, which strengthened Southey's fears of the dangerous state of mind prevalent among the urban proletariat. The first outbreak was
fairly mild. It occurred at Arnold in Nottinghamshire, in the
spring, when framework knitters removed the jack-wires
from frames owned by unpopular hosiers. They were unpopular for the good reason that they refused to enter into
agreements to maintain minimum standards of production
and quality.[2] Southey remarked that the disturbances were
serious, and referred to what he had said in *Letters from
England* about the evil consequences of a prosperity founded
upon manufactures.[3] He seems now to have convinced himself
that Rickman's faith in industrial strength was mistaken,
however inconvenient this admission might be to a militant
supporter of the war. He determined to work out his ideas
on the whole subject in the light of his developed political
creed, and the fruit of this was his *Quarterly Review* article
on the poor, which appeared at the end of 1812.

There were no disturbances in the summer of 1811, but
in November the Luddites began their work once more in
Nottinghamshire, and during the winter and spring disturbances spread to many industrial areas. It was widely
feared that in May 1812 there would be a general rising in
southern Lancashire, and although General Maitland, who
commanded the military force in the north of England, might
discount such fears, he was more cool-headed than many. A
letter of Southey's written during this winter of 1811–12
illustrates the kind of occurrence that helped to create apprehensions of a breakdown of social order. Keswick, he said,

[1] 18 Oct. 1811. See H. and H. C. Shine, *The Quarterly Review under
Gifford* (Chapel Hill, 1949), p. 26.
[2] F. O. Darvall, *Popular Disturbances* (1934), pp. 64–65.
[3] BL, c. 24, f. 161, ? Apr. 1811.

was afflicted by the fear of 'ugly fellows'—unemployed labourers from the factories in Carlisle and along the Cumberland coast. 'Every day brings bloody news from Carlisle, Cockermouth, etc.', he told Grosvenor Bedford. He asked him to send two pistols and a watchman's rattle. This last item, indeed, promised him much pleasure. Mrs. Coleridge wanted it 'to give the alarm when the ugly fellows come. But oh, Grosvenor, the glorious tunes, the solos and bravuras, that I shall play upon that noble musical instrument before any such fellow makes his appearance.' Cuthbert Southey says, in what appears to be a striking understatement, that 'these musical anticipations were fully realised'.[1] But although Southey put a cheerful face on the dangers to which he and his family were exposed, the dangers were real enough. Perhaps Shelley, who was in Keswick then, was deluded when he claimed that he was assaulted on 19 January 1812. But if so, it was a hallucination which was natural in a Keswick alarmed by rumours of 'ugly fellows', and it is difficult to believe that Shelley's neighbours thought he had imagined the attack. Southey, at any rate, had no such suspicion.[2] The terror of assault in Keswick had been exacerbated by reports over the Christmas period of the murder by a certain John Williams of a shopkeeper in the East End of London, along with his wife, baby, and servant. This multiple murder was the more horrible because Williams's technique was peculiarly ferocious (he first shattered the skull of his victim, and then cut the throat). He was, moreover, at large for nearly a fortnight afterwards, and was only arrested as the result of a second enterprise, in which three further people were killed. De Quincey gives a vivid account of the affair in his *Murder considered as one of the Fine Arts*. Southey, he says, was deeply moved, thinking it 'a private event of that order which rose to the dignity of a national event'.[3] De Quincey's recollection

---

[1] *LC*, iii. 326–7, 17 Jan. 1812.
[2] See K. N. Cameron, *The Young Shelley* (1951), p. 210. Cf. BL, c. 24, f. 189.
[3] De Quincey, *Works*, ed. Masson (Edinburgh, 1890), xiii. 76.

is confirmed by a letter which Southey wrote to Neville White on 27 December 1811. The murders brought a stigma on the nation and on human nature itself.

No circumstances which did not concern myself ever disturbed me so much. I have been more affected, more agitated, but never had so mingled a feeling of horror, and indignation, and astonishment, with a sense of insecurity too, which no man in this state of society ever felt before, and a feeling that the national character is disgraced. . . .[1]

To enter into Southey's feelings, one has only to turn up De Quincey's essay. The section on Williams is perhaps the best thing he ever wrote.[2] It was one of the rare occasions when he was thoroughly in earnest, and he evokes admirably the 'frenzy of feelings which . . . mastered the popular heart' at Christmas 1811. One passage is worth quoting here at length. It describes the moment when Williams was discovered in the actual performance of a murder, and the news that he was at work spread with incredible speed.

The frenzied movement of mixed horror and exultation—the ululation of vengeance which ascended instantaneously from the individual street, and then by a sublime sort of magnetic contagion from all the adjacent streets—can be adequately expressed only by a rapturous passage in Shelley:

> The transport of a fierce and monstrous gladness
>   Spread through the multitudinous streets, fast flying
> Upon the wings of fear:—From his dull madness
>   The starveling waked, and died in joy: the dying,
>   Among the corpses in stark agony lying,
>   Just heard the happy tidings, and in hope
> Closed their faint eyes: from house to house replying
>   With loud acclaim, the living shook heaven's cope
> And filled the startled earth with echoes.

There was something, indeed, half inexplicable in the instantaneous interpretation of the gathering shout according to its true meaning.

---

[1] *SL*, ii. 248.

[2] The Williams murders also inspired the essay *On the Knocking at the Gate in Macbeth.*

In fact, the deadly roar of vengeance, and its sublime unity, *could* point in this district only to the one demon whose idea had brooded and tyrannized, for twelve days, over the general heart. . . .[1]

It is the quotation from *The Revolt of Islam* which is of special interest. For that poem gives expression to the irresistible energy released by the popular insurgency which was either a hope or a nightmare according to one's point of view. Shelley identified himself with it, felt it as an expression of his own will. As the old hermit puts it in the fourth canto, the powers of the world are trembling, their religion laughed at, their authority cursed. These powers will be replaced by 'fearless love, and the pure law of mild equality and peace'. The image by which Shelley describes this revolution is that of a whirlpool—irresistible, and (by implication) destructive:

> as whirlpools draw
> All wrecks of Ocean to their chasm, the sway
>   Of thy strong genius, Laon, which foresaw
> This hope, compels all spirits to obey,
> Which round thy secret strength now throng in wide array.[2]

Shelley feels himself to *be* the whirlpool. No doubt Southey felt something like it when he copied out the passage from Babeuf in 1797. No doubt he would also have participated in the 'fierce and monstrous gladness' of the crowd as they hounded down John Williams. But such participation would be only a transient relief from the sense of insecurity produced by the murders, and the glimpse which they had given of the savagery to which human nature could descend. On 12 May 1812 that savagery was turned against the Prime Minister, Spencer Perceval. He was assassinated by a certain John Bellingham in the lobby of the House of Commons; and the assassin immediately became a popular hero. Southey was terrified. The crisis that he had long foreseen was suddenly upon them. The army was now 'the single plank between us

---

[1] De Quincey, *Works*, ed. Masson (Edinburgh, 1890), xiii. 112.
[2] *The Revolt of Islam*, IV. xv, lines 1544–8.

and the red sea of an English Jacquerie'.[1] Nothing could save
the country but strong government.

3. *BELLUM SERVILE*

It has been the custom to dismiss the murder of Spencer
Perceval by John Bellingham as an act of madness, and therefore without political significance. In a sense this is true:
Bellingham was not the agent of any political organization,
even one so eccentric as that which conspired in Cato Street
eight years later. In another sense it is not true. The mood
which prompted the breaking of machines could equally
prompt the shooting of prime ministers. Southey's rather
hysterical alarm had some foundation; and it may be worth
examining the Bellingham affair a little more closely.

In his study of popular disturbances in Regency England,
Mr. F. O. Darvall notes that some classes of workmen, like
colliers and navvies, who stood to gain by the increasing use
of machinery, nevertheless joined in Luddite riots. He suggests
that they wanted to be in a fight just because it was a fight.
This pugnacious state of mind made them willing to do
anything to 'protest dramatically and effectively against
existing conditions, with only a vague indefinite hope of
improving them'.[2] A dramatic and effective protest was
exactly what Bellingham wished to make. Nor was this
mental condition confined to Luddites and assassins. It is
evident enough in the *Examiner* from February to May 1812.
Ever since the King had gone irrevocably insane in 1810, the
Whigs and their allies had hoped that the Prince Regent
would appoint new ministers. By the end of February 1812 it
had become quite clear that the Prince had no intention of
dismissing Perceval's ministry, and the *Examiner* proceeded
to write an extraordinary series of violent attacks on the
Prince, on the ground of his political inconsistency. These

---

[1] BL, c. 24, f. 201. Letter to Grosvenor Bed ord, 14 May 1812.
[2] F. O. Darvall, *Popular Disturbances* (1934), p. 173.

attacks reached a climax in an article published on 22 March, which provided the basis for a prosecution for libel, and the consequent imprisonment of John and Leigh Hunt. If the threat of prosecution moderated the tone of the *Examiner* towards the Prince himself, it did not prevent a continuation of exasperated bitterness in the general temper of its political comment. This appears even in its counsels of moderation. Thus, in the issue for 10 May, there is a criticism of Burdett for his intemperate attacks on the use of military force to suppress riots. But, the paper goes on, Perceval has no right to talk self-righteously about such intemperance, he being one of the most notorious sinecurists in the kingdom, and therefore the cause of more trouble than any demagogue. The following day Perceval was assassinated. One need not suppose that the *Examiner* was inciting anyone to murder either the Prince Regent or Spencer Perceval. But to read its columns at this time is to appreciate the force of Lord Melbourne's observation that his contemporaries hated each other damnably. And this hatred found a notable voice in the London populace, who cheered Bellingham, tried to rescue him, and treasured his memory for years after his execution.[1] Cobbett explained that the public rejoicings were not at the shedding of Perceval's blood, but at the death of a man who was partly responsible for the sufferings of the country. The people who cried out 'God bless you!' to Bellingham on the scaffold were not bestowing their blessing on a murderer, 'but on an Englishman, whom they regarded (perhaps erroneously) as having been grievously ill used by the government, and who had taken vengeance into his own hands'.[2] Coleridge told Southey how, faint from heat and much walking, he went for a drink in the tap-room of a large public house, and found the customers in a state of exultation over Bellingham's crime. They drank Burdett's health, and

---

[1] The authority for this last statement is Lord Holland. See *Further Memoirs of the Whig Party 1807–21* (1905), p. 131.

[2] *Cobbett's Political Register*, xxi. 683, 30 May 1812.

followed it with such sentiments as 'This is but the beginning'
—'More of these damned scoundrels must go the same way,
and then poor people may live'—and so on.[1] Nor was this
mood confined to London. Archibald Prentice, the Manchester reformer, heard the news of Perceval's death in
Newcastle-under-Lyme. A man came running down the
street, leaping into the air, waving his hat round his head,
and shouting with frantic joy, 'Perceval is shot, hurrah!
Perceval is shot, hurrah!'[2] Crabb Robinson has left an account
of what was evidently an angry discussion of the matter.
Wordsworth was in the company of a number of respectable
dissenters two days after the assassination. The presumed
madness of Bellingham was (apparently) referred to, and
Wordsworth said that Burdett's speech in the week before
the crime was committed, accusing the soldiers of murdering
the people, might have been the 'determining motive' to
Bellingham's act. Most of the company resented this as an
attack on Burdett, and one person at least made what Crabb
Robinson regarded as a rude and offensive contradiction of
Wordsworth's assertion. This man, the son of William
Roscoe of Liverpool, said that Burdett's was a constitutional
speech, and asked what the people were to do who were
starving. 'Not murder people', said Wordsworth, 'unless
they mean to eat their hearts.' The conversation, poor
Robinson observed, had taken 'a bad turn'.[3]

Bellingham himself was a characteristic man of the age.
He was a merchant in the Russian timber trade, but had no
capital of his own. He had been in prison for debt in Russia,
and his special grievance against the British government was
that its representative there would take no action to get him
out of prison. He had managed to return to England, however,
and had worked in Liverpool as an insurance broker. Bellingham was thus a product of that commercial speculativeness

---

[1] *Letters of S. T. Coleridge* (1895), ii. 598.
[2] A. Prentice, *Historical Sketches* (1851), p. 46.
[3] E. J. Morley, *H. C. Robinson on Books and their Writers* (1938), i. 83–84.

which, for good and ill, had increased greatly in the early
nineteenth century. The mental disturbance from which he
suffered was a natural consequence of his way of life. He saw
the world in a conspiracy against his happiness. 'With the
purest of intentions', he wrote to his wife on the eve of his
execution, 'it has always been my misfortune to be thwarted,
misrepresented, and ill-used in life.' The desire to murder
was part of a general exasperation with life whose natural
conclusion was suicide. He looked forward to death, he said,
as the weary traveller looks for the promised inn, 'where he
may repose his wearied frame, after enduring the pelting of
the pitiless storm'. He told the Ordinary of Newgate that in
his life the bliss had been fleeting and illusory, the misery
permanent and real.[1] His state of mind is sympathetically
analysed by George Chalmers, who wrote an appeal for
Bellingham's widow and children. If, he says, the evils which
assail us appear 'gigantic and irremediable', and hope leaves
us, the mind will be unequal to the pressure, and will re-
linquish an insupportable existence, dragging, 'Sampson like
in its fall, the hated object of its revenge'.[2]

'Samson hath quit himself like Samson' is a sentiment which
has a strong appeal, because it combines the notoriety of a
striking action with the quietude of death. Bellingham went
complacently to his execution, feeling that he had given a
distinct and public warning to future ministers to attend to
the applications and prayers of those who suffer by oppression.
This barely concealed pleasure greatly shocked the Rev.
Daniel Wilson (afterwards Bishop of Calcutta) who visited
Bellingham in his cell the day before his execution. Wilson
hoped to arouse in him a feeling of repentance, but had little
success. The account of the interview which Wilson wrote
brings out very vividly the contrast between the stern, guilt-
ridden, humiliating religion of the clergyman, and the placid

---

[1] See *Gentleman's Magazine*, supp. to vol. 82, part 1 (1812), pp. 660 et seq.
[2] G. Chalmers, *An Appeal to the Generosity of the British Nation* (1812),
p. 13.

ROBERT SOUTHEY *circa* 1816
From a pencil sketch by Edward Nash

dignity and self-satisfaction of the assassin. What disturbed Wilson particularly was that Bellingham was in no way ignorant of the Bible, and could utter religious formulas with great facility. Wilson explained that man's transgressions against God were more numerous and more aggravated than we could possibly conceive.

I then stopped, and said to him, 'I hope I make myself understood.'

'Perfectly,' replied the prisoner: 'I know myself to be a sinner: we come into the world sinners.'

This observation was made in a civil rather than a serious tone, and gave me little hope that he deeply felt the acknowledgment he so readily made.[1]

Bellingham's self-possession was a little shaken when Wilson told him that Mrs. Perceval had prayed for him, in spite of his being the murderer of her husband. 'Her conduct was more like a Christian's than my own, certainly', he said. And later in the day a friend of Wilson's brought him to concede that he could not have been under the influence of a good spirit when he assassinated Perceval. But he did this in his customary 'unfeeling, indifferent tone', and did not abandon his own theory of himself as an instrument of God's justice.

A Wordsworth who shared the politics of the London populace might have found in Bellingham a notable example of Man's Unconquerable Mind.[2] Shelley, I think, did see him in this light. Bellingham resembles the rational Christians whom Shelley describes in *The Assassins*, a romance which he began to write in 1814, but never carried beyond the fourth chapter. The medieval sect of the Assassins, their sheikh the Old Man of the Mountain, and his deceptive Paradise, were fairly familiar to readers in the early nineteenth century.[3] Shelley transforms the story by making the Assassins

---

[1] D. Wilson, *The Substance of a Conversation with John Bellingham* (1812), p. 3.

[2] Southey himself acknowledged that Bellingham had something of greatness in him. *SL*, ii. 273. Letter to Tom Southey, 12 May 1812.

[3] Novice assassins were drugged with hashish and taken into gardens where they were entertained by beautiful women. After a few days they were drugged

wholly admirable. Their beliefs become indistinguishable from those held by Shelley himself. They had learned to identify the benignant spirit who had created them with 'the delight that is bred among the solitary rocks, and has its dwelling alike in the changing colours of the clouds and the inmost recesses of the caverns'. One way in which their benevolence expressed itself was in liquidating the pests who tyrannize over civilized society. 'The respectable man—the smooth, smiling, polished villain, whom all the city honours; whose very trade is lies and murder; who buys his daily bread with the blood and tears of men'—such parasites are destroyed by the philosophic assassin, whose manners, none the less, are imbued with 'inexpressible gentleness and benignity'. There is a certain resemblance here to Bellingham, reinforced by another passage in the second chapter of this fragment.

Secure and self-enshrined in the magnificence and pre-eminence of his conceptions, spotless as the light of heaven, he would be the victim among men of calumny and persecution. Incapable of distinguishing his motives, they would rank him among the vilest and most atrocious criminals. Great, beyond all comparison with them, they would despise him in the presumption of their ignorance. Because his spirit burned with an unquenchable passion for their welfare, they would lead him, like his illustrious master, amidst scoffs, and mockery, and insult, to the remuneration of an ignominious death.[1]

once more, and then removed. They thought they had been in paradise, and were thus encouraged to hold their lives cheap in the service of the Old Man of the Mountain. Voltaire refers to the story in the *Dictionnaire philosophique*; Erasmus Darwin mentions it in *Zoönomia*; and Southey based an episode in *Thalaba* on the accounts written by Purchas, Odoricus, and 'that undaunted liar, Sir John Maundeville'. Coleridge knew the story, as is evident from *Kubla Khan*. Shelley may have read about the sect in two papers by Falconet in the *Mémoires de l'Académie des Inscriptions*, xvii (Paris, 1751). These papers (referred to by Gibbon) contain several details which would have interested Shelley. They were not Muslims, and were said by some to be *infideles*. There was some evidence which associated them with the Jewish sect of the Essenes, and they were described by Jacques de Vitry thus: 'de Judaeis tracti sunt, sed Judaeorum ritus non observant'. They probably did not call themselves assassins, but 'Bathéniens' (their name in Egypt), which could be approximately translated 'illuminés'. Of particular interest to Shelley would be the fact that some authors accused them of incest.

[1] P. B. Shelley, *Works*, ed. R. Ingpen and W. Peck (1926–30), vi. 162–4.

In spite of the sympathy of the common people, Bellingham had much scoffing and mockery and insult to endure. In passing sentence of death upon him, the Recorder of London had laid particular emphasis on the abhorrence in which the crime of assassination was rightly held. Trelawny tells us that Shelley adopted the word *atheist* because it was a word of ill repute, and to take it up was a gesture of defiance. To sanctify the word *assassin* was a similar gesture.

Shelley expresses precisely the moral significance in Bellingham's crime that alarmed Southey. As the social order disintegrates under the strain of industrialism, the populace becomes possessed by an evil spirit of destructiveness, grotesquely masquerading under a pretence of liberality and philanthropy. One writer observed that Bellingham's plea of Not Guilty had sinister implications. His belief that he should be acquitted had been alleged as a proof of his insanity. But was it not rather a sign that he had miscalculated the extent to which 'disorganizing principles' had, as yet, perverted the respectable middle class? Bellingham's defence resolved itself into a vindication of the right of each man to murder his neighbour. 'Anarchy itself has not another step to climb.' It was only an extreme inference from that dangerous doctrine that sets the rights of nature against the obligations of law, a doctrine which had become steadily more acceptable since the American war. Perceval's murder was a sign of where all this would lead.[1]

It is clear that these apprehensions, while widely diffused in a nebulous way, were not generally felt with the intensity one finds in Southey, or even in Wordsworth, Coleridge, and Daniel Stuart of the *Courier*. Williams the murderer and Bellingham the assassin were very alarming, but not portents of moral anarchy. Even if unthinking people did cry out that the national character had been changed all at once,[2] the fact

[1] *Cursory Remarks, occasioned by the Horrible Assassination of the Right Hon. Spencer Perceval* (1812).

[2] Wordsworth, *Letters, The Middle Years*, ed. E. de Selincourt (Oxford, 1937), ii. 501, 4 June 1812.

that they *were* unthinking would enable them to recover their composure as soon as Williams and Bellingham had been forgotten. Luddites were a dangerous nuisance, and must be put down, but, after all, the threatened rising in Lancashire never happened. Mr. F. O. Darvall expresses surprise, indeed, that the disturbances of 1812 did not cause more alarm than they did, and suggests that a blessed ignorance preserved the level-headedness of the country. Southey complained to Walter Scott that the politicians were not sufficiently aware of the danger. 'They live in such a cloud of their own dust, that they cannot see the signs of the tempest gathering round them.'[1] He did his best to extend the sense of danger, but Charles Wynn, for one, did not yield to the panic. When Southey wrote a frenzied letter after the assassination, Wynn coolly commented on the poet's 'inherent enthusiasm', and pointed out that politically the disappearance of Perceval was not specially important, for Perceval's parliamentary position had been extremely precarious anyhow. When Southey foresaw the downfall of the Established Church, Wynn observed that the clergy were a very powerful body, well connected, and the loss of their property therefore most unlikely. No minister would lightly provoke them. Wynn probably conveys the prevailing temper of the House of Commons. John Rickman's letter to Southey about the assassination, while evidently dismayed, is comparatively matter-of-fact, in strong contrast to the cries of terror that Southey was uttering at this time. 'Oh my dear Wynn,' he exclaims, 'we are in a fearful state. The dragons teeth have been sown on all sides of us,—and where is the Jason who shall cut down their dreadful harvest?'[2]

The very intensity of his reaction drove Southey to an energetic search for a remedy. In a long *Quarterly Review* article, published in the number for December 1812, he developed his theory that it was the evil social condition of

[1] 10 June 1812. *Sir Walter's Post-Bag*, ed. W. Partington (1932), p. 88.
[2] NLW, 4812 D 237, 4814 D 61, 63; *Rickman*, pp. 160–1.

the industrial poor which had exposed them to the inflammatory speeches and writings of radical politicians. The politicians were aided by the weekly newspapers, which were read aloud at the ale-house for the benefit of the illiterate. He proposed severe measures against agitators, though Gifford cut out his favourite proposal of inflicting transportation on those convicted of seditious libel. Gifford, he told Grosvenor Bedford, had removed precisely those passages which pointed out with most force the danger, and indicated the most effectual means of prevention.[1] These, however, were only negative measures. Southey also urged the necessity for a scheme of parochial education on the lines worked out by Bell; for large-scale emigration; and for public works to employ the destitute. Everything in the article is touched with the urgency of a man who is desperately seeking to avert an explosion. He attacked Malthus as an odious preacher of anti-social philosophy. He observed the new dangers that came with the development of the art of unlawful organization. In the past an inflamed mob was united only by a momentary impulse of blind passion. Now, with the aid of the models of self-government provided by the Quakers, the Methodists, parish clubs, and benefit societies, a revolution could be readily effected. The Luddites and secret trade organizations were perfectly able to raise funds and sustain strike action for prolonged periods. Later writers have seen in these activities evidence of the British worker's capacity for peaceful improvement of his status. To Southey, however, they appeared to be yet another of the many causes that were interacting to produce a social earthquake.[2]

Although the article is directed to a triumphant conclusion, with a vision of the empty spaces of the world populated by

[1] BL, c. 25, f. 170, 25 Mar. 1815. Cf. *SL*, ii. 274. Letter to Tom Southey, 12 May 1812. 'I would hang about a score in a county, and send off ship loads to Botany Bay; and if there were no other means of checking the treasonable practices which are carried on in the Sunday newspapers, I would suspend the Habeas Corpus. Shut up these bellows-blowers, and the fire may, perhaps, go out.'

[2] *QR*, viii. 319–56. Southey, *Essays* (1832), i. 75–155.

British people enjoying British institutions and speaking the
English language, the savage vehemence with which it is
written betrays the fears which lay behind its composition—
fears which he does not always choose to express publicly.
Thus he admitted to his friends that he was apprehensive
about the soldiers, for their loyalty had been strained by the
flogging discipline of the army, and Burdett had been allowed
to appear as the chief opponent of that discipline. Fortunately,
by some providential infatuation, the radicals had chosen to
insult the soldiers. If they had systematically sought to
undermine their allegiance, 'the existing government would
not be worth a week's purchase, nor any throat which could
be supposed to be worth cutting, safe for a month longer'.[1]
These fears confirmed him in his belief that a dictator was
needed, but he did not see any suitable candidates for the
office, now that Perceval was dead. Lords Liverpool and
Sidmouth were out of the question; so was Nicolas Vansittart.
As for Wellesley, he was 'a vicious man, and a tyrant at
heart'.[2] Southey feared that the happiest days of England were
over, though it was possible that she might become a great
military power. His mind turned, as it had done before, to
the possibility of emigration. Portugal might prove to be a
freer country than England. Alternatively he had a strong
fancy for the post of Governor of Botany Bay. He might be
deported there anyhow, if there were a revolution.[3]

Southey did not live in a permanent state of despondency.
His state of mind was probably like that of many people in the
years after the Second World War, resigned to the unspeak-
able horror of an atomic war, occasionally frightened into a
near-panic at its apparent nearness, then putting the matter
as far out of their conscious minds as possible. Sometimes

[1] *LC*, iii. 334. Letter to Grosvenor Bedford, 14 May 1812.

[2] *SL*, ii. 274. Letter to Tom Southey, 12 May 1812. 'Wellesley' is a
conjecture, but a safe one. Cf. Wellesley's 'sensuality', NLW, 4812 D 237,
May 1812.

[3] Letter to W. Scott, 10 June 1812. *Sir Walter's Post-Bag*, ed. W. Partington
(1932), pp. 87–88.

Southey sounds almost hopeful. 'One way or another', he told Rickman in February 1813, 'I suppose this Government of ours will be destroyed in the course of twenty or thirty years,—but they will not do it quite so easily as in France.'[1] Then, three weeks later, he is moved to reproach Wynn for aiding the work of revolution by his support of the opposition, and concludes: 'What we may have to go through, before we sit down quietly in our chains, God only knows.'[2]

His alarms were connected with what he happened to be reading in the newspapers, but it is possible to exaggerate his dependence on the written word for his knowledge of what was going on. A resident of Keswick was no hermit, cut off from the world. The town is not far from the Whitehaven coal-field, and Carlisle had a considerable industrial population, much inclined to tumultuous assembly. At Keswick itself there was a cotton-twist mill owned by Blackie, Hardesty & Co. When Shelley visited Keswick in the winter of 1811–12, he observed that 'the manufacturers with their contamination have crept into the peaceful vale'. It seemed more like a suburb of London, he said, than a village of Cumberland. He asserted that children were 'frequently' found in the river 'which the unfortunate women employed at the manufactory destroy'—the manufactory is presumably the cotton-twist mill.[3] Southey seems not to have taken much interest in this specimen of the industrial system on his own doorstep. In later years he pointed out that the cottage architecture of Applethwaite was pleasanter to the eye than that at Millbeck, where Dover, Younghusband & Co. had a woollen mill. This preference moved Macaulay to scorn, and while the ugliness of industrial society is more of a valid objection than Macaulay was willing to admit, it must be granted that Southey's objections were those of a benevolent gentleman viewing the lower orders from a considerable social distance. Cuthbert

[1] HM, 19 Feb. 1813.
[2] LC, iv. 25, 12 Mar. 1813.
[3] P. B. Shelley, Works, ed. Roger Ingpen and Walter Peck (1926–30), viii. 235. Letter to Elizabeth Hitchener, 7 Jan. 1812.

Southey remarks that, long as his father had resided at Keswick, 'I do not think there were twenty persons in the lower class whom he knew by sight'.[1] Whatever the reasons for this (and imperfect sight had a good deal to do with it), the consequence was that Southey would see the industrial classes in his own area in much the same way as the wealthier people saw it in London and other large towns. The smallness of Keswick did not for him mitigate class differences. The Keswick populace were a specimen of the British populace, whose frightening insubordination he read about in the newspapers, but whom he did not know with enough intimacy to counteract the effects of panic.

His letters contain several references to local 'disaffection'. In August 1815, for example, the respectable inhabitants of Keswick arranged a victory bonfire on the top of Skiddaw, to take place on the Prince Regent's birthday. The weather was wet, so the celebration had to be postponed. Profiting by the delay, some of the 'rabble' set light to the bonfire in the early hours of the morning, when no one but themselves could see it. They also threw into the fire the cannon which had been carried up. 'This', remarked Southey, 'is a specimen of Keswick feeling.' As it would not have done for the rabble to have the satisfaction of spoiling the loyal celebrations, Southey and his friends set to work again to bring up fuel, and on 21 August they had a successful bonfire. (The occasion was marred only by Wordsworth accidentally knocking over the hot water for the punch.[2]) A year later Southey was informed of an even more disquieting circumstance. He learnt that Keswick had its own 'club of Atheists', 'who used to meet twice a week at an alehouse to enjoy the pleasures of free opinion in congenial society! The mistress of the alehouse was "of the same way of thinking",—but one of the members having married the daughter of another alewife the society has split—perhaps there may be two clubs instead of

---

[1] *LC*, vi. 13.
[2] BL, c. 25, f. 195, 14 Aug. 1815; *LC*, iv. 121–3, 23 Aug. 1815.

one.'[1] *Atheists* should perhaps be interpreted as readers of deistic literature which was once again coming into circulation. The main text was Paine's *Age of Reason*, and since Paine's religious beliefs were very closely related to his radical politics—were, indeed, the most provocative form which those politics could take—the existence of a club of freethinkers in Keswick showed that the dissemination of disorganizing principles had gone very far. This, it will be noted, is in the year 1816, by which date alarm about the possibilities of revolution had become widespread.

Unrest was closely related to distress. The main cause of distress in the years 1815 to 1820 was the general economic depression. There were considerable variations from year to year—1818 was quite prosperous—but the predominant impression is one of unemployment, low wages, and privations among some classes of workpeople unprecedented in the memory of that generation. The destitution of the silk-weavers in Spitalfields particularly shocked the people of London. At a Mansion House meeting called to consider ways of relieving distress in Spitalfields, Fowell Buxton spoke of the extreme overcrowding in workhouses, and described some harrowing cases of absolute starvation that had come to his notice. One man had been discovered amongst some willows. There were remains of life in him, said Buxton, 'but (I hardly know how to convey so loathsome an image) the vermin of all kinds had already seized upon him as their prey'. The man's story was that the last he recollected was sinking down there on Wednesday (he was found the following Saturday), overcome with weariness and hunger.[2]

Confronted with this situation, royal dukes and the Archbishop of Canterbury were willing to pay attention to the plans of Robert Owen for settling the poor in agricultural communities. John Rickman, it is true, thought him a mixture

[1] BL, c. 25, f. 302. Letter to Grosvenor Bedford, 10 Sept. 1816.
[2] *Taunton Courier*, 5 Dec. 1816.

of rogue and madman—mostly madman—and told Southey that people were only humouring him with an appearance of assent to his New View of Society. Even Rickman had to admit that the Tory journalist Dr. Stoddart had taken a fancy to him, however, and there is no doubt that the extremity of distress led the most surprising people to listen to this application of the levelling principles of 1794. The spectacle moved Hazlitt to ribald comment. Owen, he said, only secured the ear of ministers because his reform was remote, and in the meantime he provided a useful diversion against the genuine reformers by his cant against political reform and against Bonaparte. Hazlitt would begin to think there was something in Owen's New View when he had been brought up before the Lord Chief Justice or made to stand in the pillory.[1] On the other hand, Owen's conciliatory tone won the sympathy of the pantisocratic Poet Laureate. Southey was impressed that a man on good terms with ministers and the Archbishop should have levelling opinions. And in spite of his disquiet at the indiscretions to be found in his writings, he persisted in giving a general approval to Owen; this, too, in the face of Rickman's contempt for the man. He agreed with Owen's analysis of the cause of the distress: the shock given to the economy by the ending of war expenditure. (In this analysis, it may be remarked, Owen was supporting ministers against the opposition. The latter put the blame for distress on excessive government expenditure, more especially on place-men and pensioners.) Southey was further convinced by Owen of the importance of making paupers into land-workers, because to employ them in manufactures would be to increase the pressure on an already overstocked market. Owen believed that these new agricultural communities would form the nucleus of an order of society which would undermine all existing institutions. This struck Southey as over-sanguine, although he believed

---

[1] *Examiner*, 4 Aug. 1816. Cf. William Hone's article in *Hone's Reformists' Register*, 23 Aug. 1817: 'Let us alone, Mr. Owen!'

that in the long run a pantisocracy was likely to replace the system of inequality. He was constrained to tell Owen, however, that he would more easily undertake to convert the Archbishop to the Mohammedan faith than to make him assent to such principles.[1]

Nevertheless, few people would have disagreed with what Southey said in the course of his *Letter to William Smith* in 1817: 'We are far from that state in which anything resembling equality would be possible; but we are arrived at that state in which the extremes of inequality are become intolerable. They are too dangerous, as well as too monstrous, to be borne much longer.'[2] Charles Knight, later to be a powerful supporter of orthodox political economy, concurred strongly in this view. As editor of the *Windsor and Eton Express* he wrote of the evil consequences of the system of enclosure, and 'talked, as it was the fashion to talk when Southey wrote, "The nation that builds upon manufactures sleeps upon gunpowder."' By the time that he came to write his autobiography, Knight regarded his writings of these years as full of fallacies and half-truths. But he concedes that he was groping his way through thick darkness, and that there never was an economic problem more difficult to solve than that which faced England in 1816 and 1817.[3] The general conviction that a thorough remedy must be found was reinforced by an economic insecurity which extended far beyond those who were actually destitute. Tradespeople, for instance, had great difficulty in recovering small debts, which drove numbers of them out of business. An acquaintance of Robert Southey's in his Bristol days, James Jennings, owned a general store in his native village of Huntspill in Somerset, a business which had been built up by his father before him. Towards the end of the war he was forced to the conclusion that he

[1] HM, Southey to Rickman, 25 and 31 Aug. 1816. (Cuthbert Southey prints the first, with omissions, *LC*, iv. 195–7.) For Rickman's opinion, see HM, 7 Sept. 1816.

[2] Southey, *Essays* (1832), ii. 23.

[3] C. Knight, *Passages of a Working Life* (1864), i. 180–2.

could not continue in trade without serious risk of bankruptcy. In 1817 he went to live in London, and scraped a livelihood by means of miscellaneous writing and (perhaps) the money given him by a wealthy banker, Paxton. He owned some houses in south-east London, but they had become overcrowded tenements from which he had the utmost difficulty in extracting rents. It is not surprising that such a man should object to apologists for 'things as they are' who ascribed failure in business to habits of excessive drinking and thriftlessness. He believed that the problem of poor relief would be insoluble while the system of individual property remained, and was a defender of the plans of Robert Owen.[1] Multiply the history of Jennings many times over, and it becomes clear why there was such a general predisposition towards revolution, or at least a complete change, in the years after Waterloo. 'They talk of a change of Ministers,' Fanny Godwin wrote to her half-sister Mary, 'but this can effect no good; it is a change of the whole system of things that is wanted.' Fanny Godwin was not herself much inclined to welcome Owen's system of equality. Still, she confessed she would rather live with the Genevese, as described by Mary, than stay in London, with all its brilliance and vice and misery.[2] This letter was written in July 1816. The following October Fanny committed suicide. Although Mrs. Godwin's evil temper had more to do with this than anything else, the dismal letter to Mary indicates a general environment very conducive to suicide.

The anti-ministerial drift of public opinion is reflected in the newspapers. The most striking example is *The Times*. It had been vehemently ministerial in the later years of the war, mainly under the influence of Dr. Stoddart. Walter, the proprietor of the paper, became uneasy about Stoddart

[1] I have discussed Jennings's career at length in a thesis deposited in the Bodleian Library, Oxford. But see *Monthly Magazine*, June 1816, p. 391; Mar. 1817, p. 101; May 1817, p. 297; Jan. 1818, p. 499; June 1818, p. 411; and Oct. 1819, p. 201.

[2] *Life and Letters of Mary W. Shelley* (1889), i. 149–50.

during 1815, and thereafter Stoddart's influence on the editorial policy declined until, at the end of 1816, he left *The Times* altogether. In revenge he set up a *New Times*, anti-jacobin in tendency. Southey interpreted Stoddart's dismissal as a deliberate calculation on Walter's part that since Henry Hunt (the orator) was 'Lord of the Ascendant', *The Times* must swim with the stream.[1] He was not altogether right in this, because in March 1817 Walter asked Crabb Robinson to approach Southey himself to take on some of the editorial work, which was hardly a way of conciliating Henry Hunt. Southey refused because he did not want to work in London, and Thomas Barnes became effective editor in the autumn of the same year. Barnes was disposed towards reform, but it is clear that Walter appointed him because of his excellence as a professional journalist.[2] All the same, it is evident in 1816 that *The Times* was inclined to accept a good deal of the opposition criticism of ministers. In a well-mannered way it supported the cry against pensioners and place-men, the prodigious burden of taxation. It objected to the language of the 'ruthless raggamuffins' of the City of London, and of inflammatory demagogues in general. The result of this 'trimming' policy was a steady increase of circulation. Similarly, as Dr. Maccoby has shown in his study of English radicalism at this period, the *Kendal Chronicle* abandoned its ministerial politics in 1816 and took up the cause of retrenchment and reform. Although the editor had to endure some aspersions for this line of conduct, he announced that the paper had benefited by 'an accession of readers'.[3] The most striking increase was enjoyed by Cobbett's *Register*. In 1816, by an evasion of the newspaper Stamp Act, he turned it into a twopenny journal, and in this form it penetrated into every corner of the kingdom, including Keswick.

As a result, even the most poor and ignorant could talk

---

[1] *SL*, iii. 55. Letter to Charles Wynn, 27 Jan. 1817.
[2] *History of The Times* (1935), i. 157–61, 167–70.
[3] S. Maccoby, *English Radicalism 1786–1832* (1955), pp. 321–2.

about the sinking fund, standing armies, sinecures, and pensioners, and demand universal suffrage and annual parliaments. If these demands should be conceded, the miserable majority would gain political control over the comfortable minority who manipulated the administration for their own benefit. This was the *bellum servile* that haunted Southey's imagination. And it was not simply a product of his imagination. Richard Carlile's memoirs are proof enough of that. He says that he was first attracted to politics by the distress and the disturbances of 1816. He read the *Examiner* and other radical newspapers, was pleased with their general tone, 'but thought they did not go far enough with it'. He thought this, too, of Cobbett and Hone, and indeed of every thing that was printed in 1816. In the factories where Carlile was employed, 'nothing was talked of but revolution'; and he soon began to try to get more revolutionary sentiments into print.[1]

The government's notorious measures of repression, which have cast a shadow over the memory of Lord Sidmouth, were both unwise and very natural. They were a response to a situation which seemed to be slipping out of control. Habeas Corpus was temporarily suspended in 1817, six 'Gagging Acts' were passed in 1819. Southey's complaint was that far too little was done, and he would not have been satisfied with anything less than a mass-transportation of seditious journalists and the imposition of a thorough censorship. Still, he was pleased at the 'good display of force on the side of Order' which was provided by the Gagging Acts, though he added that it might have been more useful if ministers had known how to use their own power. But he could feel that the warnings which he had uttered about the dangers to be expected from a manufacturing populace had received more attention after 1815 than they had in 1812. He told Rickman that he had lived to see 'some political truths admitted, and in part acted upon, which

[1] T. C. Campbell, *The Battle of the Press* (1899), p. 12.

were regarded as visionary or perilous when first they were advanced'.[1]

Southey was greatly irritated by the countenance which many of the propertied classes gave to the cry for retrenchment and reform. These included his old foes the 'peacemongers' of the Spanish war period, the Whigs in general, and the *Edinburgh Review* in particular. Though moved by the hope of gaining office, these exploiters of sedition would be cutting their own throats if they succeeded. The Duke of Bedford was a subscriber to the fund established to reimburse the deistical publisher William Hone after his three trials for blasphemy. 'The Russells had better beware', said Southey, 'how they encourage a second church revolution,—it may undo for them what the former has done.'[2] Southey and Rickman lived in the hope that as the danger became clearer the men of property of all parties would wake up to the fact that they were faced with a 'great system for breaking up every thing'. The press, Southey thought, might well occasion such an explosion as would 'shake the whole fabric, and make all men who have any thing to lose cry out against it'.[3] This was more particularly Rickman's point of view, and he looked forward to things becoming worse before they became better. In the meantime he carried on a private war against the cant words of the age, notably 'liberality' and 'candour'. At one time he even thought of writing a commentary on such words, as a contribution to the good sense of the nation.

As one of the leading advocates of repression, Southey was intensely unpopular; and the fact that he had been a reformer exposed him to attack as a renegade. It was assumed that the government had bought him in 1813 by making him Poet Laureate. There is certainly some evidence to suggest that Southey valued this post more than might have been expected. It was a symbol of the poet's national importance—a fact which Hazlitt touched on amusingly in his review of *Carmen*

[1] HM, 14 Jan., 19 Sept. 1820.   [2] HM, 22 Jan. 1818.
[3] HM, 31 July 1820.

Nuptiale, whose proem places the Laureate crown in such a flattering light. The opening stanza refers to the superiority of the Poet's fame to the Monarch's. 'This', Hazlitt wickedly observes, 'may be very true, but not so proper to be spoken in this place. Mr. Southey may think himself a greater man than the Prince Regent, but he need not go to Carlton-house to tell him so.' Still less tactful was the Laureate's un-courtierlike boldness. George Fox the Quaker 'did not wag his tongue more saucily against the Lord's Anointed in the person of Charles II, than our Laureate here assures the daughter of his Prince, that so shall she prosper in this world and the next, as she minds what he says to her'.[1] It is possible that the idea of being Poet Laureate had long exercised a fascination on his mind, in spite of the post having been made ridiculous by his immediate predecessor, Henry James Pye. In 1793, in the course of a verse letter to Grosvenor Bedford, he related a vision in which his friend Thomas Lamb had been Prime Minister and he himself Poet Laureate.

> And (my dear Grosvenor) you will sure agree
> More innocent than Mr Pitt was he
> And votre ami as good as Mr Pye.

In another letter, written in 1796, Southey talks of making interest for the laureate's place in heaven, so that he could 'write a few hymns occasionally for the Cherubim and Seraphim that continually do cry'.[2] These are jokes, but not jokes that would have occurred to Wordsworth, who was not a predestined Poet Laureate, and only accepted the job as a kind of senile honour, an old-age pension. Southey meant to be a poet of national order, and to fight against the seditious and Satanic forces that threatened good government.

It was a sense of his responsibility as Poet Laureate that moved him, in the preface to his *Vision of Judgement,* to attack the 'Satanic school of poetry'—an attack which led to Byron's famous parody. Southey had argued that the publica-

---

[1] Hazlitt, *Works,* ed. A. R. Waller and A. Glover (1902–6), iii. 112.
[2] BL, c. 22, f. 89, 14 Dec. 1793; f. 179, 26 Feb. 1796.

tion of a lascivious book was one of the worst offences that
can be committed against the well-being of society. Byron was
evidently a principal offender, though Southey did not mention him by name. And Southey's attack is not unreasonable.
The sexuality of *Don Juan* is that of the casual adventurer.
All the same, the cold severity of Southey's denunciation is
repulsive, and reminds one that he himself never wrote anything that could properly be termed love poetry.

No one, however, complained of the Poet Laureate's lack
of sexual tenderness. It was his political views which interested
his antagonists, and his jacobin past was a severe handicap
to his aspirations as a national poet. How much so was shown
by the affair of *Wat Tyler*.[1] In 1794 Southey had left the
manuscript of this radical poetic drama with a publisher,
Ridgway, who as it happened decided not to print it.
Southey did not trouble to recover the manuscript, and it
remained in obscurity for over twenty years. It was in the
possession of a dissenting minister called Winterbotham,
who had been a friend of Ridgway's, and it was the events of
the winter of 1816–17 that eventually moved him to bring
Wat Tyler forward for publication. The violent language of
the extreme reformers—Henry Hunt warning the Prince
Regent of what happened to Charles I—aroused a good deal
of alarm, which seemed fully justified when a rather pathetic
attempt to seize arms and capture the Tower was made in
December 1816. This attempt was made at the same time as a
mass meeting in Spa-fields, addressed by Hunt. One of the
men who tried to capture the Tower, the younger Watson,
invoked the name of Wat Tyler. One of his fellow-radicals,
a man called Preston, had been compared to this fourteenth-
century rebel by the ministerial papers. (They had evidently
been reading their Burke.) Watson said that it was no bad
title;

for be it recollected, that Wat Tyler rose for the purpose of putting

---

[1] A full account of the controversy caused by *Wat Tyler* has been written by
Mr. Frank T. Hoadley. See *Studies in Philology* (1941), xxxviii. 81–96.

down an oppressive tax, and would have succeeded had he not been basely murdered by William Walworth, then Lord Mayor of London; but we have no basketwork Lord Mayors now; and if he was surrounded by thousands of his fellow countrymen, as I am, he need fear no Lord Mayor whatever. (Huzzas!)[1]

Early in the new year there were investigations and reports made by the secret committees of both Houses of Parliament. Their conclusions were published on 18 February 1817. Before that date there was much discussion of the measures necessary to deal with the spirit of disaffection, *The Times*, for example, deprecating the proposal that Habeas Corpus should be suspended. One of the weightiest contributions to the discussion on the ministerial side was an article in the thirty-first number of the *Quarterly Review*, which was published on 11 February. It analysed the state of public opinion and the nature of the reformers, and denounced the incendiary journalists who were permitted, week after week, 'to sow the seeds of rebellion, insulting the government, and defying the laws of the country'.[2] The article was by Robert Southey.[3] On the same or the following day, Sherwood, Neely, and Jones published *Wat Tyler*.

This was not the first public reminder that Southey had been a jacobin. On several occasions in 1816 the *Examiner* had been republishing some of his early poems: 'Blenheim' on 4 February, and in August and September a succession of republican 'inscriptions', and the ode 'To Horror'. Coleridge's 'Fire, Famine, and Slaughter' was also reproduced, with the explanation that it was printed from 'our Poet Laureat's Annual Anthology for 1800'. All these merely underlined the fact of apostasy. *Wat Tyler* was a richer find. The theme gained a special point from its association with the Spa-fields rioters. It was a genuine first edition, and a favourable specimen of Southey's powers as a poet. Ironically enough it provided the climax to his career as a poet whom the public

---

[1] *The Times*, 5 Dec. 1816.   [2] *QR*, xvi. 275.
[3] Much softened by Gifford. See Appendix B.

A POET MOUNTED on the COURT PEGASUS.

Southey.

1. Ap. 1817.

Aye, aye, hear him —
He is no mealy mouthed court orator
To flatter vice, and pamper lordly pride.!!

vide Wat Tyler.

AFTER *WAT TYLER*, 1817

read. *Kehama* was quite popular, *Roderick* still more so, and *Wat Tyler* went into tens of thousands. (It was even acted.) As *Wat Tyler* was a piracy, Southey made no profit out of it; but a good name is better than riches.

On 14 March 1817 the House of Commons was debating the Seditious Assemblies Bill. In the course of it, William Smith (an opposition M.P.) read out two passages, one from Southey's article on the state of public opinion, and the other from *Wat Tyler*. He slyly assumed that the author of the article was condemning the sort of seditious stuff to be found in the poetic drama, and then proposed that the latter should be suppressed and the author punished. Southey had till then taken the untimely appearance of his 'old uncle Wat' quite lightly, though he would have suppressed it if he could have got an injunction out of Lord Chancellor Eldon. 'To be sure', he told Rickman, 'it would not be desirable to have Preston or the Dr quote from John Ball upon their trials'[1]—Preston and Dr. Watson being two of the leaders at Spa-fields. He was vexed by the language his own counsel used before Eldon, talking of shame and regret, whereas, as Southey put it to Edward Nash, 'I must be a fool if I felt either'.[2] He was probably rather pleased than otherwise at his temporary notoriety, and in any case Southey's stoicism was of the kind which could endure the tooth-ache patiently.[3] Still, he must have been irritated by the continual allusions to him as a savage renegade, and when Smith made him the object of such a specific and public attack, he decided that the time had come to vindicate his conduct. The *Letter to William Smith* was the result.

Under pressure of radical criticism, Southey took pains to bring out the 'philanthropy' of his present position—his

---

[1] HM, 24 Feb. 1817.
[2] MS. in possession of Mrs. M. B. Colt. 25 Mar. 1817.
[3] Cf. the same letter: 'That such things will affect me as little as any man, you will readily believe. When my last tooth was drawing, I made a poem during the process of preparing for the operation, lancing the gum, and extracting the peccant grinder,—in praise of the key-instrument.'

belief, for example, that the extremes of inequality had become intolerable. *Wat Tyler*, he said, had been written by a poet impatient of 'all the oppressions that are done under the sun'; and he had never ceased to work for the removal of obstacles by which the improvement of mankind was impeded. Since those early days, however, he had learned not to wish for revolutions, because they led to anarchy and despotism. It is a reasonable defence so far as it goes, although understandably Southey does not admit to moods in which he sympathized with Robespierre. But reasonable or not, it did little to mend the damage caused by *Wat Tyler*. The spectacle of the Laureate's jacobin past rising in judgement against him was too diverting to be reasoned away; nor was the unconciliatory tone of the *Letter* itself calculated to impress the ordinary reader favourably. 'What man's private character did I stab?' asked Southey. 'Whom did I libel? Whom did I slander? Whom did I traduce? These miscreants live by calumny and sedition; they are libellers and liars by trade.' After this, as Hazlitt plausibly remarked, Sir Anthony Absolute's 'Damn you, can't you be cool like me?' will hardly pass for a joke.[1] Southey's most intractable difficulty, however, was the perfect timing of the publication of *Wat Tyler*. It came most opportunely to discredit a ministry which was seeking extraordinary powers against the disaffected. It contributed something towards the creation of an atmosphere in which critics were able to dismiss the apprehension of revolution as absurd. Thus, a month after the publication of *Wat Tyler*, Sydney Smith was joking with Lord Holland about ministerial fears of Hone's blasphemous parodies, of the radical Spence's plan for dividing England 'into little parcels, like a chessboard', and of the Spa-fields insurrection under Dr. Watson—'The flower and chivalry of the realm flying before one armed apothecary'. Admittedly those respectable Whigs Lords Grenville and Fitzwilliam took a different view. So did the 'sensible people' of the Lake District who, accord-

---

[1] Hazlitt, *Works*, ed. A. R. Waller and A. Glover, iii (1902–6), 226–7.

ing to Wordsworth, cried out against ministerial remissness 'in permitting the free circulation of injurious writings'.[1] But probably few of them were greatly interested in whether the Poet Laureate had been consistent in his political views.

Even so, Southey could not remain satisfied with his *Letter to William Smith*. A year later he wanted to publish a similar attack on Henry Brougham. Southey had several grounds of resentment against him. He was a demagogic Whig, a contributor to the *Edinburgh Review*, and a supporter of Lancaster's schools. On one occasion, he had called the attention of the House of Commons to an allegedly libellous comment by Southey on Whitbread in the *Edinburgh Annual Register*, arguing that it was a breach of privilege. Southey relished the prospect of publicly vindicating his criticisms of Whitbread's 'peace-mongering', but unfortunately Brougham did not after all give him the opportunity. In the summer of 1818, however, Southey thought that his chance had come. Brougham was contesting the county of Westmorland in that year's general election, and Wordsworth had taken an active part in supporting the Lowther candidates. When the poll began, on 30 June, Brougham made a speech at Appleby in the course of which he attacked 'the apostate poets, Southey and Wordsworth', who had once been poor and radical, and were now wealthy and conservative.[2] Southey thought this gave him a suitable provocation to discharge at the *Edinburgh* reviewers material that had long been accumulating. He told Grosvenor Bedford that he had 'sundry charge of small shot

---

[1] S. Smith, *Letters*, ed. N. C. Smith (Oxford, 1953), i. 274. Letter to Lord Holland, 13 Mar. 1817. Wordsworth, *Letters, The Middle Years*, ed. E. de Selincourt (Oxford, 1937), ii. 783. Letter to Daniel Stuart, 7 Apr. 1817.

[2] In a letter to Edward Nash, Southey noted that Brougham had said that 'Wordsworth had been raised by Lord Lonsdale from extreme poverty, and that it was doubtful whether he had not received parish-pay!' (MS. in possession of Mrs. M. B. Colt. 28 July 1818.) Picturesque stories of Wordsworth's poverty were current when Shelley visited the Lake District in the winter of 1811–12. Shelley told Miss Hitchener that Wordsworth 'yet retains the integrity of his independence; but his poverty is such that he is frequently obliged to beg for a shirt to his back' (P. B. Shelley, *Works*, ed. Roger Ingpen and Walter Peck (1926–30), viii. 219, 15 Dec. 1811).

ready made up for Jeffrey's posteriors'. They would do just as well for Brougham's, and Jeffrey would suffer by sympathy. A little later he reported that the manufacture of thunderbolts was going on very well, and told Rickman that he had given Brougham 'a most tremendous dressing'. (This last letter was signed 'Samson Agonistes', and he further subscribed it 'Woe be to the Philistines'.[1]) Once again, however, Samson was restrained by his friends. Grosvenor Bedford was glad that Southey had written the pamphlet and thus eased his heart; but he hoped that, having served this medicinal purpose, it would be burnt forthwith. Literary pugilism was amusing for the onlookers, who could watch the kicking and cuffing and biting and scratching in perfect safety. But it was no way to obtain either sympathy or respect. A reply would give an importance to Brougham's ridiculous attack which it lacked at present. And besides, as Bedford tactfully pointed out, there was much in Southey's pamphlet that would only cause embarrassment to himself and his friends. 'I shall sincerely lament, and so I am sure will others, if you give any thing in the tone and temper and stile of this paper to the world.'[2]

Bedford could hardly have expressed himself more strongly, and Southey yielded. He persisted, however, in thinking that Brougham's attack was essentially a matter of public concern, if only because it amounted to an incitement to the mob to stone Wordsworth and himself.[3] A sense of personal danger can often be detected in Southey's more intimate correspondence, and it is closely related to a strong feeling of his own pre-eminence. Discussing with Rickman a plan for a treatise on politics, he said that he was 'much liked in one wide circle, . . . heartily abominated in another,—and what between praise on one side and abuse on the other the book will be sent abroad with a whirlwind'. That is what his importance felt like when he was in good spirits. But a little

[1] BL, d. 47, ff. 108 and 112, 6 and 11 July 1818; HM, July 1818.
[2] BL, d. 53, f. 170, 7 Aug. 1818. See also ff. 158, 160, 166–8.
[3] HM, Southey to Rickman, 1 Aug. 1818. He later printed an extract from the MS. as a postscript to the 1821 edition of *Carmen Triumphale*.

over a month later (in January 1817) he bewails the inactivity of the government—'Are they so stupid as not to know that their throats as well as their places are at stake?' He was doing all that he could on their behalf, but it was 'under a secret apprehension that it is more likely to bring personal danger upon myself than to rouse them to exertion'.[1]

Southey's personal feuds are misunderstood if seen as merely personal. Like the ferocity of *Blackwood's* against the Cockney school of poets, they are an indication of severe social conflict. If a man feels that great forces are at work which may overwhelm him, it is some consolation to win one or two local battles. They may prove decisive. Even the most satisfying local victories on the Tory side must have seemed rather empty, however, in the events that reached a climax in the later part of 1819. The violent breaking up of the reform meeting at St. Peter's Fields, Manchester, in August, produced a situation very uncomfortable for supporters of the ministry. The action of the Manchester magistrates was widely condemned, and *The Times* commented that 'Orator' Henry Hunt had contrived to 'thrash them with their own laws'. On 13 September 1819 Hunt made a triumphal entry into London. A vast crowd gathered to see him pass through the streets, and it would not have been unreasonable to see this as the portent of vast political upheavals. One gets a hint of the atmosphere of the time from a mildly excited letter of Keats'. He connects Hunt's demonstration with the impending trial of Richard Carlile for blasphemy (Carlile had reprinted Paine's *Age of Reason*), and hazards the suggestion that the government would not dare to carry on the prosecution: 'they are affraid of his defence: it would be published in all the papers all over the Empire: they shudder at this: the Trials would light a flame they could not extinguish'.[2] Keats was wrong in his prediction, but it is interesting that he should have made the prediction at all. It

---

[1] HM, 26 Nov. 1816; BL, d. 47, f. 1, 4 Jan. 1817.
[2] *Letters of John Keats*, ed. M. B. Forman (1947), p. 407, Sept. 1819.

illustrates the kind of expectant tension that continued till
the end of the year, when the Gagging Acts to some extent
put the initiative into the hands of the government. Uncertainty was at its greatest at the end of October and the
beginning of November. On 22 October, the Lord Lieutenant
of the West Riding of Yorkshire, the Earl Fitzwilliam, was
dismissed from his post because of the part he had taken in a
county meeting which protested against the 'Peterloo Massacre'. Artillery was stationed in West Riding towns, and
troop movements were going on in most industrial areas.[1]
The yeomanry cavalry in the midland and northern counties
had been called upon to hold themselves in readiness to assist
the civil authorities in case of necessity. Amid these alarms,
Southey felt that it would be a good thing if the radicals
should bring the matter to blows soon, for they would then
be put down. 'But', he added, 'the longer revolutionary
principles are allowed to be disseminated, the greater will
be the danger,—for in the end they will make it a struggle
between youth and age, and then the weakest must go to the
wall.'[2]

'The younger rises when the old doth fall.' This letter
recalls Shakespeare's vision of moral chaos in *King Lear*; or,
to name a work closer in time, Keats's *Hyperion*. One must
bear in mind that any increase in social power by a hitherto
depressed class will usually appear to those in possession as
threatening chaos, a creeping darkness that must be contended against. This is illustrated by the documents on the
early history of trade unions in England, collected from
Home Office papers by Professor Aspinall.[3] Professor Aspinall's material is particularly interesting for the light that it
throws on the strikes of 1818. The magistrates feared that
unless the system of concerted turn-outs was put down, the
workpeople would become too powerful to be defeated. As

[1] For an authoritative account of these, see *Despatches of Arthur, Duke of
Wellington*, supp. series i. 80–86 (1867).
[2] BL, d. 47, f. 174. Letter to Grosvenor Bedford, 5 Nov. 1819.
[3] A. Aspinall, *The Early English Trade Unions* (1949).

Colonel Fletcher of Bolton-le-Moors put it: 'The danger of a
committee dictating what wages must be paid, is manifest,
and if [it] should be submitted to, a worse than universal
suffrage would succeed. It would introduce a mob oligarchy,
bearing down all the better orders of society, and would
quickly be succeeded by universal anarchy.'[1] The military
commander in the north of England, Sir John Byng, was
alarmed at the long continuance of the Lancashire cotton
workers' strike, and the unnaturally peaceable demeanour of
the unemployed. 'Their regular meeting and again dispersing
shows a system and organisation of their actions which has
some appearance of *previous tuition*.'[2] The men actually dealing
with the disturbances of 1818 were thus made uneasy by the
fears that had oppressed Southey in 1812. It was a kind of
moral sea-sickness, and Southey had a queasier stomach than
most of his contemporaries; but as the seas became more
threatening, the disquietude spread. The large, well-disci-
plined meetings that were held in the earlier part of 1819
intensified anxiety among the friends of order, and the drastic
action taken by the Manchester magistrates in August may
be understood as a desperate attempt to control the mob while
there was still time. The picture which Shelley drew of
Peterloo in *The Masque of Anarchy* corresponds very closely
to the tone of feeling found in the columns of the *Examiner*.

> Rise like Lions after slumber
> In unvanquishable number—
> Shake your chains to earth like dew
> Which in sleep had fallen on you—
> Ye are many—they are few.

In a similar triumphant strain, the *Examiner* advises reformers
on trial to plead their own cases in court:

They have seen how the very least regarded among them is
more than a match for the limited arguers on the other side. They
have seen the poor figure which is cut by every man in authority

---

[1] Ibid., p. 286, 4 Sept. 1818.
[2] Ibid., p. 250, 26 July 1818.

before whom they have been brought, whether Magistrate or Chairman, Lord Mayor or Lord Chief Justice. They have seen themselves falsely accused and imprisoned; they have seen their families and their countrymen suffering under privations always painful, sometimes intolerable and deadly; they have seen the Parliament, which might have helped them, corrupted more and more to their detriment; they have all the inducement, public and private, which men can have to persevere in a cause,—humanity, patriotism, self-interest, the universal interest, resentment, pity, knowledge, and in one word, CONSCIOUS RIGHT.

Thrice is he armed, who hath his quarrel just.[1]

If the *Examiner* felt that the weak things of the earth were being exalted, journals more extreme drew the inference that the mighty were to be put down from their seats. In the autumn of 1819 the *Black Dwarf* was urging its readers to embarrass the government by abstaining from articles that paid heavy duty.[2] Tea, for example, should be given up, and 'balm tea' or 'hay tea' used as a substitute. Roasted peas, mixed with a little mustard, made excellent coffee. Waste lands and commons should be taken over by the poor; large landowners should give up some of their surplus acres to the distressed. A modern reader will be reminded of Gandhian civil disobedience. The *Black Dwarf*, however, was scornful of 'cant' about peaceable resistance. And the issue for 27 October 1819 contains a description of the effect of mass meetings which will explain why the government was anxious to suppress them. Such meetings, says the writer, weld the people in the crowd into a unity, banishing private interest, party manoeuvre, venality, and fear. Every heart beats only for the public good. 'The spark of patriotism runs with electric swiftness from pulse to pulse, until the whole mass vibrates in unison. Then, despots, tremble, for the hour of retribution is at hand! Then the hopes of freemen burn the

---

[1] *Examiner*, 12 Sept. 1819.

[2] The threat of withholding taxes was used to exert pressure on behalf of the Reform Bill in 1832: an aim more specific and less revolutionary, however, than that advocated by the *Black Dwarf* in 1819.

brightest, for the day of liberty is near!'[1] Demogorgon would
dethrone Jupiter. Like*Hyperion*, *Prometheus Unbound* belongs
to the portentous year 1819.

The economic condition of the country added to the
uncertainty of the future. Sydney Smith, though by temperament anything but an alarmist, showed symptoms of genuine
anxiety on this account. In the summer of 1819 he had a
reasonable hope that the current slump would prove temporary; but if Britain really was 'about to cease to be the
great shop of Europe, our situation is one not to be envied'.
As the year went on his tone became gloomier. A failing
revenue, depressed commerce, a stubborn ministry—the
combination was disheartening.[2] Southey, for his part, put
much of the trouble down to the sheer dishonesty of British
traders, which put them at a disadvantage with more scrupulous firms abroad. But that was not the only trouble. Slumps
are international,

and the distress which is felt in America acts upon England. Where
this is to end Heaven knows. I am of a hopeful temper, and believe
that most evils may be overcome if they are met manfully—but
I confess that when I consider the infinite complexity of our
political system, wheel within wheel, I cannot but fear that [it] is
too complicated to go on. And I cannot conceal from myself that
there is a general tendency toward some great change, which
however it may end, must be dreadful in the process.[3]

Southey might affirm his belief that 'God's above the Devil',
but he had need of all his natural resilience to meet the threatening prospects for England as the year 1819 drew to a close.

4. THE CONSERVATIVE PRINCIPLE

The revolution did not happen. After 1819 the fear of an
imminent explosion grew weaker, and the Reform Bill

---

[1] *Black Dwarf*, iii. 695.

[2] S. Smith, *Letters*, ed. N. C. Smith (Oxford, 1953), i. 336, 340. 20 Aug.,
3 Nov. 1819.

[3] Letter to John May, 15 Dec. 1819 (MS. in the Brotherton Collection,
Leeds).

agitation of 1831 did not revive it in all its original strength.
One gets a hint of a new direction even in the great scandal
of the Queen's trial in 1820. When George IV succeeded his
father in that year, he refused to recognize his long-estranged
wife as Queen, and had her tried by the House of Lords for
immorality. The proceedings of the trial rivalled the Duke of
York's affair eleven years before in inflaming the prurience of
public curiosity, and in many ways it was a great blow to the
prestige of things established. The radicals, somewhat restricted by the Six Acts of 1819, found in defending the Queen
an unusual opportunity for combining loyalty and sedition.
It was an excellent way to embarrass George IV, but less
effective as a step towards overturning the Constitution.
Coleridge could, on this occasion, cheerfully call himself a
'Queenite', or at least an 'anti-Kingite'. Sydney Smith's
comments on the business are in a facetious vein strikingly
different from his apprehensions the previous autumn. 'Will
the people rise?' he asked Lady Mary Bennet.

Will the greater part of the House of Lords be thrown into the
Thames? Will short work be made of the Bishops? If you know,
tell me; and don't leave me in this odious state of innocence, when
you can give me so much guilty information, and make me as
wickedly instructed as yourself. And if you know that the Bishops
are to be massacred, write by return of post.

One reason for this outburst of high spirits is indicated in the
same letter. Trade and manufactures were materially improving. As a good Whig he was naturally sorry to see the
country do well under a Tory administration. 'There seems
to be a fatality which pursues us', he complained. 'When, oh
when, shall we be really ruined?'[1]

Southey, of course, was not so readily consoled. If he
should live to be seventy, he told Grosvenor Bedford on
12 November 1820, he would in all likelihood outlive the

[1] *H. C. Robinson on Books and their Writers*, ed. E. J. Morley (1938), i. 258,
8 Dec. 1820; S. Smith, *Letters*, ed. N. C. Smith (Oxford, 1953), i. 366–7,
Oct. 1820.

English Constitution and the liberties of England. And in a letter to Wynn on the following day he predicted that things would go from bad to worse, until the press had produced a revolution, or the government subdued the press. He did not, however, expect things to go from bad to worse with catastrophic suddenness, and was not alarmed, for example, by the Keswick mob's demand for an illumination in honour of the Queen. He had heard about this demand through the local tallow-chandlers, and they, he said, 'are suspicious authorities in such matters'.[1]

During the next few years he continued firmly in his belief that extraordinary dangers could be expected from a manufacturing population worked upon by determined radicals. He was not deceived by the appearance of quiet. The manufacturers were in employment, and there was no seditious movement visible, but how long would this last? There was, in fact, greater stability than Southey realized. As Professor Ashton has pointed out, the pressures that had tended to work to the disadvantage of the labouring classes during and after the great war were weakening after 1820.[2] The unfortunate James Jennings, who had to give up his grocery shop in 1817, was by 1823 established in the March of Intellect business, as secretary to the Metropolitan Literary Institution.[3] It was in 1824 that the London Mechanics' Institute began, a foundation that had many imitators, and set the tone of much future working-class agitation. The year 1820 saw the beginning of the London Magazine, a notable protest against the virulence of party politics in journalism. The first editor, John Scott, was a martyr to the cause, for he fought a duel with a representative of the editor of the Tory Blackwood's Magazine, and died from his wound. It was in the pages of the London that Charles Lamb first became a popular writer. For many years he had been deflating the

[1] BL, d. 47, f. 230, 12 Nov. 1820; SL, iii. 219, 13 Nov. 1820.

[2] Capitalism and the Historians, ed. F. A. Hayek (1954), pp. 133 et seq.

[3] See part 3 of this chapter; and my article 'The Surrey Institution and its Successor', in Adult Education (1953), xxvi. 197–208.

earnestness of his friends with audacious puns; now he did so in print through the whimsical recollections of Elia—best of all in the earnest frivolity of Mrs. Battle. Hazlitt developed from a savage radical journalist to a severe commentator on human nature in general. His most penetrating work as an essayist is the product of reflection on his experiences in the immediate post-war period. Most significant of all is the decline and transformation of the old *Monthly Magazine*, that hardy survival of the seventeen-nineties. The general miscellany was falling out of favour, and Richard Phillips, the publisher and editor, disposed of it in 1824 to Messrs. Cox and Bayliss. They at first entrusted it to the veteran jacobin John Thelwall, but at the beginning of 1826 he was dismissed, and the paper turned into an imitation of the *New Monthly Magazine*, a more purely literary journal. The pervasive, wide-ranging intellectual curiosity that was one aspect of the exhilaration of power felt in the revolutionary period had disappeared. Where it did not give way to the belles-lettres, it was replaced by a more professional interest in knowledge as a means of improving one's status.

The most dramatic movement of the March of Intellect was the London University, begun in 1828. It was the object of much Tory satire, and the disappearance of rank and titles was predicted as a necessary consequence of this innovation. Southey was suspicious, mainly because the new college was not attached to the Established Church. But he insisted that it was impossible for a people to be over-educated, and was certain that the working classes were much less improved than they could and ought to be.[1] The implicit confidence that, as he put it to Crabb Robinson once, the 'spirit of the age will act surely and safely upon the governments of Europe' to their general improvement,[2] could not have been felt in the convulsion at the time of Peterloo.

[1] See *LC*, v. 316; *QR*, xxxix. 126 et seq.
[2] H. C. Robinson, *Diary, Reminiscences, and Correspondence*, ed. T. Sadler (1872), i. 391-2, 22 Feb. 1823.

Even at the worst times, Southey had a theory of long-term optimism. It was not always of much practical consolation, but it was there. At the time of Perceval's assassination, Southey was writing a *Quarterly* article on biographies of French revolutionists. The conclusion of that article was a manful attempt to set the imminent *bellum servile* in perspective. Evil will always ultimately be subservient to good. In spite of the decline and servitude of particular nations, the human race has been and will be advancing to a better state of things. The fall of the Roman Empire must have seemed an unmitigated calamity at the time; 'yet who is there but must now acknowledge that it was expedient for the welfare of mankind that the Roman empire should be subverted?' So it would be with the evil precipitated by the French Revolution.[1] In this statement of the invincible progress of mankind, Southey is salvaging what he can of the hopes of Godwin and Condorcet. A later moment of optimism was prompted by a different theory, however. On 1 September 1818 Southey told Rickman that he had just read through Clarendon's *History of the Rebellion*, 'and the result has been rather to strengthen my hope in the conservative principles of society'.[2] Two years before Southey had justified his belief in strong government on the ground that it would be aided by the natural *vis conservatrix* in the state.[3] This idea implies a real confidence in the future. 'Conservative principles' suggests something as dynamic as anarchy itself. Order is not a bulwark, precariously held against the violence of uncontrollable life, 'hideous, dim, confused'. It is itself one of the forces far bigger than the individuals through whom they are manifested. In the *Life of Wesley*, Southey speaks of the 'great struggle between the destructive and conservative principles—between good and evil' which was taking place in his time.[4] Until the twenties, however, Southey was obsessed by the strength of

---

[1] *QR*, vii. 437–8. Cf. *LC*, iv. 88–89.   [2] *SL*, iii. 95.
[3] *QR*, xv. 573; *Essays* (1832), i. 321.
[4] *Life of Wesley* (1846 ed.), i. 286.

the destructive forces. Kehama might come to a bad end, but the end was not yet. In the words of Rickman's poor-law article in the *Quarterly* for January 1818, 'Reformed these laws must be; they cannot be reformed without exciting a struggle between the destructive and conservative principles in society, the evil and the good, the profligate against the respectable; and too many are the advantages of the former in the contest.'[1] As time went on, these advantages began to appear less formidable to the friends of order. Early in 1820, in a letter to Wynn, Southey was able to permit himself a qualified optimism. Wynn had been discussing the great changes that had taken place in Britain during the reign of George III. What, he wondered, would happen in the next thirty years? He confessed that his fears were stronger than his hopes; 'I shudder at the answer which I should conscientiously give to that question.' Southey replied that while his anticipations were of the same complexion as Wynn's, he refused to despair. 'There are many preservative principles at work; and if the press were curbed, I believe that we should weather the storm.'[2]

In the first chapter it was observed that Clarendon writes of the English civil war with much less emotional disturbance than Burke when he writes of the revolution in France. This has something to do with the difference between the two movements in sheer power: the French Revolution was the political expression of a vaster development in the economic order of Europe than had taken place in the seventeenth century. By his study of Clarendon's world, Southey was able to analyse the greater convulsion in terms of one that had been brought under control. He was able to see the course of history in a more cheering light, and could quote with approval a passage like the following from Dr. Phelan's *History of the Policy of the Church of Rome in Ireland*:

---

[1] *QR*, xviii. 304. Southey prepared Rickman's article for the press, and the phrasing here is probably his. These must be among the earliest examples in English of the term 'conservative' in something approaching its modern political sense. Cf. E. Halévy, *The Triumph of Reform* (1950), pp. 66–67 n.

[2] NLW, 4815 D 162, 4 Feb. 1820; *SL*, iii. 176, 6 Feb. 1820.

We can discover, without recurring to the voice of Revelation, that there is some mighty confluence of destinies, to which the whole human race is necessarily on its way: in the most permanent societies and most tranquil seasons a process is carried on which tends to separate man from his institutions—as, in the lapse of ages, the fixed stars themselves have deserted their primeval signs.[1]

In that last sentence Phelan captures most successfully the accent of the seventeenth-century divines. Southey deprecated the determinism that he noted in some historians of his time (Guizot for example), but 'destinies' and 'necessarily' lose their impalpable terrors when set in the context of a Jacobean metaphor. Southey, moreover, enjoyed the unselfconscious superiority with which Clarendon dissected his political opponents. In the same way he appreciated the divinity of South and Thomas Jackson. The perusal of the latter's works, he told Lord Ashley, 'always elevates me, and leaves an abiding contentment'.[2] Jackson's refutation of unbelief and misbelief, being of the early seventeenth century, was conducted in a more confident tone than that of apologists 200 years later. To immerse oneself in his work made it easier to feel convinced that the good and wise were unanimous in their support of the Church of England. Like John Henry Newman, Southey threw himself into the system of the great Anglican divines, seeking firm ground from which to contend with the wild living intellect of man.

Southey's confidence in the 'conservative principle', however, did not altogether depend on insulating himself from disturbing currents of thought in his own time. He did not forget that he had been a pantisocrat, and plans to new-model society never lost their attraction for him. For a time he interested himself in the Brighton Co-operative Society, which he learnt about through Dr. Robert Gooch in the summer of 1829. This society had been started with the help of a Dr. William King (who had also been a promoter of the

---

[1] *QR*, xxxix. 137.
[2] E. Hodder, *Life of the Seventh Earl of Shaftesbury* (1886), i. 128.

Brighton Mechanics' Institute). Capital was obtained by accumulating workmen's savings. For a time, at least, the co-operative owned a shop, a mackerel-fishing boat, and a 28-acre market garden. Moreover, King issued a monthly paper, the *Co-operator*, in which the theory and practice of the anti-competitive system were discussed. According to Gooch, its circulation was upwards of 12,000, and it was inspiring similar enterprises in other parts of the kingdom.[1] Since Southey looked kindly on Robert Owen's plans for the establishment of co-operative communities, it was natural that he should be interested in co-operative trading. He would be sympathetic, too, to King's dislike of the 'principle of competition', by which every man regarded his neighbour as a rival 'whom he must by every means in his power out-strip or supplant'.[2] John Rickman became so interested in the advantages of co-operation in improving the condition of the labouring classes that he wrote a paper for the *Co-operator*: Number 22, February 1830. He was impressed by the value of cash-trading, which would reduce prices and so raise the level of real wages. He also thought that membership of co-operative societies would produce the same material and moral advantages as membership of a religious sect. Every member attends to the advantage of the sect as a whole, and thus the sect prospers. The ultimate effect of a nation of co-operatives was obscure, but it might well break up the aristocracy of wealth and capital. This was nothing to grieve over, for the aristocracy itself would be amply compensated by greater economic security.[3] Perhaps the best published account of the Brighton society is the paper that Gooch wrote on it for the *Quarterly Review*. He argued that co-operatives would be anti-revolutionary in effect, and poked fun at those of the 'unworking classes' who feared that the extension of co-operation would compel them to work for themselves. The

[1] *LC*, vi. 50–51.

[2] *Co-operator*, No. 19, Nov. 1829. Reprinted in *Dr. William King and the Co-operator*, by T. W. Mercer (Manchester, 1922).

[3] HM, Rickman to Gooch, 24 July 1829.

great merit of the system, he said, was that it would diminish the excessive inequality prevalent in Britain. There can be no doubt that Southey concurred strongly with this view.[1]

Southey was afraid, however, that the radicals would turn such societies into an engine of mischief. Rickman was more optimistic. For the sake of expected mischief, he said, they would be patronized by the seditious. But 'if we can rest assured that Sweetness will spring from bitter Intention, by so much are we Gainers'.[2] In any event, Southey could console himself with the thought that, if revolution came, the co-operative system would be the only one from which he could expect good that would make the evils of revolution worth while.[3] As the upheaval of 1830–2 developed, however, Southey came to speak of the co-operatives as simply agencies of revolution. They had been taken up by dangerous, desperate men, and allied with the aggressive levelling system, of which Robespierre, Saint-Just, and Babeuf were the prophets. A struggle was going on in Europe between the ideas of government by authority and government by popular impulse. And this was only a prelude to the great struggle between the principle of property and that of a community of goods.[4]

But that lay in the future. In the present struggle between authority and impulse, it happened that property was sometimes on the side of impulse. The manufacturing interest, in particular, was identified with political reform. Southey had little liking for enterprising capitalists, partly because of his horror of the factory system, or (to make the same point in another way) because such people were a disintegrating force in society. They acknowledged no responsibility for their fellow-countrymen who formed the working class, treating them worse than plantation slaves when there was work, and when there was none neglecting them as though they were not

[1] QR, xli. 373–4, Nov. 1829.
[2] HM, Rickman to Southey, 25 Sept. 1829.
[3] Bodleian MS. Don. d. 86, f. 29, 11 July 1829.
[4] QR, xlv. 207–9, Apr. 1831; and p. 434, July 1831.

human beings at all. A horror of the consequences of social
disintegration repeatedly emerges from the rambling *Colloquies* between Southey and the ghost of Sir Thomas More.
This book was published in 1829, and Southey had been
writing it at intervals over the previous dozen years. It grew
out of his conviction that there were important similarities
between the age of the Reformation and Southey's own time;
and Southey believed that Sir Thomas More (apart from a
regrettable but natural prejudice in favour of Popery)
regarded the course of events in much the same way as he did
himself. Southey feared that the religious wars of the sixteenth and seventeenth centuries would be matched by new
struggles following the modern political revolutions. Such a
convulsion would be the consequence not only of the audacity
of demagogues, of a public life which had become

> the stage
> Where Hope and Youth shall ruin Fear and Age,

but also of the restless buffeting of a commercial society,
where small farmers and small shopkeepers are destroyed by
'the devouring principle of trade'.[1] This principle, radically
opposed as it is to Christianity, would be weakened by the
strengthening of Christian institutions. More particularly,
Southey favoured a high level of taxation and government
expenditure to ensure a more equitable distribution of
wealth.[2] Macaulay complained that Southey made the State
into an idol, and wanted it to be 'omniscient and omnipotent'.[3]
It is certainly true that Southey is prophetic of the modern
nation-state in both its good and its dangerous aspects: its
comparatively efficient administration, its strong influence on
economic policy, its control of education and of the dissemination of ideas. Church and State together could master the
restless buffeting that both repelled and frightened him.

Macaulay's article on the *Colloquies* in the *Edinburgh Review* is a monument of nineteenth-century optimism, and he

[1] *Colloquies* (1829), ii. 203, 253.   [2] Ibid., i. 182–94.
[3] *Edinburgh Review* (1830), l. 565.

regarded Southey as absurdly pessimistic. Coming to the *Colloquies* from Southey's earlier letters and articles, however, it is the comparative cheerfulness of the book which is striking. If Sir Thomas More utters Southeyan fears of a rising of the poor against the rich, Montesinos (as Southey here calls himself) remarks that the ghost is almost as dreadful an alarmist as the Cumberland cow which had lately uttered a republican oracle. And even when, as in the third colloquy, the tendency of the argument is deliberately sombre, the temper of the writer seems to be mournful rather than panic-stricken. This impression is strengthened by the success with which, in the course of the book, Southey evokes the countryside around Keswick. It is a tranquil work. The general drift of the argument, too, is not unhopeful. Southey is encouraged by the practical concern that is shown to better the condition of the poor. The very newspapers have their good side in deterring the powerful from abusing their power. Political upheavals are likely, and they may be terrible. But they will only suspend and not destroy the good which has been growing in Southey's lifetime.

The great reform agitation of the early thirties, therefore, came upon Southey when he was able to look at it with some detachment. This did not mean that he was not dismayed at the nearer approach of the long-dreaded revolution. Throughout the eighteen-twenties Southey was alarmed at the growing 'liberality' of the government. He was specially concerned at the prospect of the removal of disabilities from Catholics, and most of his controversial writings in these years were directed to opposing Catholic Emancipation. When Emancipation came, in 1829, he saw it as the herald of insurrection in Ireland and subversion at home.[1] He told Dr. Gooch that he had a weight at heart when he thought of what had been done, and of the seemingly inevitable consequences. And yet the thought did not move him to panic; not even to the sort of

---

[1] A point of view that becomes intelligible if one recalls the philo-Catholicism of Cobbett during the twenties.

indignation that prompted his friend Humphry Senhouse to relegate a bust of the Duke of Wellington from the dining-room to the privy. Southey told Gooch that he resigned himself to sowing good seed, hoping for the increase in better times. In the meanwhile, he said, 'I look quietly on the course of affairs, pursue my studies, and write playful verses—as if I were grown young again'.[1] There is no mistaking the note of relaxation, or of weariness. Once again Southey dallied with the idea of emigrating, if his means allowed. This time it was not the banks of the Susquehannah, or Brazil, or Portugal that tempted him, but Switzerland (one of the protestant cantons). But one feels that he is not even beginning to take the idea seriously.

Southey's greater placidity was not simply a sign that he was growing old. It also reflected the less revolutionary temper of the time. This temper is witnessed to by Richard Carlile, the atheist and radical. In the autumn of 1829 he went to a meeting of the London Radical Reform Association. Henry Hunt was there, he said, repeating the stuff he used to speak twelve or fourteen years ago. The whole proceedings were mean, tame, pointless.

You look now in vain for the energy and the daring of the Radical Reformers of 1816 to 20. There was then a general expectation that the cry of Radical Reform was to be followed by insurrection; there was then courage required to be its advocate; the country was agitated and the halter and the dungeon stared one in the face; but now, it is tame, it is hopeless, it is flat, stale, and unprofitable. I am more than ever a reformer; but I could not act with and join in the doings, the littleness, of these men, who now call themselves Radical Reformers. I seek, I crave nobler game than 'Co-operation' or that which is called Radical Reform. . . .[2]

Carlile's depression helps one to understand why the Whig leader Grey, who in 1819 went in fear of death on the scaffold, should in 1832 be able to preside over the passing of the Reform Bill.

[1] Bodleian MS. Don. d. 86, f. 30, 11 July 1829.
[2] *Lion*, iv. 451, 9 Oct. 1829.

Admittedly the events of 1830–2 were enough to raise Carlile's spirits. The succession of revolutions in Europe, the agricultural labourers' risings in the south of England, the demand for parliamentary reform focused on the unexpectedly sweeping Reform Bill of 1831—these things brought back much of the old excitement. 'The inflammable spirit is abroad', said Carlile in the *Prompter* for 18 December 1830; and through excited meetings at the Rotunda in Blackfriars, he and his associates made themselves the leaders of extreme and more violent reformers. Carlile soon found himself in prison for inciting the agricultural labourers to revolt. But from prison he issued his benediction on the Whig Reform Bill.[1]

Yet while everything seemed to point to the complete subversion of the Constitution, Southey remarked that his friends were much more cast down than he was himself. Lord Lowther appeared to have aged twenty years in a few months; Wordsworth (following the example of the notorious Marquis of Hertford) was investing all he could in the American funds; and even the pious Lord Ashley was profoundly despondent. Wynn said bravely that he would live and die where he was, but that his children would be exiles and beggars.[2] It is a novelty to find Southey writing to anyone to reassure him about a political crisis, but that is what he was doing in his letters to Ashley. Ashley was then mainly known as a young and active supporter of the old Constitution in Church and State. It was as fellow-conservatives that he and Southey first corresponded. Southey found comfort in various circumstances. The Whigs, being in power, would become conservatives *ex officio*; alternatively they would expose their incompetence so unmistakably that they would be utterly discredited. The common people would discover that they would get no benefit from reform, and the yeoman class would find that they had much to lose. Everything, in short, would

---

[1] *Prompter*, 5 Mar. 1831.
[2] NYL, 16 Apr. 1831; *SL*, iv. 225; NLW, 4815 D 265, 3 May 1831.

work through evil to good. Southey's feelings naturally
varied with the actual state of the reform agitation. At times
it looked as though the whole question would be dropped
because people had grown sick of it. At other times the hour
of crisis seemed to be at hand, and earlier hopes of deliverance
proved ill founded. But through it all, Southey remained
much calmer than he had been in the past. He told Grosvenor
Bedford that he was almost ready to believe that England
would weather the political storm because all probabilities
and appearances were against it. Nothing ever seemed to
proceed according to what would have been thought likely.
Something unexpected would occur, war with France, a
death in the cabinet, a schism among the Whigs, agricultural
insurrection, or the cholera, and prevent final disaster. 'Be
the end of these things what it may, Grosvenor, "*we's never
live to see 't*", as an old man of Grasmere, whom Betty knew,
said upon some great changes which were taking place in his
time; "*but we's, may be, hear tell*", he added; and so say I.'[1]
Southey had been grappling with the spectre of revolution so
often since 1812 that the events of 1830 to 1832 made less
impression than one would expect.

The cholera epidemic of 1831 and the following years
made a strong impression, but of a kind which reinforced his
sense of the uselessness of human anxiety. 'Against other
dangers we can make a stand, we can exert ourselves to avert
them, or to repair the ruin which they may bring on:—but
here we are helpless.'[2] Paradoxically, though, it was the
danger of cholera that moved him for the only time in his
life to take part in local affairs. He joined the Keswick Board
of Health, a body which was concerned with such matters as
finding a building to isolate cholera patients in, and preventing
unnecessary occasions of infection. (They stopped the August
races in 1832, to the indignation of local publicans.) The
precautions could not mean very much, and Southey was
haunted by the possibility that the poor of such towns as

[1] *LC*, vi. 148–9, 14 May 1831.   [2] NYL, 15 Nov. 1831.

Carlisle would break loose and spread out over the country-side. On the other hand, the epidemic had the advantage of taking people's minds off reform. A Fast Day was gratifyingly well observed in Keswick. The people there, Southey informed Ashley, shared the prevailing depravity of manners and corruption of principles. 'The existence of a Pestilence in the land brought them on that day at least into a serious state of mind. . . . I almost venture to hope that the visitation has been ordered in mercy, as a warning, rather than a chastisement. God grant that we may profit by it in time!'[1]

The warning was not heeded, at least in the way which Southey had in mind. Despite the cholera, the Reform Bill was forced through a reluctant House of Lords. Southey's one comfort was that this success of disorganizing principles could only be temporary. Some months before the final passage of the Bill, Southey told Ashley that the Citadel of the Constitution was likely to be taken by assault, but conservative forces would later recapture the ruins. Ashley would then take an active part in reconstruction. Much liberty would be lost; possibly too much.[2] In any case there was little that could be done about it. As he remarked at the beginning of the crisis, in August 1830, men had become too 'knowing' to live under the old governments. They were breaking the old bonds of subordination, and the necessary consequence would be an iron yoke. It would make little difference whether this were the despotism of an individual or of a republic. Either alternative would be destructive of freedom.[3]

Rickman, for his part, took a savage delight in foreseeing the ruin that would follow the triumph of Whig principles: the China and East India trade waning, Canada more and more discontented, the interest of the National Debt suspended, taxes unpaid, Ireland in a state of civil war, and in England the shops without customers, the factories without orders. At this point, Rickman thought, 'such frightful Con-

[1] Ibid., 10 Apr. 1832.   [2] Ibid., 7 Nov. 1831.
[3] HM, 17 Aug. 1830.

fusion will impend, that the great Majority will rush to the rescue, and the day may come when Mobs and Mob influence shall be repressed by those interested in replacing establishments on the old Basis'.[1]

One sometimes has the impression that Rickman enjoyed the prospect of ruin for its own sake. He told Southey (in July 1831) that he was so angry at the preposterous arguments used in favour of the Reform Bill that he could 'forgive almost ruin for the pleasure of seeing the accursed Whigs ruined and some of them hanged by their friends'.[2] Southey did not go to such lengths. He felt simply that it was better to fall in defence of the Constitution than dishonourably to commit political suicide. The thought of resistance to the death was more reassuring than the horrible obscurity of a future dominated by a reformed House of Commons. What that future was likely to hold was indicated, Rickman argued, by John Cam Hobhouse's 'villainous Vestry Bill'. This Bill proposed to relieve the smaller tradespeople from the poor rates, at the expense of the larger house occupiers. It was a Bill concocted by the small tradesmen of Westminster, who were at least as 'civilized and politically learned' as tradesmen elsewhere. Their 'first political essay is an organized Robbery of the Upper Classes—Ex pede disce Diabolum'.[3]

Between them, Rickman and Southey made one concerted attempt to direct the movement of public opinion into a more conservative channel. They planned a sequel to the *Colloquies on Society* which Southey had published in 1829. The main weakness of this book had been that there was not in fact very much argument in it. Sometimes More and Montesinos raise their voices a little. More sternly chides his host for presuming that Britain was now exempt from war, pestilence, and famine; and Southey accepts the rebuke with a willing and humble mind, lamenting at the same time that in these

<hr>

[1] HM, 22 Mar. 1832.
[2] Ibid., 16 July 1831.
[3] Ibid., 2 Apr. 1831.

days the authority of elder and wiser minds should be so undervalued. But the general tone of the colloquies is one of placid exposition. There is little doubt that this would have been remedied in the second series. It took its origin from Rickman's disagreement with some of the ideas in the published *Colloquies*. He took the trouble to send Southey his objections to the hope of perpetual peace, which Montesinos had uttered at the close of the last colloquy.[1] Then, during 1830, Rickman began to assemble material for some kind of attack on reformers, much as in earlier years he had prepared 'dissertations' for use by Southey in the *Quarterly Review*. At the end of the year, Southey stayed with Rickman in London, and it was then that the plan for new colloquies was worked out. Over the next few months Rickman sent Southey his dissertations to be worked into conversation form, and by the early summer of 1831 they had enough to make it worth setting up in proof. At this point they decided to circulate the proofs to friends to make comments in the margin. Southey employed Henry Taylor and his father (who was secretary to the Parliamentary Commission of Inquiry into the Poor Laws) to put arguments for the reforming political economists. He also showed the proofs to Wordsworth. Coleridge was avoided, because 'he would travel from Dan to Beersheba in the margin'.[2]

Besides Rickman and Southey it was necessary to have a third participant in the discussions to put the reforming point of view which it was the main object of the colloquies to confute. They christened him Neocritus, and Rickman warned Southey against making him a feeble advocate of his cause. Southey himself caught enough of Rickman's robust spirit to urge him to contradict and add what he pleased to the draft of one of the colloquies which he sent him.[3] The topics dealt with included parliamentary reform, the Corn Laws and agriculture, free trade, the national debt and taxation, the

---

[1] Ibid., 11 Nov. 1829.   [2] Ibid., 1 May 1831.
[3] Ibid., Rickman to Southey, 17 Jan. 1831; Southey to Rickman, 27 Mar. 1831.

poor laws, and the newspapers. Southey put forward his favourite project of electoral reform, borrowed from the *cortes* of Spain, that of indirect election. He also had the idea of putting some seats in the Commons up for auction, to be purchased on the same principle as commissions in the army. The money so obtained would be given to a national fund to finance some good cause. It would have been amusing to read the comments of Neocritus on this scheme. Southey and Rickman wrote eagerly, with hopes of influencing public opinion when people had grown weary of the Reform Bill. But the Bill was destined to go through, and when this became clear there seemed little point in proceeding with the book. Murray, who had been entrusted with the publication of the new colloquies, was extremely dilatory in his dealings with Southey at this time. Had he been quicker, one volume at least might have been published. As it is, no part of the work seems to have survived, although it is clear that much of it was set up in proof.

With the passing of the Reform Bill, Southey found himself in an unfamiliar political world, in which the struggles of his own generation were becoming increasingly remote. Fortunately he found new scope for his political interests in two causes: the protection of British agriculture, and the promotion of factory reform. The last political article he wrote for the *Quarterly Review* was an examination of the Corn-Law controversy. (It began with some observations on Ebenezer Elliott's *Corn-Law Rhymes*, which, however, the editor cut out.[1]) The main argument of the article was that food was too important to be left to the chances of the foreign market, and therefore it was worth subsidizing home agriculture. The repeal of the Corn Laws would enable manufacturers to compete with greater effect in foreign countries, but Southey questioned whether this was a desirable policy. For one thing it increased international ill-feeling. He related

[1] This section of the article was later printed in a posthumous collection of Elliott's work. See *More Verse and Prose* (1850), ii. 81–116.

how, when some lead-mines were opened in the United States, British dealers exported large quantities of lead to that country and sold it at a loss in order to ruin the new mining company. The American government then put a duty on all imported lead, except bullets. At once the British firms took advantage of the exception, and proceeded as before, having cast the lead into bullets for the purpose of passing through the customs. Manœuvres of this kind, said Southey, were a natural consequence of the love of lucre; but they did harm by giving Britain a bad reputation—

a dislike not arising from mere envy, but from a resentful sense of injury inflicted by what may be called commercial invasion,—by a spirit which, whether it displays itself in avarice or in ambition, in the love of conquest or the lust of gain, in a cotton-king or a military emperor, is a manifestation of the same principle.[1]

Systematic attempts to force British manufactures on foreign markets would defeat their own purpose. It would arouse national feelings, and national policies would justly be directed towards thwarting this commercial aggression. Further, Southey believed that commerce was ruinous if it rendered countries dependent on each other for the necessaries of life. In this, as in other questions, Southey was apprehensive of anything that could not be kept under control. The State must keep the means of subsistence within its power, or run into formidable peril.

The article ended with a plea for a reform of the factory system, in the course of which he was able to commend a remark of that old incendiary William Cobbett. Cobbett had argued that the prosperity of a few capitalists was not a proof of the prosperity of the country as a whole. Southey emphasized the contrast between the capitalists and their workpeople, returning to a theme which he had first elaborated in *Letters from England* over a quarter of a century before. The manufacturing system had raised armies of miserably poor people, who knew that their condition was worse than it

[1] *QR*, li. 256, Mar. 1834.

need be, and who had the power, if not to improve their state, then to cause a social cataclysm.

It carries in itself the sure cause of its own terrible destruction. That physical force which it has brought together as an instrument of lucration—a part of its machinery—will one day explode under high pressure; and the words of the poet will then have a new and appalling interpretation—

Labor omnia vincit
Improbus, et duris urgens in rebus egestas.[1]

Reform of working conditions might avert this catastrophe, and, happily, reformers were at work. One of the most active was a man after Southey's own heart, Michael Sadler. He entered the House of Commons in order to oppose Catholic Emancipation; he wrote against the population theory of Malthus, and tried to secure the extension of the Poor Law to Ireland; he spoke and voted against the Reform Bill; and he forced upon the attention of Parliament the condition of children in factories. In 1832 he introduced a Bill to regulate their labour, and his speech on this occasion gave the Commons some uncomfortable moments. He described the cruel discipline to which the children were subjected. They were, for example, beaten with thongs, and to illustrate the point he produced some specimens. One thong was fixed in a handle, 'the smack of which, when struck upon the table, resounded through the House'. Sadler pointed out that it was quite equal to breaking an arm, 'but that the bones of the young are, as I have before said, pliant'.[2] Sadler did not persuade the House to pass his Bill, but he secured a formal inquiry into the employment of children. The report of this inquiry shocked Southey as much as anything he had ever read. 'For one or two nights', he told Lord Ashley, 'it disturbed my sleep, in a way that no book ever did before.'[3]

[1] *QR*, li. 279. The lines are from Virgil, *Georgics*, i. 145–6. 'Unwearying labour overcomes every difficulty, and want spurring men on in times of hardship' (A. H. Bryce trans.).
[2] *Memoirs of the Life and Writings of Michael Thomas Sadler* (1842), p. 375. Cf. *Hansard's Parliamentary Debates*, 3rd series, xi. 367, 16 Mar. 1832.
[3] NYL, 23 Mar. 1833.

Sadler lost his seat in the general election after the Reform Bill became law, and Ashley was approached to take over the promotion of factory legislation in the Commons. He agreed to do this, and Southey proceeded to take an almost paternal interest in Ashley's new work. He gave him advice about the fraudulent Sunday schools that existed in some factories, and sent him the section of the unpublished colloquies which dealt with the factory system. Sadler's report, indeed, made the latter out of date. He had known that the system was an intolerable evil, he told Ashley, but had no conception, till he read the report, of the positive cruelty connected with it. He advised Ashley not to occupy himself exclusively with the factory question, lest he should wear himself out as Clarkson did over the slave trade. For this reason Southey was specially anxious that Ashley should not visit the industrial areas. The painful things he would see would be too strongly impressed on his memory; they would be *burnt in.* 'The reflection would be more heart-sickening than it now is, that so much misery,—so much evil—must remain after all that can be done to lessen it.'[1]

Southey's political pilgrimage ends in sombre resignation. He could still be angry, especially when the conservatives in the House of Commons failed to give united support to factory reform. On this issue, he told Caroline Bowles, 'the Conservatives as a party have manifested an equal want of sense and principle'. They had neither head nor heart, and so could not take advantage of a popular cause.[2] Nothing was to be hoped of such infatuated politicians, and he quietly waited for the storm to burst. His main confidence was in the Church of England. He believed that it was spiritually stronger than it had been at any time since the days of Laud, and therefore well prepared for whatever trial it might have to endure.[3] Little as Southey might sympathize with the

[1] Ibid., 11 May 1833.
[2] *Correspondence of Robert Southey with Caroline Bowles*, ed. E. Dowden (1881), p. 274, 14 Apr. 1833. Cf. NYL, 6 Apr. 1833.
[3] NYL, 14 Oct. 1833; *LC*, vi. 222, 16 Nov. 1833. Cf. John Keble's letter to Southey, 1833. National Library of Scotland MS. 2529, f. 2.

Tractarian Movement as it developed, he participated whole-
heartedly in the sentiment which initiated the Movement—
the desire to take firm counter-action against the enemies of
the Church. John Henry Newman returned from Italy in the
summer of 1833, stirred up by the Whig government's
suppression of some Irish bishoprics. He was convinced that
he had a work to do in England, a work of deliverance from
triumphant secularism. His sense of mission seemed foreshadowed for him in Southey's *Thalaba*, a poem for which he
had 'an immense liking'. Many years later Father Henry
Ryder said that it attracted Newman

as the picture of a life-long vocation with its mysterious isolation
ever at war with the social instincts of the hero; its irrepressible
onward movement despite its grave oriental quietude; its asceticism;
its succession of pictures, which so full of colour never glitter, have
nothing of the impressionist about them; the tremendous catastrophe in which the hero dying achieves his victory, without
earthly recompense. It was his picture of what he trusted the
Movement and his share in the Movement would have been.[1]

If Lord Ashley was in some measure the heir of Southey's
concern with social reform, the poet's lonely contention with
the powers of darkness was repeated, more momentously, in
Newman's attempt to awaken the Church of England to her
vocation.

[1] W. Ward, *Life of John Henry Cardinal Newman* (1912), ii. 355.

IV ∿ APOSTATE?

In many ways Southey anticipates the Victorian social prophets, awakening the country's conscience to intolerable social evils, condemning the cold philosophy of selfishness which condoned those evils. If he was a conservative, he was of the same school as Sadler, Oastler, and Lord Ashley. He has a place of honour in Max Beer's *History of British Socialism*, and would have felt much sympathy with Engels's denunciation of 'the brutal indifference, the unfeeling isolation of each in his private interest' which characterized the England of his day. Engels, for his part, would have appreciated Southey's contempt for those bourgeois 'whose souls can hardly be conceived of as any thing else than glands for secreting lucre'.[1] One can make a fair case for the view that Southey's rejection of political reform was in no way a surrender to Leviathan, that he was on the contrary a sturdy champion of the rights of man, 'essentially the friend of the poor, the young, and the defenceless'.[2] It could even be argued that not being a political reformer was a positive incentive to searching out ways and means of specific social reform. He could not ease his conscience by saying that all would be well once the revolution was achieved, the Reform Bill passed. Something had to be done, and done at once if disaster were to be avoided.

Yet Southey does not impress the imagination in the same

---

[1] F. Engels, *The Condition of the Working-Class in England in 1844* (1892), p. 24; Southey, *Colloquies* (1829), ii. 142.
[2] E. Hodder, *Life and Work of the Seventh Earl of Shaftesbury* (1886), i. 262. (Ashley, writing after Southey's death.)

way as such men as Carlyle, or Dickens, or Kingsley, or
Ruskin. His preoccupation with public order, his determina-
tion to prevent any shift in the balance of power within the
country, weakened him as an advocate of reform. Thus, in
writing of Ireland he certainly proposes a heavy tax on
absentee landlords, and the introduction of the English poor
laws. But the whole force of his argument is directed towards
repression. With whatever remedies a dangerous madman
is to be treated, he writes, 'the beginning must be to secure
him in a strait-waistcoat'. Southey was naturally confident
of the benevolence of his own intentions towards the patient,
but one can hardly blame the patient for not sharing this
confidence. The majority of Irishmen, says Southey, 'suppose
that Catholic Emancipation is to put an end to tithes, taxes,
and rent'; and on his own admission the draining away of
rents from Ireland was a major grievance. The Irish might be
ferocious, bigoted, or lawless, but they were seeking redress
for substantial wrongs. To advocate repression was not the
way to inspire confidence that a genuine policy of social
reform was intended. There can be no question that Southey
himself wanted such a policy. But he laboured to produce a
political situation in which anything of the sort would have
been highly improbable.[1]

Southey's conservatism allied him with people who cared
little for his humanitarian principles. His collaboration with
John Rickman is an interesting example of this. While Rickman was, in his own way, a reformer too (as his interest
in the Brighton co-operative society shows), he considered
much of Southey's thinking to be sentimental. Rickman had
no misgivings about the manufacturing system, and no
patience with Robert Owen. He tolerated the slave trade,
and was suspicious of schemes for the education of the poor.
He did not share Southey's regret over the disappearance of
peasant farming. Southey writes almost in the manner of
Charles Hall and Cobbett on the handsome farms and miser-

[1] *QR* (1828), xxxviii. 572, 597–8; *Essays* (1832), ii. 397, 441–3.

able labourers of modern England. Rickman, on the other hand, in his article on the poor laws (which Southey prepared for the *Quarterly* of January 1818) takes some pains to argue that 'cottage farms' are an aberration of economic amateurs. In order to maintain the present state of civilization, it is essential to have the greatest possible surplus of agricultural produce. This depends on the best use being made of labourers and working cattle, and any arable farm should be large enough to employ one tolerable plough team. Southey's comment on this kind of reasoning was that a statistical gain may be morally a loss.[1] The two men differed even more radically in their view of human nature. Southey dismissed with contempt what one may call the materialist analysis. Referring to the evil results of the unrestrained avarice of landlords, he remarks in passing that 'a set of miserable sciolists have maintained that selfishness is the foundation of all our virtues as well as of all our vices . . .'.[2] Some eighteen months after this was published, when sending Southey material for the poor-law article, Rickman placed himself emphatically among such miserable sciolists.

In my last I do not think I said strongly enough that Selfishness, the care of Self—both in high and low is the only effectual Motive which causes or can cause the well being of all the orders of Society —and that what is called Liberality,—if it be deemed other than an *exception* from the Rules of Selfishness and private property—must for the same reason go to ruin all human well-being.[3]

In the war against the destructives, Rickman was too formidable an ally for Southey to wish to weaken the force of his arguments. So his economic views passed unaltered into the review of Pasley's book on military policy; and in preparing Rickman's poor-law article for the *Quarterly*, Southey was countenancing a sterner attitude towards the poor, in marked contrast to the earlier paternalism which his own articles had fostered.[4] Not that he allowed Rickman to

---

[1] *QR*, xviii. 278–9; ibid., xxxvii. 555; *Essays* (1832), ii. 237.
[2] *QR*, xv. 567; *Essays* (1832), i. 309–10.   [3] HM, 10 Nov. 1817.
[4] Cf. H. A. Boner, *Hungry Generations* (New York, 1955), p. 208.

bludgeon him out of his opinions, as a firm letter on the
subject of Robert Owen proves.[1] But Rickman was not the
man to encourage Southey in a generous, warm-hearted concern for human dignity.

Southey's difficulties were increased by his hostility to
many reformers. However much he detested the practice of
flogging in the army and navy, he was disinclined to swell
a chorus of protest led by Cobbett and Burdett. He could,
indeed, congratulate Grey Bennet for his exposure of the
state of Newgate prison, and for his work on behalf of the
factory children, at the same time as he deplored Bennet's
alliance with 'that principle of evil which is at work night and
day for the destruction of laws, monarchy, religion, and social
order'.[2] But sometimes his zeal for reform was clearly damped
by its subversive associations. His increasing antagonism to
Sir Samuel Romilly led to considerable changes in his attitude
to penal reform. Before 1810 he had strongly supported
Romilly's efforts to humanize punishments. In the *Edinburgh
Annual Register for 1808* (which he was writing in the winter
of 1809–10) he reported Romilly's speech in support of a
Bill to abolish the death penalty for stealing five shillings
from a shop, and described it as 'able, impressive, and important'. Southey expressed the hope that Romilly's efforts
would lead to extensive and beneficial changes in the whole
system of criminal laws. He mentioned that a society had been
formed to work for the total abolition of the death penalty,
and while he did not commit himself to any point of view on
the question, he said that the society itself must undoubtedly
do some good. The attempt to reform the penal code would
be opposed by no one 'except those who are in all cases for
the old *mumpsimus*'.[3] Romilly, however, was associated with

[1] *SL*, iii. 45–46, 14 Sept. 1816.
[2] *QR* (1818), xix. 113–14; *Essays* (1832), ii. 173–4.
[3] *Edinburgh Annual Register for 1808*, part 1, pp. 152–7. *Mumpsimus*: 'In
allusion to the story of an illiterate English priest, who when corrected for
reading 'quod in ore *mumpsimus*' in the Mass, replied, 'I will not change my
old mumpsimus for your new sumpsimus''.' (*N.E.D.*)

the defeatist Whigs over the war in Spain. Rickman disliked him intensely, calling him a 'detestable Misanthrope and Anarchist'.[1] The result was that Southey ceased to favour any penal reform of Romilly's making. In the *Edinburgh Annual Register for 1810* (written early in 1812) Southey insisted on the weight of legal authority opposed to Romilly. He emphasized the Solicitor-General's argument against restricting the judges' discretionary power (one could not make precise punishments for each particular offence in advance). As Southey put it in a letter written later in 1812, there never was a grosser absurdity than the notion that you could uniformly fit the law to the offence. He was impatient of Romilly's pretensions to be considered a philosophical lawyer. 'The men of practice deprecate his experiments, and I am certain that those who understand any thing of the nature of man and society despise the pseudo-philosophy from which they spring.' Southey's repudiation of Romilly is strongly expressed in the *Register* for 1811. There he condemns him as one who would change the whole character of the legal system: the very ground of his praise in the *Register* for 1808.[2]

In spite of this reversal of opinion, Southey continued to believe that punishments under British law often offended the common sense of justice. The punishment of death was misapplied whenever it produced compassion for the criminal. Moreover, the purposes of strong government were sometimes better served by clemency than by severity. Machine-breakers should be transported to Botany Bay, and for life too, but not hanged. 'Governments are never aware how much they may gain by affecting this kind of generosity.'[3] It is probable that this concern with political expediency was only a façade behind which the philanthropist hid himself. As soon as the obnoxious Romilly was dead, he could once again

[1] HM, Rickman to Southey, 6 Mar. 1811.
[2] *Edinburgh Annual Register for 1810*, part 1, pp. 232–40; ibid. for 1811, part 1, pp. 151–63. BM MS. Adds. 30928, f. 124, 29 Oct. 1812.
[3] BL, d. 47, f. 7. Letter to G. C. Bedford, 20 Jan. 1817.

permit his reforming instinct free expression. He hoped that
Wynn would take up the work, for he would conduct it 'with
more judgment and upon better principles than Sir Samuel'.[1]
In the event it was Peel who succeeded Romilly, and Southey
pronounced a retrospective blessing in the *Quarterly Review*
on his 'unostentatious, well-considered legal reforms'.[2]

Southey here bears witness to the persistence of his humanitarian views. But his tone is hardly one to stir men to action.
To seek improvement dutifully within the established order
of things is to cut oneself off from the kind of energy which
actually produces reforms. In his more philosophical moods,
indeed, Southey was quite willing to acknowledge this. He
told John Taylor Coleridge on one occasion that there was
'a most pernicious set of opinions mixed up both with the
Bible and the Missionary Societies', just as there had been
with the movement for the abolition of the slave trade. None
the less, one could not have the good which these movements
did without the evil; 'and it is no little advantage when the
men who hold those opinions direct some of their restless
zeal into a useful channel'.[3] It was in this light that he came
to view Methodism. Wesley and Whitefield, he said, were
easy to ridicule, and their fanaticism might excite sorrow and
indignation. They nevertheless 'set the mind and the soul in
action; the stirring which they excited continues to widen
and increase, and to produce good and evil'.[4] Much of the
evil, too, might have been avoided if the bishops in Wesley's
time had all been as enlightened as Berkeley, and been willing
to accept men from the lower classes as missionaries and
catechists. Then Wesley and Whitefield, 'instead of being
inflamed and exasperated by ill-judged and illegal resistance',
might have been conciliated into becoming the Dominic and
the Loyola of the English Church, the founders of an order

[1] *SL*, iii. 108. Letter to G. C. Bedford, 1 Jan. 1819. Cf. NLW, 4813 D 305.
Letter to C. W. W. Wynn, 22 Dec. 1818.
[2] *QR* (1831), xliv. 280.
[3] BM MS. Adds. 47553, f. 57, 30 Jan. 1825.
[4] *QR* (1809), i. 195.

and not of a schism.[1] This magnanimous attitude was, however, connected with the fact that by Southey's time the most violent enthusiasms of Methodism had been left behind. It is true that in the *Annual Review for 1803* he writes with unmitigated hostility about the Methodist plot to seize power within the Church, and inaugurate a reign of ignorance, fanaticism, intolerance, and persecution.[2] But as the years went by, Methodism gave him no such cause for alarm as the radicals did after 1810, and the movement emerged as a friend to order rather than a menace, especially since atheism and sedition had become such dangerous allies. It even seemed to him to be ripening towards reunion with the Established Church.[3]

By contrast, the radicalism of the Regency period and after was raw, dynamic, threatening. No one could be sure what would come of it. In its more exalted moods it looked towards a total disruption of the existing order of society. The fundholders' mansions were doomed to ruin, the large farms would be broken up. Parliament, said John Cam Hobhouse, would never reform itself, but the people would break through their unnatural bondage with as much ease as Samson broke through the green withes with which the Philistines tried to bind him. The great day was not far distant (Hobhouse was speaking in May 1819), 'the bloated carcase . . . seems about to burst—the system is dissolving, it is falling to pieces on all sides'.[4] Or again, in 1818 a radical journal advocated the non-payment of taxes as a weapon of revolution. Taxation, it argued, is the spring that supports the present system,

and the people are the masters of this *spring*, and whenever they choose to interrupt the current the machine will stop for want of

---

[1] *QR* (1816), xv. 227; *Essays* (1832), i. 232.

[2] *Annual Review for 1803*, p. 210. See also above, Chap. II, pp. 70–71.

[3] Southey was involved in an attempt to form a group of Church Methodists. *LC*, v. 159–66. See also the closing paragraph of the *Life of Wesley*; and *Correspondence with Caroline Bowles*, ed. E. Dowden (1881), pp. 175–6.

[4] *Champion*, 30 May 1819.

the principle that had maintained it in motion. The more taxes the
people of any country pay, the greater is the power they possess
over their Rulers. . . . Undoubtedly, there never was a Government
over which the nation had so much *virtual* controul; they hold the
reins completely of our political Pegasus; and it is on their breath
that the aerial fabric depends.[1]

The very confusion of metaphor here conveys something of
the exhilaration of the writer. The name of the journal was
the *Gorgon*, and Shelley may have had it in mind when he
gave the name of Demogorgon to the mysterious and irresistible power from the abyss which dethrones Jupiter.[2] Such
journalism was a kind of democratic gorgon to freeze the
blood of borough-mongering exploiters of the poor—or
rather, to be more exact, their blood was frozen by the effects
of the *Gorgon* on the populace:

> That maddening wine of life, whose dregs they drain
> To deep intoxication; and uplift,
> Like Maenads who cry loud, Evoe! Evoe!
> The voice which is contagion to the world.[3]

It would never have occurred to Southey, after his conversion to conservatism, to allow for the possibility that resistance to Demogorgon might be ill judged, and that this awful
power might be the means of bringing about desirable social
change. A modern reader, looking back on early trades
unions and political associations with the detachment readily
acquired after 150 years, may see in them the preventives of
violent revolution. Were they not examples of the British
genius for self-government? But to Southey they were simply
a frightening sign of imminent revolution. In the old days,
he said, when mobs were inflamed with sedition, 'they were
a headless multitude, bound together only by the momentary

---

[1] *Gorgon*, 8 Aug. 1818, pp. 92–93.

[2] The actual name *Demogorgon* he probably learnt from his friend J. F.
Newton. See Newton's *Three Enigmas* (1821), p. 75. He may also have seen
it in the notes to *Madoc in Wales*, section iv. See Southey, *Poetical Works*
(1837–8), v. 150.

[3] *Prometheus Unbound*, ii. iii. 7–10.

union of blind passion; they are now an organised association, with their sections, their secret committees, and their
treasury'.[1] Southey could find some justification for his panic
in the language of many radicals. Even more alarming was
the temper of the radical he had known best: himself.

Southey held it against Hazlitt that he believed the love of
liberty to consist in the hatred of tyrants; that to be a true
jacobin a man must be a good hater.[2] But if ever there was
a good hater, it was Southey. His very philanthropy was a
fierce crusade against evil, breaking the bones of the wicked.
He had, his son writes, an abhorrence of cruelty of any kind,
and his cheek would glow, and his eye darken and almost
flash fire, when he chanced to witness or hear of it. 'I saw',
said Southey once, 'five or six men on Sunday stoning a dog
to death—and I heard the dog's cries—and I wished I had
been the Exterminating Angel.'[3] On that particular occasion
(it was in 1796) he felt some misgivings about his indignant
feelings. In later years he became less scrupulous. His epics
are full of this fierce spirit. Thalaba, 'the Destroyer', knowing
that he cannot fly the dangers of the Paradise of Sin, but that
the dangers can be conquered, shatters the sorcerer's skull as
effectively as Southey thought he had cracked the vermin
Malthus. Roderick exulting in the field of battle as he tramples
down his enemies gives one a fair notion of how Southey
appeared to himself in his controversies with Brougham,
William Smith, and Lord Byron.

Southey naturally attributed his own temper to his antagonists. He opposed the Catholic emancipators so strongly
because he felt that if *he* were a Catholic his whole heart and
soul would be bent upon the overthrow of the Protestant
Establishment.[4] Even in his most conservative days, he
remained capable of responding to the jacobin fervour. As he

---

[1] *QR* (1812), viii. 345; *Essays* (1832), i. 125–6.
[2] *QR* (1817), xvi. 550; *Essays* (1832), ii. 103. Cf. Hazlitt, *Works*, ed. A. R.
Waller and A. Glover (1902–6), iii. 175–6.
[3] *LC*, vi. 236–7; BL, c. 22, f. 201. Letter to G. C. Bedford, 26 July 1796.
[4] *LC*, vi. 37.

describes the common topics of radical denunciation, his words take on an unconscious eloquence. The common people, he says, listen to Cobbett's *Register* and other papers in tap-rooms and pot-houses, and hear that there is neither common sense nor common honesty in the government: 'that the liberty of the press has been destroyed, and they are, in fact, living under military law; that they are a flogged nation,—and flogging is only fit for beasts,—and beasts they are,—and like beasts they deserve to be treated, if they submit patiently to such wrongs and insults'.[1] Southey himself had once despised the poor for their patience under oppression,[2] and his faith in the good sense and honesty of the government was a late development. It is, therefore, significant that he follows this evocation of the jacobin temper with a comment that might have come from the most crusted Tory in England. Such things, he observes, are listened to by 'men already profligate and unprincipled, needy because they are dissolute, and discontented because they are needy'. Only a few pages before this contemptuous outburst, he had described the attractions of the tavern fireside to the miserable inhabitants of city cellars and garrets. If such unfortunate people become depraved, he said, 'ought we to wonder at this, when their better faculties have never been brought into action?'[3] But sympathetic understanding of this kind could not survive a breath of his own former hostility to the established order. He knew that there were men at large who hoped to dash down Moloch-idols, Samson-like, and burst their fetters.[4] Those who thought in this way were weak, mistaken, insane, or wicked, and must be resisted at all costs. In such a crisis, Southey had no leisure to play the Victorian Sage.

Yet his understanding of the mood to which the Cobbetts

---

[1] *QR*, viii (1812), 342; *Essays* (1832), i. 121.

[2] BL, c. 22, f. 204, 2 Aug. 1796; and see Chap. II, p. 49 above.

[3] *QR*, viii (1812), 339–40; *Essays* (1832), i. 116.

[4] Southey, *Poetical Works* (1837–8), i. 338. *Vision of the Maid of Orleans*, iii. 227–8.

and Shelleys appealed undoubtedly gave the impulse to his concern for social reform, his interest in practical philanthropy. Long after he had become a *Quarterly* reviewer, a partisan of ministers, he insisted that much good might have come from the generous feeling that was abroad at the time of the French Revolution—if it had been properly directed.[1] That was the difficulty. Southey put the blame for the devastating consequences of the revolution upon the lack of able men, coupled with the fact that the heart of France had been corrupted. But one may well wonder how far the ablest men, the purest hearts, could have controlled the social revolution in Europe at the end of the eighteenth century. A character in *Roderick* uses words that can be aptly applied to Southey's own time. 'Our portentous age', says Prince Pelayo,

> As with an earthquake's desolating force,
> Hath loosen'd and disjointed the whole frame
> Of social order.[2]

In such a world other people often appear rather as embodiments of that desolating force than as hoping and suffering human beings like ourselves. Our security, our very identity, is threatened, and we must keep a hold on ourselves, no matter what happens to anyone else. Normal moral standards are put under a severe strain, if they do not break down altogether.

Pelayo's words are spoken to the wavering Count Eudon, forerunner of Whigs and peace-mongers. Mediation and compromise are not to be thought of; safety lies in dauntless fortitude and readiness for battle. Only the sense of power, the thought of instant action and deliverance, can revive the heart in adversity—that, and religion, which promises a world closer to the heart's desire than the world of mortal life.[3] Another character in the same poem, Adosinda, finds her support in hatred. She is spared from the massacre of her family in order to feed the lust of a Moorish captain.

[1] *History of the Peninsular War* (1823), i. 14.   [2] *Roderick*, xiii. 177–9.
[3] Ibid., sections xiii and xiv.

The very horror of that monstrous thought
Saved me from madness; I was calm at once,—
Yea comforted and reconciled to life:
Hatred became to me the life of life,
Its purpose and its power.[1]

One finds a mental condition resembling Adosinda's in
Engels, when he said that the English working man, treated
as a chattel, could 'save his manhood only in hatred and
rebellion against the bourgeoisie'. Perhaps the best analysis of
this state of mind was made by William Godwin, in his novel
St. Leon. The hero, imprisoned by the Inquisition, enjoys his
encounters with the spy because combat restored to him the
sense of his own identity. 'I secretly defied his arts, and
amused myself with baffling his most cunning devices. . . . I
therefore felt that I was his superior, and, which was a
sensation I had not lately been accustomed to, that I was
somebody.'[2]

Adosinda, St. Leon, and the English working man engage
our sympathy because they are sufferers. If the charge of
apostasy sticks to Southey, it is because he *is* accustomed to
the sensation of being somebody. Like Ladurlad in *The Curse
of Kehama*, he feels that he bears a charmed life,

                                   which may defy
       All weapons,—and the darts that whizz around,
       As from an adamantine panoply
       Repell'd, fall idly to the ground.[3]

It is Southey's self-righteousness and egotism that alienate
most readers. They are appalled by his assumption that

---

[1] *Roderick*, iii. 324–8.
[2] F. Engels, *Condition of the Working Class in England in 1844* (1892),
p. 212; W. Godwin, *St. Leon*, chap. 31. Cf. Charles Lamb's observation on
Coleridge's *Ancient Mariner*: 'The Ancient Marinere undergoes such Trials, as
overwhelm and bury all individuality or memory of what he was, like the state
of a man in a Bad dream, one terrible peculiarity of which is: that all conscious-
ness of personality is gone.' Letter to Wordsworth, 30 Jan. 1801. *Letters*,
ed. E. V. Lucas (1935), i. 240.
[3] *Curse of Kehama*, viii. 117–20.

political reformers and religious unbelievers deserve either pity or punishment or both. His belief in his own greatness as a poet now seems impertinent, and his habit of stealing the limelight in laureate poems downright ludicrous. But to view Southey in this way is to miss the poignancy of his predicament. It was intolerable to him to feel that he might be helpless in this portentous age. He stoutly held to his conviction that most evils might be overcome if they were met manfully, and to some extent he enjoyed the sensation of manful resistance for its own sake. Hence his pugnacious support for the war against Napoleonic France. It was a war of light against darkness, and the failure of Whigs and radicals to accept this judgement did more than anything else to make him a Tory. His confidence in the correctness of his opinions and in the distinction of his poetry is all part of this need to feel that his way was clear amid the dangers of the world, and that he had the power to take it.

Southey's radicalism throve mainly in an atmosphere of withdrawal, whether on the imagined banks of the Susque-hannah or on the shore of Derwentwater. His ideal reformer was the clergyman who performs his duties with fatherly care, and is rewarded by the filial devotion of his parishioners. His heart warmed to the story of the Alsatian pastor J. F. Oberlin, who raised a poverty-stricken parish in the Vosges to some degree of prosperity, building a bridge with volunteer labour, improving agriculture, and developing education. 'The march of intellect', said Southey, 'has never proceeded so rapidly to the music of *Ça ira*, as it did to Oberlin's psalm tunes.' Not that Oberlin had any quarrel with *Ça ira*. He sympathized with the French Revolution, and Southey approved of his feeling. Did it not once seem as though some great improvement in society was about to be effected?—

that an end would be put to the enormities of civil and ecclesiastical usurpation; that the abuses of existing systems would be abated; and that the institutions of society, which hitherto had added more or less in every part of Christendom to the miseries of life, would thenceforth be mainly directed towards improving the moral and intellectual condition of mankind?[1]

These hopes might still retain their meaning in a remote valley in the Vosges, and in Keswick too Southey might console himself with some sober hopes for the welfare of mankind. But in the main arena of European life, amid the bitter contentions of national politics, it was difficult to retain this generous spirit.

At no period did Southey ever feel hopes for human progress as sanguine as those expressed by Wordsworth in *The Prelude*, the sense that a benignant spirit was abroad which might not be withstood. Southey's general attitude is well expressed in his *Hymn to the Penates*, in lines where he recalls the hours he passed at Oxford,

> when the noise
> Of lewd Intemperance on my lonely ear
> Burst with loud tumult, as recluse I sate,
> Musing on days when man should be redeem'd
> From servitude, and vice, and wretchedness.[2]

The musings were remote from the actual state of the world, and the loneliness of the poet underlines the length of time that will be needed to fulfil his pious hopes. His visions of happiness are always in some kind of retreat from the world— for example the complete seclusion enjoyed by Monnema and her two children in the *Tale of Paraguay*, or the inoffensive life of the Jesuit settlements in Paraguay, described in the same poem. He tells his cousin Margaret Hill that, if he had Merlin's power, he would withdraw with her to an island whose coral reef would keep off visiting mariners.

> In such a blessed isle
> We might renew the days of infancy,
> And Life like a long childhood pass away,
> Without one care.[3]

To some extent (so far as is practicable in this life) he

---

[1] *QR* (1831), xliv. 365, 369–70.
[2] Southey, *Poetical Works* (1837–8), ii. 275.   [3] Ibid. ii. 237.

realized this scheme of happiness in Keswick. He found solace in his family, in rural beauty, above all in the world of books. In his retreat he was kind, considerate, and cheerful, an admirable father, the tactful head of a household that sometimes required diplomatic management. Mrs. Coleridge was not the easiest person to have in the family, but he kept her in order with a skilful mixture of genial firmness and sympathy. An incident he relates in a letter to Danvers suggests both what he had to put up with, and the way he dealt with it.

We have nothing to do with the Miseries of Human Life here— except indeed Mrs Coleridge—who threw a glass of water over the table cloth one day at dinner, when it was not quite summer weather with her, and groaned out to herself in an audible whisper— '*nothing but misery!*' An exclamation of which I have not failed often to remind her.[1]

Observers as different as Shelley, John Stuart Mill, and Carlyle agree that Southey was a man of considerable charm. But the charm depended on his resolute exclusion of the world of conflict and insecurity. He had no love for the 'severe contentions of friendship', the violent arguments such as those with which Bernard Shaw and Sidney and Beatrice Webb used to exercise themselves.[2] He never let himself be drawn into a disputatious conversation, and if such a conversation developed, his habit was to content himself with giving 'a quiet and good-humoured indication of the view in which he rested'.[3] No trace here of the literary warrior who so eagerly discharged thunderbolts at the *Edinburgh Review*!

If Southey only ventured into the world in order to do battle there, it was because he would otherwise have found

---

[1] BM MS. Adds. 30928, f. 82, 13 Jan. 1807.

[2] Cf. G. B. Shaw, *Times Literary Supplement*, 20 Oct. 1945. Mrs. J. R. Green 'was so startled at our first after-dinner discussion that she could not believe that we could remain on speaking terms after it, and was relieved to find next morning that it had not made the smallest change in our personal relations and was part of our daily routine'.

[3] *LC*, vi. 4–5.

it too terrifying to contemplate. That he kept his nerve as
well as he did was mainly thanks to a naturally buoyant
temperament. It sustained him in the ceaseless literary labour
by which he kept his own family and Coleridge's, and,
moreover, enabled him to turn to work as a relief from dis-
agreeable feelings, as an anodyne. 'Whenever anything
distresses me', he said, 'I fly to hard employment, as many
fly to the bottle.'[1] It is not surprising that what he wrote in
these conditions does not usually give direct expression to his
distresses. He was careful not to allow impressions to sink
in too deeply, for his senses were perilously acute, and ideas
could have the vividness and apparent reality of actual
experience. He kept his dangerous imagination under control
by variety of employment. 'I fly from one thing to another,
each new train of thought neutralising, as it were, the last.'[2]

Southey's verse and prose both suffer from this unwillingness to explore and reassess experience. His *Life of Wesley*,
for example, admirable though it is as an impartial and
efficient narrative, is marred by its rather facile explanations
of the causes of Methodism. His evangelical reviewers were
on strong ground when they objected to his fondness for
calling in mental disease to explain the oddities of Wesley's
and Whitefield's converts. To call a state of mind diseased is
to empty it of meaning. Southey was scornful of the doctrine
of catastrophic *new birth*. When preached with vehement
sincerity, it was certainly capable of producing a 'powerful
effect upon weak minds, ardent feelings, and disordered
fancies'.[3] But this did not awaken in Southey any suspicion
that the power of the doctrine might spring from deeper
psychological causes than animal magnetism, his favourite
hypothesis.

He used to complain that Coleridge never came to the

---

[1] *SL*, i. 294, 7 Dec. 1804.

[2] J. Holland and J. Everett, *Memoirs of James Montgomery* (1854), ii. 320,
2 Jan. 1812.

[3] *Life of Wesley* (1846 ed.), i. 211. The same patronizing temper informs
his fragmentary *Life of George Fox*. See *Friends' Quarterly* (1955), ix. 37–38.

point, but wasted time nosing every nettle along the hedge. 'My way is', he said, 'when I see my object, to dart at it like a greyhound.'[1] It is this quality which makes him such an excellent *Quarterly* reviewer. One cannot mistake the masterful way in which he habitually expounds his themes. But the poet is impoverished. His language is usually unevocative, not shaped by the pressure of passive feeling. Thus, when he describes the after-sunset glow in *Madoc*, it may not at first be obvious just what has gone wrong:

> Still on the light,
> The last green light that lingers in the west,
> Their looks are fasten'd, till the clouds of night
> Roll on, and close in darkness the whole heaven.[2]

A phrase has been lifted here from Coleridge's *Dejection*, and a comparison with that poem shows what has happened. 'Though I should gaze for ever', says Coleridge, 'on that green light that lingers in the west'—and the light does linger. Southey's verse moves on with its usual rapidity. Admittedly there are passages which are not open to this criticism, for example a description in *Roderick* of a deep mountain valley. The scene is impressed on the reader with unusual inwardness, particularly its heat and silence, broken only by the sound of the river below,

> Long in the distance heard, which nearer now,
> With endless repercussion deep and loud,
> Throbb'd on the dizzy sense.[3]

In general, however, Southey was impatient to be on the move, seeking the moment of vengeance and battle.

One of the rare occasions when his assurance deserted him was in the writing of the second part—'The Vision'—of *The Poet's Pilgrimage to Waterloo*. His language here takes on a sombre power which shows what he might have achieved

---

[1] *SL*, ii. 188–9, 29 Jan. 1810; and see K. Coburn, *Inquiring Spirit* (1951), p. 143.

[2] *Madoc in Aztlan*, xxvi. 259–62.

[3] *Roderick*, xvi. 130–2.

if he had been more like the pedlar in Wordsworth's *Excursion*, who

> could *afford* to suffer
> With those whom he saw suffer.[1]

He visited the famous battlefield in the early autumn of 1815, in order to collect material for a laureate poem. He carried with him a letter for Richard Carbonell, a wounded soldier whose parents lived in Keswick. But Carbonell was dead when he arrived. This was bad enough, but the condition of the wounded soldiers whom he saw was even more of a shock. 'I had never before seen the real face of war so closely', he said, 'and God knows! a deplorable sight it is.'[2] He eased his heart by execrations against Bonaparte, the cause of all the trouble; but this gave only partial relief. 'The shaken mind felt all things insecure'[3] and in the second part of the poem Southey explores the insecurity by means of a Spenserian allegory. He was travelling over a vast, dreary plain, with innumerable crowds of people. Behind them were the wrecks of human history, before them blank mist.

> Yet thither, as some power unseen impelled,
> My blind involuntary way I held.[4]

He found himself again on the battlefield. Perplexed and grieved, he was called aside by a grave personage, who stood on a tower. Its foundations were in a ruinous state, but farther up it seemed more presentable. The grave personage proved to be an apologist for materialism. Southey replied to his arguments by appealing to the peace that supports the heroic mind through all the troubles of life. But this only moved the old man to a declamation which weighed on Southey's mind like a burden. The movement of history reveals no purpose.

[1] *Excursion*, i. 370–1.
[2] *Journal of a Tour to the Netherlands in the autumn of 1815*, ed. W. Robertson Nicoll (1903), p. 66.
[3] *Poet's Pilgrimage*, i. iv. 39.
[4] Ibid. ii. i. 4.

The winds which have in viewless heaven their birth,
  The waves which in their fury meet the clouds,
The central storms which shake the solid earth,
  And from volcanoes burst in fiery floods,
Are not more vague and purportless and blind,
Than is the course of things among mankind![1]

Southey is only recalled from the despair into which this vision of life plunges him by the voice, sweet as a mother's, of the Heavenly Muse. He springs from the tower, and is carried gently to the Sacred Hill. There he is rebuked by Urania for listening to the tempter. Although progress is slow, she says, it is none the less progress. She conducts the doubting poet to a beautiful glade, where his spirit is soothed. She tells him that the stream which flows there comes from the Well of Life, flowing from the Rock of Ages. The Cross of Christ stands in the rock, and by it grows a tree, a descendant of the Tree of Knowledge. Urania bids the poet taste the bitter, wholesome fruit. He does so.

The bitterness was even as of death;
I felt a cold and piercing thrill pervade
  My loosened limbs, and losing sight and breath,
To earth I should have fallen in my despair,
Had I not clasped the Cross and been supported there.

My heart, I thought, was bursting with the force
  Of that most fatal fruit; soul-sick I felt,
And tears ran down in such continuous course,
  As if the very eyes themselves should melt.
But then I heard my heavenly teacher say,
Drink, and this mortal stound will pass away.

I stoopt and drank of that divinest Well,
  Fresh from the Rock of Ages where it ran.
It had a heavenly quality to quell
  My pain: . . . I rose a renovated man,
And would not now when that relief was known
For worlds the needful suffering have foregone.[2]

---

[1] Ibid. II. ii. 20.   [2] Ibid. II. iii. 43–45.

Southey is now able to see the work of providence in history. Nations prosper according to their virtue: hence the infinite importance of defeating Bonaparte, who would have darkened the light that Europe is now free to carry into every part of the earth. The poem ends with a vision of the good which a righteous Britain may do.

The optimistic conclusion returns us to the normal world of Southey's poetry. It is the expression of doubt, bewilderment, and prostration which is unusual, and impressive. Characteristically the mood is repressed, not wrestled with. The water of life has a heavenly quality to *quell* the pain. The bitterness of death is anaesthetized, and the evil suggestions of the tempter are forcibly thrust out. Southey's poem differs strikingly in this respect from the revised version of Keats's *Hyperion*, although both are descriptions of the same kind of experience. Keats, alone in Moneta's temple, comes near to death, but is able to climb the steps of the altar and so saves himself. The life pours into him again, and, grateful but perplexed, he watches a re-enactment of the fall of Saturn. While Southey's consolation depends on a conviction that everything in the long run works out for good, Keats does not view the overthrow of the old gods as suffering justified by the greater good which follows.[1] For him the miseries of the world are misery, and will not let him rest.

There is a counterpart to Southey's dialogue with the evil prophet in his correspondence with Rickman. Rickman had objected to his using words like 'holy' and 'righteous' about the Spanish rising against Napoleon. The Creator seemed concerned only with general results, 'careless (so to speak) of the individual, even sometimes of a whole species of animals (the mammoth for example)'. Southey agreed that individuals, species, and nations might be sacrificed to general results; but 'the belief that Good is stronger than Evil sets all right upon the great scale, and all is set right for individuals

---

[1] Oceanus puts this view in the second book of *Hyperion*, but the meaning of the poem as a whole, especially in the revised version, is much more complex.

also in a future state'.[1] All is set right. It would have
broken Southey's heart not to believe this, and yet no educated person in his time could have quite the unselfconscious
assurance of the ages of faith. To cling to traditional certi-
tudes was to avert attention from what one knew was there.
The howling deserts of infidelity had to be crossed if one
were to reach the firm lands of faith beyond. It is no accident
that John Henry Newman, perhaps the most formidable of
the Victorian apologists for orthodox Christianity, was one
who made no attempt to ignore that howling desert. He
looked into the busy world, and confessed that he saw no
reflection of its creator there. And having made this drastic
concession, he turned it into an argument for the 'terrible
aboriginal calamity' of the Fall.[2] The reader may not in
fact accept Newman's reasoning; but it is reasoning which
takes into account experience profoundly difficult to reconcile
with religious belief, and it has an accent of conviction not
to be found in Southey.

He depended on his physical buoyancy to the end. He
suffered a terrible blow in 1834 when his wife became insane,
but he contrived to apply his old remedy of work. Henry
Taylor reflected afterwards that this probably proved fatal to
him; 'having a strength of heart and intellectual energy
which he had never known to fail, he was led to use them to a
degree which human nature will not bear'.[3] Carlyle, who met
him a few times after Mrs. Southey had died in 1837,
describes him as still talking and listening well, able to
respond with enthusiasm to the newly published *French
Revolution*. But his look was careworn, 'his eyes especially
were as if full of gloomy bewilderment and incurable sorrow'.
On one occasion they talked of Shelley, that ghost of Southey's
youth. 'A haggard existence that of his', said Carlyle; and
Southey replied, 'It *is* a haggard existence!' Still, even now
the buoyancy remained, as Carlyle's account of their last

[1] *Rickman*, 169–72.   [2] Newman's *Apologia pro Vita Sua*, chap. v.
[3] BL, d. 9, f. 218, 24 Aug. 1839.

conversation shows. They spoke of the approach of a violent democratic revolution, of the decay of all morality and nobility with its ultimate penalty of social ruin. Carlyle remarked that their perfect consent on these matters gave an animation to the dialogue, which he remembered as copious and pleasant.

Southey's last word was in answer to some tirade of mine about universal Mammon-worship, gradual accelerating decay of mutual humanity, of piety and fidelity to God or man, in all our relations and performances,—the whole illustrated by examples, I suppose; —to which he answered, not with levity, yet with a cheerful tone in his seriousness, 'It will not, and it cannot come to good!'[1]

William Gilbert certainly knew how to cast a horoscope. Southey walked through desolation until he succumbed to sheer fatigue. In 1839, three and a half years before his death, his mind quietly gave way.

[1] Carlyle, *Reminiscences*, ed. C. E. Norton (1887), ii. 293–4.

APPENDIX A

Southey's Religious Beliefs after 1811

SOUTHEY enjoys a reputation for theological orthodoxy, partly on the strength of his championship of the Church of England against Catholics and dissenters, partly because of such articles as that in the *Quarterly Review* on the progress of infidelity. His denunciations of unbelief are violent, and he is fervent in his advocacy of a reverent submission to Christian doctrine and discipline. Positive religion, he says, quoting from J. E. M. Portalis, 'is a dyke, a rampart, which alone can secure us against the torrent of false and, more or less, dangerous opinions, which the delirium of human reason would invent'.[1] Southey's political conservatism was accompanied by a growing respect for what Portalis calls the deposit of Christian doctrine. Not only did he find much that was congenial to him in such seventeenth-century divines as Jackson and South, but he seems also to have been influenced by such contemporary Christian apologists as John Miller and Christopher Benson to accept the main tenets of orthodoxy.

None the less, Southey's reverent submission to authority was not unconditional, and his more orthodox readers found little satisfaction in him as a defender of the faith. *The Book of the Church* had a reassuring title, and it was the fulfilment of a sound enough plan, long entertained by Southey, to write the lives of the 'heroes of our religion'. Wycliffe and Tindale, Latimer and Ridley should, Southey thought, be as popular as Admiral Blake, Marlborough, and Nelson.[2] As the *British Review* was quick to point out, however, Southey's account of these heroes was infected with heresy. In the course of the book he fell foul of several of the Thirty-Nine Articles. He sympathized with Pelagius, and indirectly attacked St. Paul's teaching on faith. He seemed to think that Romanism would be an

[1] *QR* (1823), xxviii. 525. Cf. J. E. M. Portalis, *De l'usage et de l'abus de l'esprit philosophique* (Paris, 1820), ii. 184.

[2] *QR* (1810), iv. 513.

excellent religion if it were stripped of its ecclesiastical abuses, and if the popes were men like Fénelon.[1] Even more disquieting was the *Life of Wesley*. The *Eclectic Review* described it as 'a sort of digest and manual' of the 'current mass of contumelious "liberality"'. It particularly reprehended the tendency to refer belief in divine inspiration to mental disease, or to enthusiasm. And it remarked that Southey's objections to the 'oddities' of Methodism often concealed an objection to Christianity itself. To protest against the doctrine that good works cannot be performed before justification is to protest against more than John Wesley; it is to be at odds with the official doctrine of the Church of England. The evangelical Anglican journal, the *Christian Observer*, made the same general criticism, and particularly censured Southey's scepticism about the existence of the Devil. ('We should be glad to see Mr. Southey adopt, in some future edition, a more orthodox title for that spirit who "goeth about seeking whom he may devour", than the "personified principle of evil".') This same journal said that rumours of Southey's heterodoxy, 'even as to the divinity and atonement of Christ, and the reality of spiritual influences', were widely current. He should declare his faith boldly. An equivocal witness was of no value in times when the established religion was so rudely assailed.[2]

What did Southey actually believe? In 1814 he made an unusually detailed confession of faith to Grosvenor Bedford, who had complained that there was too much 'religious feeling' in one of the laureate odes, and that he ran the danger of being considered either an 'enthusiast' or a hypocrite. Southey's reply was this:

I am neither enthusiast nor hypocrite, but a man deeply and habitually religious in all my feelings, according to my own views of religion; which views differ from those of the Church which I defend, in material points;—otherwise I should be in that church. I am too old to bring my own opinions upon this subject into discussion unnecessarily; but when I am conversing with persons in whose zeal I can sympathize I take scrupulous care that they may not misunderstand me, and imagine that because we agree in feeling we agree also in points of faith. But there is no occasion to do this in public. I write religiously because I write as I feel. *Not* being of the Church, I hold the Church Establishment one of our greatest, perhaps the greatest of our blessings; and conscientiously desire to strengthen and support it. *Not* believing in the

[1] *British Review*, xxii. 315–44 (Aug. 1824).
[2] *Eclectic Review*, N.S., xv. 1 et seq. (Jan. 1821); *Christian Observer*, xix. 747 et seq. (Nov. 1820).

inspiration of the Bible, but believing in the faith which is founded upon it, I hold its general circulation as one of the greatest benefits which can be conferred upon mankind. *Not* believing that men are damned for not being Christians I believe that Christianity is a divine religion, and that it is our duty to diffuse it. See whether whatever I write in my own person is not consistent with this exposition.—The consequence naturally is that I am exposed to a double imputation, of enthusiasm from those who believe less,—of irreligion from those who believe more.[1]

This letter suggests that Shelley's account of Southey's beliefs in 1811–12 is quite probably correct. He was surprised to find the *Quarterly* reviewer so unorthodox. 'Southey calls himself a Christian, but he does not believe that the Evangelists were inspired. . . . He rejects the Trinity, and thinks that Jesus Christ stood precisely in the same relation to God as himself.'[2] Under the influence of Shelley's arguments, Southey may have been pressed into more heresies than usual. But the impression left by Shelley's account of his conversations is that on this occasion Southey merely stated his real beliefs without reserve. The young atheist must not be allowed to suppose that religion necessarily entailed theological nonsense. It is not difficult to believe that Southey assented to Shelley's definition of the deity as 'the mass of infinite *intelligence*' (it was no worse than some others). Long after 1811 he held to his belief that evil was the product of human institutions. 'Southey', said Shelley, with obvious delight, 'is no believer in original sin: he thinks that which appears to be a taint of our nature is in effect the result of unnatural political institutions: there we agree. He thinks the prejudices of education, and sinister influences of political institutions, adequate to account for all the Specimens of vice which have fallen within his observation.'[3]

Shelley was disappointed that Southey did not accept what he considered to be the necessary consequences of such beliefs. He was rather irritated by Southey's conviction that age and experience would bring Shelley round to his point of view. None the less, the conversations with Southey did have some effect. Some time after his visit to Keswick, Shelley was walking in the country with Thomas Love Peacock. They passed a pleasant-looking vicarage,

---

[1] BL, c. 25, f. 144, 29 Dec. 1814.

[2] Shelley, *Works*, ed. R. Ingpen and W. Peck (1926–30), viii. 223. Letter to Elizabeth Hitchener, 26 Dec. 1811.

[3] Ibid. 227–8. Letter to Elizabeth Hitchener, 2 Jan. 1812.

and Shelley suddenly remarked to Peacock, 'I feel strongly inclined to enter the Church'. Peacock was surprised, as well he might be, and Shelley explained that assent to the supernatural part of faith was 'merely technical'. He was more of a disciple to the moral doctrines of Christianity than many who made an ostentatious profession of faith.

And consider for a moment how much good a good clergyman may do. In his teaching as a scholar and a moralist; in his example as a gentleman and a man of regular life; in the consolation of his personal intercourse and of his charity among the poor, to whom he may often prove a most beneficent friend when they have no other to comfort them. It is an admirable institution that admits the possibility of diffusing such men over the surface of the land. And am I to deprive myself of the advantages of this admirable institution because there are certain technicalities to which I cannot give my adhesion, but which I need not bring prominently forward?

Peacock merely commented that Shelley would find more restraint in the office than would suit his aspirations, and there the matter dropped.[1] Southey was not the only man from whom Shelley could have derived such a view of the Church. But the parallel between what he said to Peacock and what Southey was writing to Grosvenor and Horace Bedford in 1796 and 1797 is so striking that mere coincidence can almost certainly be ruled out. The probability is that on that fine summer morning, in congenial surroundings, an idea expressed to him by Southey suddenly took possession of his mind.

Southey described himself at this time as a *seeker*, 'a sheep without a fold, but not without a shepherd'.[2] He was himself of no visible church, but felt that he belonged to the communion of saints— the communion which included papist, protestant, and heathen. Southey's position then, and for many years afterwards, was close to that of such 'rational churchmen' as Bishop Watson and Sydney Smith; but it was not one that could comfortably be held by a member of the Church of England. As late as 1860 the controversy over *Essays and Reviews* showed that those who denied the plenary inspiration of scripture and the doctrine of eternal punishment were only Anglicans by courtesy of the Privy Council. The ecclesiastical

---

[1] T. L. Peacock, *Works*, ed. Henry Cole (1875), iii. 408.
[2] J. Holland and J. Everett, *Memoirs of James Montgomery* (1854), ii. 298. Southey to Montgomery, 6 May 1811.

court which tried two of the contributors to *Essays and Reviews* for heresy was convinced that these two doctrines were essential. This conviction was not confined to the more traditionalist communions. In 1825, Joseph John Gurney, a Quaker, published a volume of *Essays on the Evidences, Doctrines, and Practical Operation of Christianity*. He wrote this book in order to set out plainly the doctrines that all Christian people hold in common. (It was a companion volume to one describing the tenets peculiar to the Society of Friends.) Southey was much impressed by the book. He thought that if the author had been a clergyman, it would have shown him to be worthy of a bishopric. But he differed from him on two points, and explained the grounds of his difference in a letter to Gurney. Gurney had argued that the whole of the Old Testament should be regarded as equally inspired because Jesus and the Apostles, in their quotations from it, made no 'invidious distinctions' between the various books. The whole was appealed to as a paramount authority. Southey suggested that, so far as the historical books of the Old Testament were concerned, it was enough to argue for their authenticity. To claim more was to place an unnecessary stumbling-block in the unbeliever's path. 'There are external difficulties, and there is, in my apprehension, a moral and internal evidence which it is far more difficult to set aside. For while the theology is pure, being that of the Mosaic dispensation, the moral feeling is that of a ferocious people.'

Southey goes on to express his disbelief in the doctrine of eternal torments for the wicked. He could believe that the wicked were annihilated, and that in this sense they had to endure an eternal punishment. 'But for an eternity of torments—I *cannot* believe it,— and God forgive me if I am wrong, but I cannot in this case call upon him to help mine unbelief.'[1]

Southey never changed his mind on this question. Towards the end of his life he considered himself to be a member of the Church of England, but his zeal for the Church never included an indiscriminate zeal for its doctrines. As late as June 1837 he took the trouble to assure Henry Taylor that he utterly disbelieved the doctrine of eternal torments.[2] Because he did not wish to disturb 'established delusions', however, but only to defend established

---

[1] Friends' House Library, London: Gurney Letters, iii. 422. 4 Jan. 1826. Cf. J. B. Braithwaite, *Memoirs of J. J. Gurney* (1854), i. 292–3. Gurney's reply is in the National Library of Scotland, MS. 2528, ff. 46–47, 7 Jan. 1826.

[2] BL, d. 9, f. 39, 21 June 1837.

truths,[1] Southey did not obtrude his theological reservations in his published writings.

Much of Southey's religious belief can be described as a christianized faith in the holiness of the heart's affections and in man's unconquerable mind. Methodism ventured into emotional depths from which he recoiled, and he had no love for the 'ravings and raptures' of enthusiasts. But as the *Life of Wesley* shows, there was one kind of enthusiasm with which he could sympathize generously. The passages which describe the sufferings of Methodists at the hands of the mob are invariably told with great spirit, and Southey fully appreciates John Nelson's feelings when taken captive through the streets of York:

> We were guarded through the city . . . but it was as if hell were moved from beneath to meet me at my coming. The streets and windows were filled with people, who shouted and huzzaed, as if I had been one that had laid waste the nation. But the Lord made my brow like brass, so that I could look on them as grasshoppers, and pass through the city as if there had been none in it but God and myself.[2]

Perhaps this was what Southey felt like after the publication of *Wat Tyler*. He also had an evident sympathy with Wesley's formidable authority over the Methodists, even though he was sometimes critical of the way in which Wesley was 'inflated' with his power. He admired the way Wesley obtained from his early disciples unhesitating, cheerful, and devoted obedience. Nor was he condemning Wesley when he referred to his 'aspiring presages' of the 'extensive influence which his life and labours would produce upon mankind'.[3] There was some resemblance here between the founder of Methodism and the Poet Laureate who took his office with such unprecedented seriousness. To use Carlyle's language, the Hero-Poet could respect the Hero-Reformer.

To one doctrine, at least, Southey was passionately attached—the belief in personal immortality. As his wife, hopelessly insane, lay dying, he wrote that there had been times in his life when his heart would have been broken if this doctrine had not supported him. 'At this moment it is worth to me more than all the world could give.'[4]

---

[1] *LC*, v. 236. Letter to Henry Taylor, 22 Oct. 1825.

[2] *Life of Wesley* (1846 ed.), i. 398.

[3] Ibid. 136. Coleridge, indeed, was moved to question whether Southey ought to be so tolerant of Wesley's restless, ambitious energy. Ibid., p. 338 n.

[4] BL, d. 9, f. 83; *LC*, vi. 346. The correspondent was Henry Taylor.

APPENDIX B[1]

The Prose-Gelder at Work: Southey's article on Parliamentary Reform in the Quarterly Review, October 1816

SOUTHEY complained that Gifford had done everything in his power to render this article spiritless and worthless. It had been transformed into a mere pamphlet on behalf of the ministry.

> Gifford *dares* not speak my opinions,—and for this I do not blame him,—he is rather to be pitied,—or the Ministry are to be pitied who dare not even *hear* the advice of one of their most strenuous and most disinterested advocates. But what Devil is it that makes him garble my sentences as well as my arguments! Look at p. 239—about the Ed. Rev. and Balaam, and see what he has made of the allusion! I do not write to him immediately, because I am really too much offended at these impertinent mutilations.—This matter I thought had been put upon a proper footing. But it shall be so in future; and I will have him distinctly understand that I will not submit, like a schoolboy, to have my compositions corrected in this manner.—Ideots that they are! they call upon me to fight their battles,—and then carefully take off the edge of my sword.[2]

As it happens, he restored the true text of this paper when he reprinted some of his articles in 1832, so that one can see how far his complaints were justified. To take Balaam's ass first. Southey had written that during the Peninsular War, the wise men of the North (that is, the *Edinburgh Review*) had come forward, 'like the son of Beor, to take up their prophecy in behalf of the Moabite; the beast upon which Balaam was mounted could have prophesied as wisely,—and would not have been more out of tune; for the voice of the country was in accord with its honour and its duty . . .' Gifford seems to have thought that this rudeness at the expense of a rival review was imprudent, and the *Quarterly*'s text contains no hint

---

[1] See p. 162, n. 3.
[2] BL, d. 47, f. 11. Letter to G. C. Bedford, 12 Feb. 1817.

of a joke. 'And we had our wise men of the North, who came forward, like the son of Beor, to take up their prophecy in behalf of the Moabite; but the voice of the country was in accord with its own honour and its duty. . . .'[1] One can understand Southey's wrath, for any shrewd hit at the *Edinburgh* was dear to him. But this, after all, was a detail. There are several other examples of this sort, but they are not worth particularizing.

More substantial is the omission of a passage on page 332 of the 1832 text. Southey was arguing that the war against France in 1793 was unquestionably popular. He mentioned the Birmingham riots of 1791 as an instance of the rabble's politics at the time. Moreover, people were then tried for sedition and 'convicted upon evidence scandalously insufficient'. Nothing about Birmingham or sedition trials appears in the corresponding page of the *Quarterly Review*.[2]

Again, on page 385 of the 1832 text, Southey assumes that at some time large towns then unrepresented in the House of Commons would have the privilege of electing M.P.s extended to them. This concession to the spirit of reform was carefully removed. A little later, on page 388, Southey argues that the sale of a certain number of seats in Parliament should be made legal, on the same basis as commissions in the army and navy. Gifford excised this too.[3]

A different kind of omission is that of an appeal to the followers of Spence to try out their theories of co-operation in practice on a small scale. If they are well-meaning men (and Southey is prepared to allow that they have the makings of a harmless and useful sect) 'they will attempt to demonstrate the utility of their schemes in a manner that will bring no injury to others'. But the Spenceans must understand that a subversive cry of 'No Landlords!' cannot be tolerated.[4] Gifford may have been alarmed by the partial countenance that the *Quarterly Review* would have been giving a revolutionary organization if this passage had been allowed to stand. The final omission, on the other hand, was clearly dictated by a desire to avoid the charge of undue severity. Southey concluded his article by calling for the revival of Lord Grenville's Bill against seditious assemblies, and for a new law to make transportation or banishment the punishment for seditious libel. This was replaced by some

---

[1] *Essays* (1832), i. 353; *QR*, xvi. 239–40.
[2] Ibid., pp. 332; 228.   [3] Ibid., pp. 385; 257. 388; 258.
[4] Ibid., pp. 411–12; 271.

plaintive paragraphs protesting that government cannot take responsibility for evils that have been caused by bad weather and the difficulties of adapting the economy to the conditions of peace. 'They cannot stay the pestilence; but they can take care that, while it rages, the city is not plundered.'[1]

1 Ibid., pp. 421–2; 276–8.

INDEX

Q

PRINTED IN GREAT BRITAIN
AT THE UNIVERSITY PRESS, OXFORD
BY VIVIAN RIDLER
PRINTER TO THE UNIVERSITY